AF327140

MASTERWORKS OF
HISTORY

VOLUME 2

43-92
184-190

MASTERWORKS SERIES

Editorial Board

Alvin Johnson, LL.D.

PRESIDENT EMERITUS, THE NEW SCHOOL
FOR SOCIAL RESEARCH

Robert Andrews Millikan, Sc.D.

CHAIRMAN OF THE EXECUTIVE COUNCIL,
CALIFORNIA INSTITUTE OF TECHNOLOGY

Alexander Maclaren Witherspoon, Ph.D.

ASSOCIATE PROFESSOR OF ENGLISH,
YALE UNIVERSITY

MASTERWORKS OF HISTORY

VOLUME 2

BEDE: ECCLESIASTICAL HISTORY OF THE
ENGLISH NATION

MACAULAY: HISTORY OF ENGLAND FROM
THE ACCESSION OF JAMES II

BANCROFT: HISTORY OF THE UNITED STATES

CHARLES AND MARY BEARD:
THE RISE OF AMERICAN CIVILIZATION

EDITED BY JOSEPH REITHER

McGraw-Hill Book Company

New York • St. Louis • San Francisco • London • Düsseldorf
Kuala Lumpur • Mexico • Montreal • Panama • São Paulo
Sydney • Toronto • Johannesburg • New Delhi • Singapore

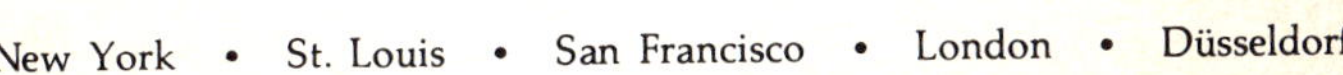

Masterworks of History, Volume II

Copyright 1948 by Copeland & Lamm, Inc. All rights reserved. Printed in the United States of America. No part of this publication may be reproduced, stored in a retrieval system, or transmitted, in any form or by any means, electronic, mechanical, photocopying, recording, or otherwise, without the prior written permission of the publisher.

First McGraw-Hill Paperback Edition, 1973

07-040811-4

1 2 3 4 5 6 7 8 9 MU MU 7 9 8 7 6 5 4 3

CONTENTS

THE ECCLESIASTICAL HISTORY OF THE ENGLISH NATION

by

THE VENERABLE BEDE

CONTENTS

The Ecclesiastical History of the English Nation

BEDE

673-735

THE SPIRIT which pervades Bede's work is the spirit of the religion that he preached. His serenity, his compassion, his humility, his faith, are but a few of the qualities which reflect the spiritual strength which gradually gained dominion over the minds of primitive and civilized men alike.

The Roman conquest of Britain was begun by Julius Caesar in 57 B.C., and was continued by degrees until Claudius's expedition in A.D. 43, decisively established the Roman hold and began the Romanization of the indigenous population. In A.D. 78, Agricola began the conquest of the north which was completed by Hadrian, whose protective wall fixed the boundary between Scotland and Roman Britain. By the middle of the fourth century Britain was thoroughly Romanized. However, early in the fifth century, when the Germans began to pour into Gaul, the Roman garrisons were withdrawn from Britain and many Romans fled to the continent for safety. The island was thus exposed to the increasing piratical raids of the Scots (from Ireland), which had begun around A.D. 350, and the invasions of the Jutes, Angles, and Saxons. Roman civilization in Britain was completely destroyed by the Germanic invaders. Toward the end of the sixth century there emerged seven Germanic kingdoms, three of them Saxon (Essex, Wessex, Sussex), one Jutish (Kent), and three Angle (East Anglia, Mercia, and Northumbria).

It was in the Jutish Kingdom of Kent that Augustine the Monk landed in 597 and began the conversion of its ruler to Christianity. Shortly thereafter Northumbria, which had also been converted, assumed the hegemony of the seven kingdoms (*Heptarchy*). However, in 633 the heathen Mercians gained dominance and overwhelmed the Roman Church, introducing a period of anarchy. There then began a reconversion of Britain from two directions.

The conversion of Ireland to Christianity, probably begun by the fourth century, was completed by St. Patrick in the fifth century. In the sixth century the conversion of Scotland was begun in 563 when St. Columba landed at Iona from Ireland and established there a monastery. Oswald, who succeeded to the throne of Northumbria, found refuge with the monks of Iona during his exile. In 633 he invited them to send a missionary to reconvert his people. The Scottish monk Aidan accordingly established a monastery and bishopric in Northumbria and thus began the reconversion of Britain which was practically completed by 670. Along with Christianity went the spread of education, which laid the basis for the eighth-century Anglo-Saxon renaissance of which Bede is perhaps the most distinguished representative.

However, the Church in Ireland had long been out of touch with Rome, and some of its practices differed from those of the Roman Church. If the unity of Western Christendom was to be preserved, it was necessary that these differences be reconciled. This is the issue with which Bede concerns himself at such length. The date of Easter, the harmonization of the Irish and Roman calendars, uniformity with respect to the tonsure, and other such matters were merely incidents which pointed the larger issue.

Of the life of Bede little is known beyond what he tells of himself in a brief biographical note at the conclusion of his *Ecclesiastical History*. He was educated at the monasteries of Wearmouth and Jarrow within which he passed his life. His works fall into three classifications; scientific, historical, and theological, but it is upon the *Ecclesiastical History* that his present fame rests. Its early popularity and influence were broadened when Alfred the Great had the work translated from Latin into Anglo-Saxon. Bede's researches in preparation for his history were extensive. He searched the records of monasteries and churches, consulted the historical compilations of predecessors and contemporaries, examined oral tradition, and checked his facts by reference to records in church institutions in Gaul and in the Vatican. His history is still the chief source of our present knowledge of the period covered.

THE ECCLESIASTICAL HISTORY OF THE ENGLISH NATION

BOOK ONE

I. Of the Situation of Britain and Ireland

BRITAIN, an island in the ocean, formerly called Albion, is situated between the north and west, facing, though at a considerable distance, the coasts of Germany, France, and Spain, which form the greatest part of Europe. It extends 800 miles in length towards the north, and is 200 miles in breadth, except where several promontories extend further in breadth, by which its compass is made to be 3675 miles. Britain excels for grain and trees, and is well adapted for feeding cattle and beasts of burden. It also produces vines in some places, and has plenty of land and water-fowls of several sorts; it is remarkable also for rivers abounding in fish, and plentiful springs. It has the greatest plenty of salmon and eels; seals are also frequently taken, and dolphins, as also whales; besides many sorts of shell-fish, such as muscles, in which are often found excellent pearls of all colours, red, purple, violet, and green, but mostly white. There is also a great abundance of cockles, of which the scarlet dye is made; a most beautiful colour, which never fades with the heat of the sun or the washing of the rain; but the older it is, the more beautiful it becomes. It has both salt and hot springs, and from them flow rivers which furnish hot baths, proper for all ages and sexes, and arranged according. For water, as St. Basil says, receives the heating quality, when it runs along certain metals, and becomes not only hot but scalding. Britain has also many veins of metals, as copper, iron, lead, and silver; it has much and excellent jet, which is black and sparkling, glittering at the fire, and when heated, drives away serpents; being warmed with rubbing, it holds fast whatever is applied to it, like amber. The island was formerly embellished with twenty-eight noble cities, besides innumerable castles, which were all strongly secured with walls, towers, gates, and locks. And, from its lying almost under the North Pole, the nights are light in summer, so that at midnight the beholders are often in doubt whether the evening twilight still continues, or that of the morning is coming on; for the sun, in the night, returns under the earth, through the northern regions at no great distance from them. For this reason the days are of a great length in summer, as, on the contrary, the nights are in winter, for the sun then withdraws into the southern parts, so that the nights are eighteen hours long. Thus the nights are extraordinarily short in summer, and the days in winter, that is, of only six equinoctial hours. Whereas, in Armenia, Macedonia, Italy, and other countries of the same latitude, the longest day or night extends but to fifteen hours, and the shortest to nine.

This island at present, following the number of the books in which the Divine law was written, contains five nations, the English, Britons, Scots, Picts, and Latins, each in its own peculiar dialect cultivating the sublime study of Divine truth. The Latin tongue is, by the study of the Scriptures, become common to all the rest. At first this island had no other inhabitants but the Britons, from whom it derived its name, and who, coming over into Britain, as is reported, from Armorica, possessed themselves of the southern parts thereof. When they, beginning at the south, had made themselves masters of the greatest part of the island, it happened, that the nation of the Picts, from Scythia, as is reported, putting to sea, in a few long ships, were driven by the winds beyond the shores of Britain, and arrived on the northern coast of Ireland, where, finding the nation of the Scots, they begged to be allowed to settle among them, but could not succeed in obtaining their request. Ireland is the greatest island next to Britain, and lies to the west of it; but as it is shorter than Britain to the north, so, on the other hand, it runs out far beyond it to the south, opposite to the northern parts of Spain, though a spacious sea lies between them. The Picts, as has been said, arriving in this island by sea, desired to have a place granted them in which they might settle. The Scots answered that the island could not contain them both; but "We can give you good advice," said they, "what to do; we know there is another island, not far from ours, to the eastward, which we often see at a distance, when the days are clear. If you will go thither, you will obtain settlements; or, if they should oppose you, you shall have our assistance." The Picts, accordingly, sailing over into Britain, began to inhabit the northern parts thereof, for the Britons were possessed of the southern. Now the Picts had no wives, and asked them of the Scots; who would not consent to grant them upon any other terms, than that when any difficulty should arise, they should choose a king from the female royal race rather than from the male: which custom, as is well known, has been observed among the Picts to this day. In process of time, Britain, besides the Britons and the Picts, received a third nation, the Scots, who, migrating from Ireland under their leader, Reuda, either by fair means, or by force of arms, secured to themselves those settlements among the Picts which they still possess. From the name of their commander, they are to this day called Dalreudins; for, in their language, Dal signifies a part.

Ireland, in breadth, and for wholesomeness and serenity of climate, far surpasses Britain; for the snow scarcely ever lies there above three days: no man makes hay in the summer for winter's provision, or builds stables for his beasts of burden. No reptiles are found there, and no snake can live there; for, though often carried thither out of Britain, as soon as the ship comes near the shore, and the scent of the air reaches them, they die. On the contrary, almost all things in the island are good against poison. In short, we have known that when some persons have been bitten by serpents, the scrapings of leaves of books that were brought out of Ireland, being put into water, and given them to drink, have immediately expelled the spreading poison, and assuaged the swelling. The island abounds in milk and honey, nor is there any want of vines, fish, or fowl; and it is remarkable for deer and goats. It is properly the country of the Scots, who, migrating from thence, as has been said, added a third nation in Britain to the Britons and the Picts.

II. Caius Julius Caesar, the First Roman That Came into Britain

Britain had never been visited by the Romans, and was, indeed, entirely unknown to them before the time of Caius Julius Caesar, who, in the year 693 after the building of Rome, but the sixtieth year before the incarnation of our Lord, was consul with Lucius Bibulus, and afterwards while he made war upon the Germans and the Gauls, which were divided only by the river Rhine, came into the province of the Morini, from whence is the nearest and shortest passage into Britain. Here, having provided about eighty ships of burden and vessels with oars, he sailed over into Britain; where, being first roughly handled in a battle, and then meeting with a violent storm, he lost a considerable part of his fleet, no small number of soldiers, and almost all his horses. Returning into Gaul, he put his legions into winter-quarters, and gave orders for building six hundred sail of both sorts. With these he again passed over early in spring into Britain, but, whilst he was marching with a large army towards the enemy, the ships, riding at anchor, were, by a tempest either dashed one against another, or driven upon the sands and wrecked. Forty of them perished, the rest were, with much difficulty, repaired. Caesar's cavalry was, at the first charge, defeated by the Britons, and Labienus, the tribune, slain. In the second engagement, he, with great hazard to his men, put the Britons to flight. Thence he proceeded to the river Thames, where an immense multitude of the enemy had posted themselves on the farthest side of the river, under the command of Cassibellaun, and fenced the bank of the river and almost all the ford under water with sharp stakes: the remains of these are to be seen to this day, apparently about the thickness of a man's thigh, and being cased with lead, remain fixed immovably in the bottom of the river. This, being perceived and avoided by the Romans, the barbarians, not able to stand the shock of the legions, hid themselves in the woods, whence they grievously galled the Romans with repeated sallies. In the meantime, the strong city of Trinovantum, with its commander Androgeus, surrendered to Caesar, giving him forty hostages.

Many other cities, following their example, made a treaty with the Romans. By their assistance, Caesar at length, with much difficulty, took Cassibellaun's town, situated between two marshes, fortified by the adjacent woods, and plentifully furnished with all necessaries. After this, Caesar returned into Gaul, but he had no sooner put his legions into winter-quarters, than he was suddenly beset and distracted with wars and tumults raised against him on every side.

III.   *Claudius, the Second of the Romans Who Came into Britain*

In the year of Rome 798, Claudius, fourth emperor from Augustus, being desirous to approve himself a beneficial prince to the republic, and eagerly bent upon war and conquest, undertook an expedition into Britain, which seemed to be stirred up to rebellion by the refusal of the Romans to give up certain deserters. He was the only one, either before or after Julius Caesar, who had dared to land upon the island; yet, within a very few days, without any fight or bloodshed, the greatest part of the island was surrendered into his hands. He also added to the Roman empire the Orcades, which lie in the ocean beyond Britain, and then, returning to Rome the sixth month after his departure, he gave his son the title of Britannicus. This war he concluded in the fourth year of his empire, which is the forty-sixth from the incarnation of our Lord. In which year there happened a most grievous famine in Syria, which in the Acts of the Apostles is recorded to have been foretold by the prophet Agabus. Vespasian, who was emperor after Nero, being sent into Britain by the same Claudius, brought also under the Roman dominion the Isle of Wight, which is next to Britain on the south, and is about thirty miles in length from east to west, and twelve from north to south; being six miles distant from the southern coast of Britain at the east end, and three only at the west. Nero, succeeding Claudius in the empire, attempted nothing in martial affairs; and, therefore, among other innumerable detriments brought upon the Roman state, he almost lost Britain; for under him two most noble towns were there taken and destroyed.

IV.   *Diocletian and How He Persecuted the Christians*

In the year of our Lord's incarnation 286, Diocletian, the thirty-third from Augustus, and chosen emperor by the army, reigned twenty years, and created Maximian, surnamed Herculius, his colleague in the empire. In their time, one Carausius, of very mean birth, but an expert and able soldier, being appointed to guard the seacoasts, then infested by the Franks and Saxons, acted more to the prejudice than to the advantage of the commonwealth; and from his not restoring to its owners the booty taken from the robbers, but keeping all to himself, it was suspected that by intentional neglect he suffered the enemy to infest the frontiers. Hearing, therefore, that an order was sent by Maximian that he should be put to death, he took upon him the imperial robes, and possessed himself of Britain, and having most valiantly retained it for the space of seven years, he was at length put to death by the treachery of his associate, Allectus. The usurper, having thus got the island from Carausius, held it three years, and was then vanquished by Asclepiodotus, the captain of the Praetorian bands, who thus at the end of ten years restored Britain to the Roman empire. Meanwhile, Diocletian in the east, and Maximian Herculius in the west, commanded the churches to be destroyed, and the Christians to be slain. This persecution was the tenth since the reign of Nero, and was more lasting and bloody than all the others before it; for it was carried on incessantly for the space of ten years, with burning of churches, out-lawing of innocent persons, and the slaughter of martyrs. At length, it reached Britain also, and many persons, with the constancy of martyrs, died in the confession of their faith.

V. The Church in Britain Enjoys Peace

When the storm of persecution ceased, the faithful Christians, who, during the time of danger, had hidden themselves in woods and deserts, and secret caves, appearing in public, rebuilt the churches which had been levelled with the ground; founded, erected, and finished the temples of the holy martyrs, and, as it were, displayed their conquering ensigns in all places; they celebrated festivals, and performed their sacred rites with clean hearts and mouths. This peace continued in the churches of Britain until the time of the Arian madness, which, having corrupted the whole world, infected this island also, so far removed from the rest of the globe, with the poison of its arrows; and when the plague was thus conveyed across the sea, all the venom of every heresy immediately rushed into the island, ever fond of something new, and never holding firm to anything.

At this time, Constantius, who, whilst Diocletian was alive, governed Gaul and Spain, a man of extraordinary meekness and courtesy, died in Britain. This man left his son Constantine, born of Helen his concubine, emperor of the Gauls. Eutropius writes, that Constantine, being created emperor in Britain, succeeded his father in the sovereignty. In his time the Arian heresy broke out, and although it was detected and condemned in the Council of Nice, yet it nevertheless infected not only all the churches of the continent, but even those of the islands, with its pestilent and fatal doctrines.

VI. The Britons Ravaged by the Scots and Picts

From that time, the south part of Britain, destitute of armed soldiers, of martial stores, and of all its active youth, which had been led away by the rashness of the tyrants, never to return, was wholly exposed to rapine, as being totally ignorant of the use of weapons. Whereupon they suffered many years under two very savage foreign nations, the Scots from the west, and the Picts from the north. We call these foreign nations, not on account of their being seated out of Britain, but because they were remote from that part of it which was possessed by the Britons; two inlets of the sea lying between them, one of which runs in far and broad into the land of Britain, from the Eastern Ocean, and the other from the Western, though they do not reach so as touch one another. The Eastern has in the midst of it the city Giudi. The Western has on it, that is, on the right hand thereof, the city Alcluith, which in their language signifies the Rock Cluith, for it is close by the river of that name.

On account of the irruption of these nations, the Britons sent messengers to Rome with letters in mournful manner, praying for succours, and promising perpetual subjection, provided that the impending enemy should be driven away. An armed legion was immediately sent them, which, arriving in the island, and engaging the enemy, slew a great multitude of them, drove the rest out of the territories of their allies, and having delivered them from their cruel oppressors, advised them to build a wall between the two seas across the island, that it might secure them, and keep off the enemy; and thus they returned home with great triumph. The islanders raising the wall, as they had been directed, not of stone, as having no artist capable of such a work, but of sods, made it of no use.

But the former enemies, when they perceived that the Roman soldiers were gone, immediately coming by sea, broke into the borders, trampled and overran all places, and like men mowing ripe corn, bore down all before them. Hereupon messengers are again sent to Rome, imploring aid, lest their wretched country should be utterly extirpated, and the name of a Roman province, so long renowned among them, overthrown by the cruelties of barbarous foreigners, might become utterly contemptible. A legion is accordingly sent again, and, arriving unexpectedly in autumn, made great slaughter of the enemy, obliging all those that could escape, to flee beyond the sea; whereas before, they were wont yearly to carry off their booty without any opposition. Then the Romans declared to the Britons, that they could not for the future undertake such troublesome expeditions for their sake, advising them rather to handle their weapons like men, and undertake themselves the charge of engaging their enemies, who would not prove too powerful for them, unless they were deterred by cowardice; and, thinking that it might be some help to the allies, whom they were forced to abandon, they built a strong stone wall from sea to sea, in a straight line between the towns that had been there built for fear of the enemy, and not far from the trench of Severus. This famous wall, which is still to be seen, was built at the public and private expense, the Britons also lending their assistance. It is eight feet in breadth, and twelve in height, in a straight line from east to west, as is still visible to beholders. This being finished, they gave that dispirited people good advice, with patterns to furnish them with arms. Besides, they built towers on the seacoast to the southward, at proper distances, where their ships were, because there also the irruptions of the barbarians were apprehended, and so took leave of their friends, never to return again.

After their departure, the Scots and Picts, understanding that they had declared they would come no more, speedily returned, and growing more confident than they had been before, occupied all the northern and farthest part of the island, as far as the wall. Hereupon a timorous guard was placed upon the wall, where they pined away day and night in the utmost fear. On the other side, the enemy attacked them with hooked weapons, by which the cowardly defenders were dragged from the wall, and dashed against the ground. At last, the Britons, forsaking their cities and wall, took to flight and were dispersed. The enemy pursued, and the slaughter was greater than on any former occasion; for the wretched natives were torn in pieces by their enemies, as lambs are torn by wild beasts. Thus, being expelled from their dwellings and possessions, they saved themselves from starvation, by robbing and plundering one another, adding to the calamities occasioned by foreigners, by their own domestic broils, till the whole country was left destitute of food, except such as could be procured in the chase.

VII. *The Britons, Compelled by Famine, Drove the Barbarians out of Their Territories*

In the meantime, the aforesaid famine distressing the Britons more and more, and leaving to posterity lasting memorials of its mischievous effects, obliged many of them to submit themselves to the depredators; though others still held out, confiding in the Divine assistance, when none was to be had from men. These continually made excursions from the mountains, caves, and woods, and, at length, began to inflict severe losses on their enemies, who had been for so many years plundering the country. The Irish robbers thereupon returned home, in order to come again soon after. The Picts, both then and afterwards, remained quiet in the farthest part of the island, save that sometimes they would do some mischief, and carry off booty from the Britons.

When, however, the ravages of the enemy at length ceased, the island began to abound with such plenty of grain as had never been known in any age before; with plenty, luxury increased, and this was immediately attended with all sorts of crimes; in particular, cruelty, hatred of truth, and love of falsehood; in so much that if any one among them happened to be milder than the rest, and inclined to truth, all the rest abhorred and persecuted him, as if he had been the enemy of his country. Nor were the laity only guilty of these things, but even our Lord's own flock, and his pastors also, addicting themselves to drunkenness, animosity, litigiousness, contention, envy, and other such like crimes, and casting off the light yoke of Christ. In the meantime, on a sudden, a severe plague fell upon that corrupt generation, which soon destroyed such numbers of them that the living were scarcely sufficient to bury the dead; yet those that survived could not be withdrawn from the spiritual death, which their sins had incurred, either by the death of their friends, or the fear of their own. Whereupon, not long after, a more severe vengeance, for their horrid wickedness, fell upon the sinful nation. They consulted what was to be done, and where they should seek assistance to prevent or repel the cruel and frequent incursions of the northern nations; and they all agreed with their King Vortigern to call over to their aid, from the parts beyond the sea, the Saxon nation; which, as the event still more evidently showed, appears to have been done by the appointment of our Lord Himself, that evil might fall upon them for their wicked deeds.

VIII.   *The Angles Invited into Britain*

In the year of our Lord 449, Martian being made emperor with Valentinian, and the forty-sixth from Augustus, ruled the empire seven years. Then the nation of the Angles, or Saxons, being invited by the aforesaid king, arrived in Britain with three long ships, and had a place assigned them to reside in by the same king, in the eastern part of the island, that they might thus appear to be fighting for their country, whilst their real intentions were to enslave it. Accordingly they engaged with the enemy, who were come from the north to give battle, and obtained the victory; which, being known at home in their own country, as also the fertility of the country, and the cowardice of the Britons, a more considerable fleet was quickly sent over, bringing a still greater number of men, which, being added to the former, made up an invincible army. The newcomers received of the Britons a place to inhabit, upon condition that they should wage war against their enemies for the peace and security of the country, whilst the Britons agreed to furnish them with pay. Those who came over were of the three most powerful nations of Germany—Saxons, Angles, and Jutes. From the Jutes are descended the people of Kent, and of the Isle of Wight, and those also in the province of the West-Saxons who are to this day called Jutes, seated opposite to the Isle of Wight. From the Saxons, that is, the country which is now called Old Saxony, came the East-Saxons, the South-Saxons, and the West-Saxons. From the Angles, that is, the country which is called Anglia, and which is said, from that time, to remain desert to this day, between the provinces of the Jutes and the Saxons, are descended the East-Angles, the Midland-Angles, Mercians, all the race of the Northumbrians, that is, of those nations that dwell on the north side of the river Humber, and the other nations of the English. The two first commanders are said to have been Hengist and Horsa. Of whom Horsa, being afterwards slain in battle by the Britons, was buried in the eastern parts of Kent, where a monument, bearing his name, is still in existence. In a short time, swarms of the aforesaid nations came over into the island, and they began to increase so much, that they became terrible to the natives themselves who had invited them. Then, having on a sudden entered into league with the Picts, whom they had by this time repelled by the force of their arms, they began to turn their weapons against their confederates. At first, they obliged them to furnish a greater quantity of provisions; and, seeking an occasion to quarrel, protested, that unless more plentiful supplies were brought them, they would break the confederacy, and ravage all the island; nor were they backward in putting their threats in execution. In short, the fire kindled by the hands of these pagans, proved God's just revenge for the crimes of the people. They plundered all the neighbouring cities and country, spread the conflagration from the Eastern to the Western sea, without any opposition, and covered almost every part of the devoted island. Public as well as private structures were overturned; the priests were everywhere slain before the altars; the prelates and the people, without any respect of persons, were destroyed with fire and sword; nor was there any to bury those who had been thus cruelly slaughtered. Some of the miserable remainder, being taken in the mountains, were butchered in heaps. Others, spent with hunger, came forth and submitted themselves to the enemy for food, being destined to undergo perpetual servitude, if they were not killed even upon the spot. Some, with sorrowful hearts, fled beyond the seas. Others, continuing in their own country, led a miserable life among the woods, rocks, and mountains, with scarcely enough food to support life, and expecting every moment to be their last.

IX.   *The Britons' First Victory over the Angles*

When the victorious army, having destroyed and dispersed the natives, had returned home to their own settlements, the Britons began by degrees to take heart, and gather strength, sallying out of the lurking places where they had concealed themselves, and unanimously imploring the Divine assistance, that they might not utterly be destroyed. They had at that time for their leader, Ambrosius Aurelius, a modest man, who alone, by chance, of the Roman nation had survived the storm, in which his parents, who were of the royal race, had perished. Under him the Britons revived, and offering battle to the victors, by the help of God, came off victorious. From that day, sometimes the natives, and sometimes their enemies, prevailed.

X.   *The Britons Wasted Themselves by Civil Wars*

In Britain, there was some respite from foreign, but not from civil war. There still remained the ruins of cities destroyed by the enemy, and abandoned; and the natives, who had escaped the enemy, now fought against each other. However, the kings, priests, private men, and the nobility, still remembering the late calamities and slaughters, in some measure kept within bounds; but when these died, and another generation succeeded, which knew nothing of those times, and was only acquainted with the present peaceable state of things, all the bonds of sincerity and justice were so entirely broken that there was not only no trace of them remaining, but few persons seemed to be aware that such virtues had ever existed. Among other most wicked actions, not to be expressed, which their own historian, Gildas, mournfully takes notice of, they added this —that they never preached the faith to the Saxons, or English, who dwelt amongst them; however, the goodness of God did not forsake his people, whom He foreknew, but sent to the aforesaid nation much more worthy preachers, to bring it to the faith.

XI. *How Pope Gregory Sent Augustine to Preach to the English Nation*

In the year of our Lord 582, Maurice, the fifty-fourth from Augustus, ascended the throne, and reigned twenty-one years. In the tenth year of his reign, Gregory, a man renowned for learning and behaviour, was promoted to the apostolical see of Rome, and presided over it thirteen years, six months and ten days. He, being moved by Divine inspiration, in the fourteenth year of the same emperor, and about the one hundred and fiftieth after the coming of the English into Britain, sent the servant of God, Augustine, and with him several other monks, who feared the Lord, to preach the word of God to the English nation. They having, in obedience to the pope's commands, undertaken that work, were, on their journey, seized with a sudden fear, and began to think of returning home, rather than proceed to a barbarous, fierce, and unbelieving nation, to whose very language they were strangers; and this they unanimously agreed was the safest course. In short, they sent back Augustine, who had been appointed to be consecrated bishop in case they were received by the English, that he might, by humble entreaty, obtain of the holy Gregory, that they should not be compelled to undertake so dangerous, toilsome, and uncertain a journey. The pope, in reply, sent them a hortatory epistle, persuading them to proceed in the work of the Divine word, and rely on the assistance of the Almighty. The purport of which letter was as follows:—

"Gregory, the servant of the servants of God, to the servants of our Lord. Forasmuch as it had been better not to begin a good work, than to think of desisting from that which has been begun, it behoves you, my beloved sons, to fulfil the good work, which, by the help of our Lord, you have undertaken. Let not, therefore, the toil of the journey, nor the tongues of evil speaking men, deter you; but with all possible earnestness and zeal perform that which, by God's direction, you have undertaken; being assured, that much labour is followed by an eternal reward. When Augustine, your chief, returns, whom we also constitute your abbat,

humbly obey him in all things; knowing, that whatsoever you shall do by his direction, will, in all respects, be available to your souls. Almighty God protect you with his grace, and grant that I may, in the heavenly country, see the fruits of your labour."

XII. *Augustine First Preached to King Ethelbert*

Augustine, thus strengthened by the confirmation of the blessed Father Gregory, returned to the work of the word of God, with the servants of Christ, and arrived in Britain. The powerful Ethelbert was at that time king of Kent; he had extended his dominions as far as the great river Humber, by which the Southern Saxons are divided from the Northern. On the east of Kent is the large Isle of Thanet containing according to the English way of reckoning, 600 families, divided from the other land by the river Wantsum. In this island landed the servant of our Lord, Augustine, and his companions, being, as is reported, nearly forty men. They had, by order of the blessed Pope Gregory, taken interpreters of the nation of the Franks, and sending to Ethelbert, signified that they were come from Rome, and brought a joyful message, which most undoubtedly assured to all that took advantage of it everlasting joys in heaven, and a kingdom that would never end, with the living and true God. The king having heard this, ordered them to stay in that island where they had landed, and that they should be furnished with all necessaries, till he should consider what to do with them. For he had before heard of the Christian religion, having a Christian wife of the royal family of the Franks, called Bertha; whom he had received from her parents, upon condition that she should be permitted to practise her religion with the Bishop Luidhard, who was sent with her to preserve her faith. Some days after, the king came into the island, and sitting in the open air, ordered Augustine and his companions to be brought into his presence. For he had taken precaution that they should not come to him in any house, lest, according to an ancient superstition, if they practised any magical arts, they might impose upon him, and so get the better of him. But they came furnished with Divine, not with magic virtue, bearing a silver cross for their banner, and the image of our Lord and Saviour painted on a board; and singing the litany, they offered up their prayers to the Lord for the eternal salvation both of themselves and of those to whom they were come. When he had sat down, pursuant to the king's commands, and preached to him and his attendants there present, the word of life, the king answered thus:—"Your words and promises are very fair, but as they are new to us, and of uncertain import, I cannot approve of them so far as to forsake that which I have so long followed with the whole English nation. But because you are come from far into my kingdom, and, as I conceive, are desirous to impart to us those things which you believe to be true, and most beneficial, we will not molest you, but give you favourable entertainment, and take care to supply you with your necessary sustenance; nor do we forbid you to preach and gain as many as you can to your religion." Accordingly he permitted them to reside in the city of Canterbury, which was the metropolis of all his dominions, and, pursuant to his promise, besides allowing them sustenance, did not refuse them liberty to preach.

XIII. St. Augustine in Kent

As soon as they entered the dwelling-place assigned them, they began to imitate the course of life practised in the primitive church; applying themselves to frequent prayer, watching and fasting; preaching the word of life to as many as they could; despising all worldly things, as not belonging to them; receiving only their necessary food from those they taught; living themselves in all respects conformably to what they prescribed to others, and being always disposed to suffer any adversity, and even to die for that truth which they preached. In short, several believed and were baptized, admiring the simplicity of their innocent life, and the sweetness of their heavenly doctrine. There was on the east side of the city a church dedicated to the honour of St. Martin, built whilst the Romans were still in the island, wherein the queen, who, as has been said before, was a Christian, used to pray. In this they first began to meet, to sing, to pray, to say mass, to preach, and to baptize, till the king, being converted to the faith, allowed them to preach openly, and build or repair churches in all places.

When he, among the rest, induced by the unspotted life of these holy men, and their delightful promises, which, by many miracles, they proved to be most certain, believed and was baptized, greater numbers began daily to flock together to hear the word, and, forsaking their heathen rites, to associate themselves, by believing, to the unity of the church of Christ. Nor was it long before he gave his teachers a settled residence in his metropolis of Canterbury, with such possessions of different kinds as were necessary for their subsistence.

XIV. St. Augustine Receives Answer to the Doubts He Had Proposed

In the meantime, Augustine, the man of God, repaired to Arles, and, pursuant to the orders received from the holy Father Gregory, was ordained archbishop of the English nation, by Aetherius, archbishop of that city. Then returning into Britain, he sent Laurentius the priest, and Peter the monk, to Rome, to acquaint Pope Gregory, that the nation of the English had received the faith of Christ, and that he was himself made their bishop. At the same time, he desired his solution of some doubts that occurred to him. He soon received proper answers to his questions, which we have also thought fit to insert in this our history—

The First Question of Augustine, Bishop of the Church of Canterbury.—Concerning bishops, how they are to behave themselves towards their clergy? or into how many portions the things given by the faithful to the altar are to be divided? and how the bishop is to act in the church?

Gregory, Pope of the City of Rome, answers.—Holy Writ, which no doubt you are well versed in, testifies, and particularly St. Paul's Epistle to Timothy, wherein he endeavours to instruct him how he should behave himself in the house of God; but it is the custom of the apostolic see to prescribe rules to bishops newly ordained, that all emoluments which accrue, are to be divided into four portions;—one for the bishop and his family, because of hospitality and entertainments; another for the clergy; a third for the poor; and the fourth for the repair of churches. But in regard that you, my brother, being brought up under monastic rules, are not to live apart from your clergy in the English church, which, by God's assistance, has been lately brought to the faith; you are to follow that course of life which our forefathers did in the time of the primitive church, when none of them said anything that he possessed was his own, but all things were in common among them.

But if there are any clerks not received into holy orders, who cannot live continent, they are to take wives, and receive their stipends abroad; because we know it is written, that out of the same portions above-mentioned a distribution was made to each of them according to every one's wants. Care is also to be taken of their stipends, and provision to be made, and they are to be kept under ecclesiastical rules, that they may live orderly, and attend to singing of psalms, and, by the help of God, preserve their hearts, and tongues, and bodies from all that is unlawful. But as for those that live in common, why need we say anything of making portions, or keeping hospitality and exhibiting mercy? in as much as all that can be spared is to be spent in pious and religious works, according to the commands of Him who is the Lord and Master of all, "Give alms of such things as you have, and behold all things are clean unto you."

Augustine's Second Question.—Whereas the faith is one and the same, why are there different customs in different churches? and why is one custom of masses observed in the holy Roman church, and another in the Gallican church?

Pope Gregory answers.—You know, my brother, the custom of the Roman church in which you remember you were bred up. But it pleases me, that if you have found anything, either in the Roman, or the Gallican, or any other church, which may be more acceptable to Almighty God, you carefully make choice of the same, and sedulously teach the church of the English, which as yet is new in the faith, whatsoever you can gather from the several churches. For things are not to be loved for the sake of places, but places for the sake of good things. Choose, therefore, from every church those things that are pious, religious, and upright, and when you have, as it were, made them up into one body, let the minds of the English be accustomed thereto.

Augustine's Third Question.—I beseech you to inform me, what punishment must be inflicted, if any one shall take anything by stealth from the church?

Gregory answers.—You may judge, my brother, by the person of the thief, in what manner he is to be corrected. For there are some, who, having substance, commit theft; and there are others, who transgress in this point through want. Wherefore it is requisite that some be punished in their purses, others with stripes; some with more severity, and some more mildly. And when the severity is more, it is to proceed from charity, not from passion; because this is done to him who is corrected, that he may not be delivered up to hell-fire. For it behoves us to maintain discipline among the faithful, as good parents do with their carnal children, whom they punish with stripes for their faults, and yet design to make those their heirs whom they chastise; and they preserve what they possess for those whom they seem in anger to persecute. This charity is, therefore, to be kept in mind, and it dictates the measure of the punishment, so that the mind may do nothing beyond the rule of reason. You may add that they are to restore those things which they have stolen from the church. But, God forbid, that the church should make profit from those earthly things which it seems to lose, or seek gain out of such vanities.

Augustine's Fourth Question.—Whether two brothers may marry two sisters, which are of a family far removed from them?

Gregory answers.—This may lawfully be done; for nothing is found in holy writ that seems to contradict it.

Augustine's Fifth Question.—To what degree may the faithful marry with their kindred? and whether it is lawful for men to marry their stepmothers and relations?

Gregory answers.—A certain worldly law in the Roman commonwealth allows, that the son and daughter of a brother and sister, or of two brothers, or two sisters, may be joined in matrimony; but we have found, by experience, that no offspring can come of such wedlock; and the Divine Law forbids a man to "uncover the nakedness of his kindred." Hence of necessity it must be the third or fourth generation of the faithful, that can be lawfully joined in matrimony; for the second, which we have mentioned, must altogether abstain from one another. To marry with one's stepmother is a heinous crime, because it is written in the Law, "Thou shalt not uncover the nakedness of thy father": now the son, indeed, cannot uncover his father's nakedness; but in regard that it is written, "They shall be two in one flesh," he that presumes to uncover the nakedness of his stepmother, who was one flesh with his father, certainly uncovers the nakedness of his father. It is also prohibited to marry with a sister-in-law, because by the former union she is become the brother's flesh. For which thing also John the Baptist was beheaded, and ended his life in holy martyrdom.

But for as much as there are many of the English, who, whilst they were still in infidelity, are said to have been joined in this execrable matrimony, when they come to the faith they are to be admonished to abstain, and be made to know that this is a grievous sin. Let them fear the dreadful judgment of God, lest, for the gratification of their carnal appetites, they incur the torments of eternal punishment. Yet they are not on this account to be deprived of the communion of the body and blood of Christ, lest they seem to be punished for those things which they did through ignorance before they had received baptism. For at this time the Holy Church chastises some things through zeal, and tolerates some through meekness, and connives at some things through discretion, that so she may often, by this forbearance and connivance, suppress the evil which she disapproves. But all that come to the faith are to be admonished not to do such things. And if any shall be guilty of them, they are to be excluded from the communion of the body and blood of Christ. For as the offence is, in some measure, to be tolerated in those who did it through ignorance, so it is to be strenuously prosecuted in those who do not fear to sin knowingly.

XV. *Pope Gregory Writes to the Bishop of Arles*

Thus far the answers of the holy Pope Gregory to the questions of the most reverend prelate, Augustine. But the epistle, which he says he had written to the bishop of Arles, was directed to Vergilius, successor to Aetherius, the copy whereof follows—

"To his most reverend and holy brother and fellow bishop, Vergilius; Gregory, servant of the servants of God. If our common brother, Bishop Augustine, shall happen to come to you, I desire your love will, as is becoming, receive him so kindly and affectionately that he may be supported by the honour of your consolation, and others be informed how brotherly charity is to be cultivated. And, since it often happens that those who are at a distance, sooner than others, understand the things that need correction, if any crimes of priests or others shall happen to be laid before you, you will, in conjunction with him, sharply inquire into the same. And do you both act so strictly and carefully against those things which offend God, and provoke his wrath, that for the amendment of others, the punishment may fall upon the guilty, and the innocent may not suffer an ill name."

XVI. *Pope Gregory Writes to the Abbot Mellitus*

The holy father, Gregory, sent letters worthy to be preserved in memory, wherein he plainly shows what care he took of the salvation of our nation. The letter was as follows—

"To his most beloved son, the Abbot Mellitus; Gregory, the servant

of the servants of God. We have been much concerned, since the departure of our congregation that is with you, because we have received no account of the success of your journey. When, therefore, Almighty God shall bring you to the most reverend Bishop Augustine, our brother, tell him what I have, upon mature deliberation on the affair of the English, determined upon, viz., that the temples of the idols in that nation ought not to be destroyed; but let the idols that are in them be destroyed; let holy water be made and sprinkled in the said temples, let altars be erected, and relics placed. For if those temples are well built, it is requisite that they be converted from the worship of devils to the service of the true God; that the nation, seeing that their temples are not destroyed, may remove error from their hearts, and knowing and adoring the true God, may the more familiarly resort to the places to which they have been accustomed. And because they have been used to slaughter many oxen in the sacrifices to devils, some solemnity must be exchanged for them on this account, as that on the day of the dedication, or the nativities of the holy martyrs, whose relics are there deposited, they may build themselves huts of the boughs of trees, about those churches which have been turned to that use from temples, and celebrate the solemnity with religious feasting, and no more offer beasts to the Devil, but kill cattle to the praise of God in their eating, and return thanks to the Giver of all things for their sustenance; to the end that, whilst some gratifications are outwardly permitted them, they may the more easily consent to the inward consolations of the grace of God. For there is no doubt that it is impossible to efface every thing at once from their obdurate minds; because he who endeavours to ascend to the highest place, rises by degrees or steps, and not by leaps. Thus the Lord made Himself known to the people of Israel in Egypt; and yet He allowed them the use of the sacrifices which they were wont to offer to the Devil, in his own worship; so as to command them in his sacrifice to kill beasts, to the end that, changing their hearts, they might lay aside one part of the sacrifice, whilst they retained another; that whilst they offered the same beasts which they were wont to offer, they should offer them to God, and not to idols; and thus they would no longer be the same sacrifices."

XVII. *Pope Gregory Exhorts Augustine*

At which time he also sent Augustine a letter concerning the miracles that he had heard had been wrought by him; wherein he admonishes him not to incur the danger of being puffed up by the number of them. The letter was in these words—

"I know, most loving brother, that Almighty God, by means of your affection, shows great miracles in the nation which He has chosen. Wherefore it is necessary that you rejoice with fear, and tremble whilst you rejoice, on account of the same heavenly gift; viz., that you may rejoice because the souls of the English are by outward miracles drawn to inward grace; but that you fear, lest, amidst the wonders that are wrought, the weak mind may be puffed up in its own presumption, and as it is externally raised to honour, it may thence inwardly fall by vainglory.

"It remains, therefore, most dear brother, that amidst those things, which through the working of our Lord, you outwardly perform, you always inwardly strictly judge yourself, and clearly understand both what you are yourself, and how much grace is in that same nation, for the conversion of which you have also received the gift of working miracles. And if you remember that you have at any time offended our Creator, either by word or deed, that you always call it to mind, to the end that the remembrance of your guilt may crush the vanity which rises in your heart. And whatsoever you shall receive, or have received, in relation to working miracles, that you consider the same, not as conferred on you, but on those for whose salvation it has been given you."

XVIII. *Pope Gregory to King Ethelbert*

"*To the most glorious Lord, and his most excellent son, Ethelbert, king of the English, Bishop Gregory.* Almighty God advances all good men to the government of nations, that He may by their means bestow the gifts of his mercy on those over whom they are placed. This we know to have been done in the English nation, over whom your glory was therefore placed, that by means of the goods which are granted to you, heavenly benefits might also be conferred on the nation that is subject to you. Therefore, my illustrious son, do you carefully preserve the grace which you have received from the Divine goodness, and hasten to promote the Christian faith, which you have embraced, among the people under your subjection; multiply the zeal of your uprightness in their conversion; suppress the worship of idols; overthrow the structures of the temples; edify the manners of your subjects by much cleanness of life, exhorting, terrifying, soothing, correcting, and giving examples of good works, that you may find Him your rewarder in heaven, whose name and knowledge you shall spread abroad upon earth. For He also will render the fame of your honour more glorious to posterity, whose honour you seek and maintain among the nations.

"For even so Constantine, our most pious emperor, recovering the Roman commonwealth from the perverse worship of idols, subjected the same with himself to our Almighty God and Lord Jesus Christ, and was himself, with the people under his subjection, entirely converted to Him. Whence it followed that his praises transcended the fame of former princes; and he as much excelled his predecessors in renown as he did in good works.

"I have sent you some small presents, which will not appear small, when received by you with the blessing of the holy apostle, Peter. May Almighty God, therefore, perfect in you his grace which He has begun, and prolong your life here through a course of many years, and after a time receive you into the congregation of the heavenly country. May heavenly grace preserve your excellency in safety."

XIX. *Ethelfrid Expels the Scots*

At this time, Ethelfrid, a most worthy king, and ambitious of glory, governed the kingdom of the Northumbrians, and ravaged the Britons more than all the great men of the English, in so much that he might be compared to Saul, once king of the Israelites, excepting only this, that he was ignorant of the true religion. For he conquered more territories from the Britons, either making them tributary, or driving the inhabitants clean out, and planting English in their places, than any other king or tribune. To him might justly be applied the saying of the patriarch blessing his son in the person of Saul, "Benjamin shall ravin as a wolf; in the morning he shall devour the prey, and at night he shall divide the spoil." Hereupon, Aedan, king of the Scots that inhabit Britain, being concerned at his success, came against him with an immense and mighty army, but was beaten by an inferior force, and put to flight; for almost all his army was slain at a famous place, called Degsastan, that is, Degsastone. In which battle also Theodbald, brother to Ethelfrid, was killed, with almost all the forces he commanded. This war Ethelfrid put an end to in the year 603 after the incarnation of our Lord, the eleventh of his own reign, which lasted twenty-four years, and the first year of the reign of Phocas, who then governed the Roman empire. From that time, no king of the Scots durst come into Britain to make war on the English to this day.

BOOK TWO

I. *Death of St. Augustine*

IN THE year of our Lord 604, Augustine, archbishop of Britain, ordained two bishops, viz. Mellitus and Justus; Mellitus to preach to the province of the East-Saxons, who are divided from Kent by the river Thames, and border on the Eastern sea. Their metropolis is the city of London, which is situated on the banks of the aforesaid river, and is the mart of many nations resorting to it by sea and land. When this province also received the word of truth, by the preaching of Mellitus, King Ethelbert built the church of St. Paul, in the city of London, where he and his successors should have their episcopal see. As for Justus, Augustine ordained him bishop in Kent, at the city which the English nation named Rhofescestir, from one that was formerly the chief man of it, called Rhof. It was almost twenty-four miles distant from the city of Canterbury to the westward, and contains a church dedicated to St. Andrew, the apostle. King Ethelbert, who built it, bestowed many gifts on the bishops of both those churches, as well as on that of Canterbury, adding lands and possessions for the use of those who were with the bishops.

After this, the beloved of God, Father Augustine, died, and his body was deposited without, close by the church of the apostles, Peter and Paul, by reason that the same was not yet finished, nor consecrated, but as soon as it was dedicated, the body was brought in, and decently buried in the north porch thereof; wherein also were interred the bodies of all the succeeding archbishops, except two only.

II. Death of Kings Ethelbert and Sabert

In the year of our Lord's incarnation 616, which is the twenty-first year after Augustine and his companions were sent to preach to the English nation, Ethelbert, king of Kent, having most gloriously governed his temporal kingdom fifty-six years, entered into the eternal joys of the kingdom which is heavenly.

King Ethelbert died on the 24th day of the month of February, twenty-one years after he had received the faith, and was buried in St. Martin's porch within the church of the blessed apostles Peter and Paul, where also lies his queen, Bertha. Among other benefits which he conferred upon the nation, he also, by the advice of wise persons, introduced judicial decrees, after the Roman model; which, being written in English, are still kept and observed by them. Among which, he in the first place set down what satisfaction should be given by those who should steal anything belonging to the church, the bishop, or the other clergy, resolving to give protection to those whose doctrine he had embraced.

But after the death of Ethelbert, the accession of his son Eadbald proved very prejudicial to the new church; for he not only refused to embrace the faith of Christ, but was also defiled with such a sort of fornication as the apostle testifies was not heard of, even among the Gentiles; for he kept his father's wife. By both which crimes he gave occasion to those to return to their former uncleanness, who, under his father, had, either for favour, or through fear of the king, submitted to the laws of faith and chastity. Nor did the perfidious king escape without Divine punishment and correction; for he was troubled with frequent fits of madness, and possessed by an evil spirit. This confusion was increased by the death of Sabert, king of the East-Saxons, who departing to the heavenly kingdom, left three sons, still pagans, to inherit his temporal crown. They immediately began to profess idolatry, which, during their father's reign, they had seemed a little to abandon, and they granted free liberty to the people under their government to serve idols.

III. *The Reign of King Edwin*

The nation of the Northumbrians, that is, the nation of the Angles that live on the north side of the river Humber, with their king, Edwin, received the faith through the preaching of Paulinus. This Edwin, as a reward of his receiving the faith, and as an earnest of his share in the heavenly kingdom, received an increase of that which he enjoyed on earth, for he reduced under his dominion all the borders of Britain that were provinces either of the aforesaid nation, or of the Britons, a thing which no British king had ever done before; and he in like manner subjected to the English the Mevanian islands. The first whereof, which is to the southward, is the largest in extent, and most fruitful, containing nine hundred and sixty families, according to the English computation; the other above three hundred.

The occasion of this nation's embracing the faith was, their aforesaid king, being allied to the kings of Kent, having taken to wife Ethelberga, otherwise called Tate, daughter to King Ethelbert. He having by his ambassadors asked her in marriage of her brother Eadbald, who then reigned in Kent, was answered, "That it was not lawful to marry a Christian virgin to a pagan husband, lest the faith and the mysteries of the heavenly King should be profaned by her cohabiting with a king that was altogether a stranger to the worship of the true God." This answer being brought to Edwin by his messengers, he promised in no manner to act in opposition to the Christian faith, which the virgin professed; but would give leave to her, and all that went with her, men or women, priests or ministers, to follow their faith and worship after the custom of the Christians. Nor did he deny but that he would embrace the same religion, if, being examined by wise persons, it should be found more holy and more worthy of God.

Hereupon the virgin was promised, and sent to Edwin, and pursuant to what had been agreed on, Paulinus, a man beloved of God, was ordained bishop, to go with her, and by daily exhortations, and celebrating the heavenly mysteries, to confirm her and her company, lest they should be corrupted by the company of the pagans. Paulinus was ordained bishop by the Archbishop Justus, on the 21st day of July, in the year of our Lord 625, and so he came to King Edwin with the aforesaid virgin as a companion of their union in the flesh. But his mind was wholly bent upon reducing the nation to which he was sent to the knowledge of truth; according to the words of the apostle, "To espouse her to one husband, that he might present her as a chaste virgin to Christ." Being come into that province, he laboured much, not only to retain those that went with him, by the help of God, that they should not revolt from the faith, but, if he could, to convert some of the pagans to a state of grace by his preaching. But, as the apostle says, though he laboured long in the word, "The god of this world blinded the minds of them that believed not, lest the light of the glorious Gospel of Christ should shine unto them."

The next year there came into the province a certain assassin, called Eumer, sent by the king of the West-Saxons, whose name was Cuichelm, in hopes at once to deprive King Edwin of his kingdom and his life. He had a two-edged dagger, dipped in poison, to the end that if the wound were not sufficient to kill the king it might be performed by the venom. He came to the king on the first day of Easter, at the river Derwent, where then stood the regal city, and being admitted as if to deliver a message from his master, whilst he was in an artful manner delivering his pretended embassy, he started on a sudden, and drawing the dagger from under his garment, assaulted the king; which Lilla, the king's beloved minister, observing, having no buckler at hand to secure the king from death, interposed his own body to receive the stroke; but the wretch struck so home, that he wounded the king through the knight's body. Being then attacked on all sides with swords, he in that confusion also slew another soldier, whose name was Forthhere.

On that same holy night of Easter Sunday, the queen had brought forth to the king a daughter, called Eanfled. The king, in the presence of Bishop Paulinus, gave thanks to his gods for the birth of his daughter; and the bishop, on the other hand, returned thanks to Christ, and endeavoured to persuade the king, that by his prayers to Him he had obtained that the queen should bring forth the child in safety, and without much pain. The king, delighted with his words, promised, that in case God would grant him life and victory over the king by whom the assassin had been sent, he would cast off his idols, and serve Christ; and as a pledge that he would perform his promise, he delivered up that same daughter to Paulinus, to be consecrated to Christ. She was the first baptized of the nation of the Northumbrians, on Whitsunday, with twelve others of her family. At that time, the king, being recovered of the wound which he had received, marched with his army against the nation of the West-Saxons; and having begun the war, either slew or subdued all those that he had been informed had conspired to murder him. Returning thus victorious unto his own country, he would not immediately and unadvisedly embrace the mysteries of the Christian faith, though he no longer worshipped idols, ever since he made the promise that he would serve Christ; but thought fit first at leisure to be instructed, by the venerable Paulinus, in the knowledge of faith, and to confer with such as he knew to be the wisest of his prime men, to advise what they thought was fittest to be done in that case. And being a man of extraordinary sagacity, he often sat alone by himself a long time, silent as to his tongue, but deliberating in his heart how he should proceed, and which religion he should adhere to.

IV. *King Edwin Is Persuaded by a Vision*

A heavenly vision, which the Divine Mercy was pleased once to reveal to this king, when he was in banishment at the court of Redwald, king of the Angles, was of no little use in urging him to embrace and understand the doctrines of salvation. Paulinus, therefore, perceiving that it was a very difficult task to incline the king's lofty mind to the humility of the way of salvation, and to embrace the mystery of the cross of life, and at the same time using both exhortation with men, and prayer to God, for his and his subjects' salvation; at length, as we may suppose, it was shown him in spirit what was the vision that had been formerly revealed to the king. Nor did he lose any time, but immediately admonished the king to perform the vow which he made, when he received the oracle, promising to put the same in execution, if he was delivered from the trouble he was at that time under, and should be advanced to the throne.

The king, hearing these words, answered that he was both willing and bound to receive the faith which he taught; but that he would confer about it with his principal friends and counsellers, to the end that if they also were of his opinion, they might all together be cleansed in Christ the Fountain of Life. Paulinus consenting, the king did as he said; for, holding a council with the wise men, he asked of every one in particular what he thought of the new doctrine, and the new worship that was preached?

One of the king's chief men, approving of his words and exhortations, presently added: "The present life of man, O king, seems to me, in comparison of that time which is unknown to us, like to the swift flight of a sparrow through the room wherein you sit at supper in winter, with your commanders and ministers, and a good fire in the midst, whilst the storms of rain and snow prevail abroad; the sparrow, I say, flying in at one door, and immediately out at another, whilst he is within, is safe from the wintry storm; but after a short space of fair weather, he immediately vanishes out of your sight, into the dark winter from which he had emerged. So this life of man appears for a short space, but of what went before, or what is to follow, we are utterly ignorant. If, therefore, this new doctrine contains something more certain, it seems justly to deserve to be followed." The other elders and king's councillors, by Divine inspiration, spoke to the same effect.

V. *King Edwin and His Nation Become Christians*

King Edwin, with all the nobility of the nation, and a large number of the common sort, received the faith, and the washing of regeneration, in the eleventh year of his reign, which is the year of the incarnation of our Lord 627, and about one hundred and eighty after the coming of the English into Britain. He was baptized at York, on the holy day of Easter, being the 12th of April, in the church of St. Peter the Apostle, which he himself had built of timber, whilst he was catechising and instructing in order to receive baptism. In that city also he appointed the see of the bishopric of his instructor and bishop, Paulinus. But as soon as he was baptized, he took care, by the direction of the same Paulinus, to build in the same place a larger and nobler church of stone, in the midst whereof that same oratory which he had first erected should be enclosed. Having therefore laid the foundation, he began to build the church square, encompassing the former oratory. But before the whole was raised to the proper height, the wicked assassination of the king left that work to be finished by Oswald his successor. Paulinus, for the space of six years from that time, that is, till the end of the reign of that king, by his consent and favour, preached the word of God in that country, and all that were pre-ordained to eternal life believed and were baptized. Among whom were Osfrid and Eadfrid, King Edwin's sons, who were both born to him, whilst he was in banishment, of Quenberga, the daughter of Cearl, king of the Mercians.

So great was then the fervour of the faith, as is reported, and the desire of the washing of salvation among the nation of the Northumbrians, that Paulinus at a certain time coming with the king and queen to the royal country-seat, which is called Adgefrin, stayed there with them thirty-six days, fully occupied in catechising and baptizing; during which days, from morning till night, he did nothing else but instruct the people resorting from all villages and places, in Christ's saving word; and when instructed, he washed them with the water of absolution in the river Glen, which is close by. This town, under the following kings, was abandoned, and another was built instead of it, at the place called Melmin.

VI. *Letters to the Scots concerning the Observance of Easter*

Pope Honorius wrote to the Scots [Irish], whom he had found to err in the observance of Easter, earnestly exhorting them not to think their small number wiser than all the ancient and modern churches of Christ, throughout the world; and not to celebrate a different Easter, contrary to the Paschal calculation, and the synodical decrees of all the bishops upon earth. Likewise John, who succeeded Severinus, successor to the same Honorius, being yet but pope elect, sent to them letters of great authority and erudition for correcting the same error; evidently showing that Easter Sunday is to be found between the fifteenth moon and the twenty-first, as was proved in the Council of Nice. He also in the same epistle admonished them to be careful to crush the Pelagian heresy, which he had been informed was reviving among them.

VII. *Edwin Being Slain, Paulinus Returns into Kent*

Edwin reigned most gloriously seventeen years over the nations of the English and the Britons, six whereof, as has been said, he also was a servant in the kingdom of Christ. Cadwalla, king of the Britons, rebelled against him, being supported by Penda, a most warlike man of the royal race of the Mercians, and who from that time governed that nation twenty-two years with various success. A great battle being fought in the plain that is called Heathfield, Edwin was killed on the 12th of October, in the year of our Lord 633, being then forty-seven years of age, and all his army was either slain or dispersed. In the same war also, before him, fell Osfrid, one of his sons, a warlike youth; Eanfrid, another of them, compelled by necessity, went over to King Penda, and was by him afterwards, in the reign of Oswald, slain, contrary to his oath. At this time a great slaughter was made in the church or nation of the Northumbrians; and the more so because one of the commanders, by whom it was made, was a pagan, and the other a barbarian, more cruel than a pagan; for Penda, with all the nation of the Mercians, was an idolater, and a stranger to the name of Christ; but Cadwalla, though he bore the name and professed himself a Christian, was so barbarous in his disposition and behaviour, that he neither spared the female sex, nor the innocent age of children, but with savage cruelty put them to tormenting deaths, ravaging all their country for a long time, and resolving to cut off all the race of the English within the borders of Britain. Nor did he pay any respect to the Christian religion which had newly taken root among them; it being to this day the custom of the Britons not to pay any respect to the faith and religion of the English, nor to correspond with them any more than with pagans. King Edwin's head was brought to York, and afterwards into the church of St. Peter the Apostle, which he had begun, but which his successor Oswald finished, as has been said before. It was deposited in the porch of St. Gregory, Pope, from whose disciples he had received the word of life.

The affairs of the Northumbrians being in confusion, by reason of this disaster, without any prospect of safety except in flight, Paulinus, taking with him Queen Ethelberga, whom he had before brought thither, returned into Kent by sea, and was honourably received by the Archbishop Honorius and King Eadbald.

BOOK THREE

I. How Edwin's Successors Lost Both Faith and Kingdom

EDWIN being slain in battle, the kingdom of the Deira, to which province his family belonged, and where he first began to reign, devolved on Osric, the son of his uncle Elfric, who, through the preaching of Paulinus, had also received the faith. But the kingdom of the Bernicians—for into these two provinces the nation of the Northumbrians was formerly divided—was possessed by Eanfrid, the son of Ethelfrid, who derived his origin from the royal family of that province. For all the time that Edwin reigned, the sons of the aforesaid Ethelfrid, who had reigned before him, with many of the nobility, lived in banishment among the Scots or Picts, and were there instructed according to the doctrine of the Scots, and received the grace of baptism. Upon the death of the king, their enemy, they returned home, and Eanfrid, as the eldest of them, mentioned above, became king of the Bernicians. Both those kings, as soon as they obtained the government of their earthly kingdoms, renounced and lost the faith of the heavenly kingdom, and again delivered themselves up to be defiled by the abominations of their former idols.

But soon after, the king of the Britons, Cadwalla, slew them both, through the rightful vengeance of Heaven, though the act was base in him. He first slew Osric, the next summer; for, being besieged by him in a strong town, he sallied out on a sudden with all his forces, by surprise, and destroyed him and all his army. After this, for the space of a year, he reigned over the provinces of the Northumbrians, not like a victorious king, but like a rapacious and bloody tyrant, and at length brought to the same end Eanfrid, who unadvisedly came to him with only twelve chosen soldiers, to sue for peace. To this day, that year is looked upon as unhappy, and hateful to all good men; as well on account of the apostasy of the English kings, who had renounced the faith, as of the outrageous tyranny of the British king. Hence it has been agreed by all who have written about the reigns of the kings, to abolish the memory of those perfidious monarchs, and to assign that year to the reign of the following king, Oswald, a man beloved by God. This last king, after the death of his brother Eanfrid, advanced with an army, small, indeed, in number, but strengthened with the faith of Christ; and the impious commander of the Britons was slain, though he had most numerous forces, which he boasted nothing could withstand, at a place in the English tongue called Denisesburn, that is, Denis's-brook.

II. King Oswald, Asking a Bishop of the Scottish Nation, Had Aidan Sent Him

The same Oswald, as soon as he ascended the throne, being desirous that all his nation should receive the Christian faith, whereof he had found happy experience in vanquishing the barbarians, sent to the elders of the Scots, among whom himself and his followers, when in banishment, had received the sacrament of baptism, desiring they would send him a bishop, by whose instruction and ministry the English nation, which he governed, might be taught the advantages, and receive the sacraments of the Christian faith. Nor were they slow in granting his request; but sent him Bishop Aidan, a man of singular meekness, piety, and moderation; zealous in the cause of God, though not altogether according to knowledge; for he was wont to keep Easter Sunday according to the custom of his country, which we have before so often mentioned, from the fourteenth to the twentieth moon; the northern province of the Scots, and all the nation of the Picts, celebrating Easter then after that manner, and believing that they therein followed the writings of the holy and praiseworthy Father Anatolius; the truth of which every skilful person can discern. But the Scots which dwelt in the South of Ireland had long since, by the admonition of the bishop of the Apostolic See, learned to observe Easter according to the canonical custom.

On the arrival of the bishop, the king appointed him his episcopal see in the isle of Lindisfarne, as he desired. Which place, as the tide flows and ebbs twice a day, is enclosed by the waves of the sea like an island; and again, twice in the day, when the shore is left dry, becomes contiguous to the land. The king also humbly and willingly in all cases giving ear to his admonitions, industriously applied himself to build and extend the church of Christ in his kingdom; wherein, when the bishop, who was not skilful in the English tongue, preached the gospel, it was most delightful to see the king himself interpreting the word of God to his commanders and ministers, for he had perfectly learned the language of the Scots during his long banishment. From that time many of the Scots came daily into Britain, and with great devotion preached the word to those provinces of the English, over which King Oswald reigned, and those among them that had received priest's orders, administered to them the grace of baptism. Churches were built in several places; the people joyfully flocked together to hear the word; money and lands were given of the king's bounty to build monasteries; the English, great and small, were, by their Scottish masters, instructed in the rules and observance of regular discipline; for most of them that came to preach were monks. Bishop Aidan was himself a monk of the island called Hii, whose monastery was for a long time the chief of almost all those of the northern Scots, and all those of the Picts, and had the direction of their people. That island belongs to Britain, being divided from it by a small arm of the sea, but had been long since given by the Picts, who inhabit those parts of Britain, to the Scottish monks, because they had received the faith of Christ through their preaching.

III. *When the Nation of the Picts Received the Faith*

In the year of our Lord 565, when Justin, the younger, the successor of Justinian, had the government of the Roman empire, there came into Britain a famous priest and abbat, a monk by habit and life, whose name was Columba, to preach the word of God to the provinces of the northern Picts, who are separated from the southern parts by steep and rugged mountains; for the southern Picts, who dwell on this side of those mountains, had long before, as is reported, forsaken the errors of idolatry, and embraced the truth, by the preaching of Ninias, a most reverend bishop and holy man of the British nation, who had been regularly instructed at Rome, in the faith and mysteries of the truth; whose episcopal see, named after St. Martin the bishop, and famous for a stately church (wherein he and many other saints rest in the body), is still in existence among the

English nation. The place belongs to the province of the Bernicians, and is generally called the White House, because he there built a church of stone, which was not usual among the Britons.

Columba came into Britain in the ninth year of the reign of Bridius who was the son of Meilochon, and the powerful king of the Pictish nation, and he converted that nation to the faith of Christ, by his preaching and example, whereupon he also received of them the aforesaid island for a monastery, for it is not very large, but contains about five families, according to the English computation. His successors hold the island to this day; he was also buried therein, having died at the age of seventy-seven, about thirty-two years after he came into Britain to preach. Before he passed over into Britain, he had built a noble monastery in Ireland, which, from the great number of oaks, is in the Scottish tongue called Dearmach—The Field of Oaks. From both which monasteries, many others had their beginning through his disciples, both in Britain and Ireland; but the monastery in the island where his body lies, is the principal of them all.

That island has for its ruler an abbat, who is a priest, to whose direction all the province, and even the bishops, contrary to the usual method, are subject, according to the example of their first teacher, who was not a bishop, but a priest and monk; of whose life and discourses some writings are said to be preserved by his disciples. But whatsoever he was himself, this we know for certain, that he left successors renowned for their continency, their love of God, and observance of monastic rules. It is true they followed uncertain rules in their observance of the great festival, as having none to bring them the synodal decrees for the observance of Easter, by reason of their being so far away from the rest of the world; wherefore they only practised such works of piety and chastity as they could learn from the prophetical, evangelical, and apostolical writings. This manner of keeping Easter continued among them for the space of 150 years, till the year of our Lord's incarnation 715.

IV.   How the Controversy Arose about the Due Time of Keeping Easter

In the meantime, Bishop Aidan being dead, Finan, who was ordained and sent by the Scots, succeeded him in the bishopric, and built a church in the Isle of Lindisfarne, the episcopal see; nevertheless, after the manner of the Scots, he made it, not of stone, but of hewn oak, and covered it with reeds; and the same was afterwards dedicated in honour of St. Peter the Apostle, by the reverend Archbishop Theodore. Eadbert, also bishop of that place, took off the thatch, and covered it, both roof and walls, with plates of lead.

At this time, a great and frequent controversy happened about the observance of Easter; those that came from Kent or France affirming that the Scots kept Easter Sunday contrary to the custom of the universal church. Among them was a most zealous defender of the true Easter, whose name was Ronan, a Scot by nation, but instructed in ecclesiastical truth, either in France or Italy, who, disputing with Finan, convinced many, or at least induced them to make a more strict inquiry after the truth; yet he could not prevail upon Finan, but, on the contrary, made him the more inveterate by reproof, and a professed opposer of the truth, being of a hot and violent temper. James, formerly the deacon of the venerable Archbishop Paulinus, kept the true and Catholic Easter, with all those that he could persuade to adopt the right way. Queen Eanfleda and her followers also observed the same as she had seen practised in Kent, having with her a Kentish priest that followed the Catholic mode, whose name was Romanus. Thus it is said to have happened in those times that Easter was twice kept in one year; and that when the king having ended the time of fasting, kept his Easter, the queen and her followers were still fasting, and celebrating Palm Sunday. This difference about the observance of Easter, whilst Aidan lived, was patiently tolerated by all men, as being sensible, that though he could not keep Easter contrary to the custom of those who had sent him, yet he industriously laboured to practise all works of faith, piety, and love, according to the custom of all holy men; for which reason he was deservedly beloved by all; even by those who differed in opinion concerning Easter, and was held in veneration, not only by indifferent persons, but even by the bishops, Honorius of Canterbury, and Felix of the East Angles.

But after the death of Finan, who succeeded him, when Colman, who was also sent out of Scotland, came to be bishop, a greater controversy arose about the observance of Easter, and the rules of ecclesiastical life. Whereupon this dispute began naturally to influence the thoughts and hearts of many, who feared, lest having received the name of Christians, they might happen to run, or to have run, in vain. This reached the ears of King Oswy and his son Alfrid; for Oswy, having been instructed and baptized by the Scots, and being very perfectly skilled in their language, thought nothing better than what they taught. But Alfrid, having been instructed in Christianity by Wilfrid, a most learned man, who had first gone to Rome to learn the ecclesiastical doctrine, and spent much time at Lyons with Dalfin, archbishop of France, from whom also he had received the ecclesiastical tonsure, rightly thought this man's doctrine ought to be preferred before all the traditions of the Scots. For this reason he had also given him a monastery of forty families, at a place called Rhypum; which place, not long before, he had given to those that followed the system of the Scots for a monastery; but for as much as they afterwards, being left to their choice, prepared to quit the place rather than alter their opinion, he gave the place to him, whose life and doctrine were worthy of it.

Agilbert, bishop of the West Saxons, above-mentioned, a friend to King Alfrid and to Abbat Wilfrid, had at that time come into the province of the Northumbrians, and was making some stay among them; at the request of Alfrid, made Wilfrid a priest in his monastery. He had in his company a priest, whose name was Agatho. The controversy being there started, concerning Easter, or the tonsure, or other ecclesiastical affairs, it was agreed that a synod should be held in the monastery of Streaneshalch, which signifies the Bay of the Lighthouse, where the Abbess Hilda, a woman devoted to God, then presided; and that there this controversy should be decided. The kings, both father and son, came thither, Bishop Colman with his Scottish clerks, and Agilbert with the priests Agatho and Wilfrid, James and Romanus were on their side; but the Abbess Hilda and her followers were for the Scots, as was also the venerable Bishop Cedd, long before ordained by the Scots, as has been said above, and he was in that council a most careful interpreter for both parties.

King Oswy first observed, that it behoved those who served one God to observe the same rule of life; and as they all expected the same kingdom in heaven, so they ought not to differ in the celebration of the Divine mysteries; but rather to inquire which was the truest tradition, that the same might be followed by all; he then commanded his bishop, Colman, first to declare what the custom was which he observed, and whence it derived its origin. Then Colman said, "The Easter which I keep, I received from my elders, who sent me bishop hither; all our forefathers, men beloved of God, are known to have kept it after the same manner; and that the same may not seem to any contemptible or worthy to be rejected, it is the same which St. John the Evangelist, the disciple beloved of our Lord, with all the churches over which he presided, is recorded to have observed." Having said thus much, and more to the like effect, the king commanded Agilbert to show whence his custom of keeping Easter was derived, or on what authority it was grounded. Agilbert answered, "I desire that my disciple, the priest Wilfrid, may speak in my stead; because we both concur with the other followers of the ecclesiastical tradition that are here present, and he can better explain our opinion in the English language, than I can by an interpreter."

Then Wilfrid, being ordered by the king to speak, delivered himself thus:—"The Easter which we observe, we saw celebrated by all at Rome, where the blessed apostles, Peter and Paul, lived, taught, suffered, and were buried; we saw the same done in Italy and in France, when we travelled through those countries for pilgrimage and prayer. We found the same practised in Africa, Asia, Egypt, Greece, and all the world, wherever the church of Christ is spread abroad, through several nations and tongues, at one and the same time; except only these and their accomplices in obstinacy, I mean the Picts and the Britons, who foolishly, in these two remote islands of the world, and only in part even of them, oppose all the rest of the universe." When he had so said, Colman answered, "It is strange that you will call our labours foolish, wherein we follow the example of so great an apostle, who was thought worthy to lay his head on our Lord's bosom, when all the world knows him to have lived most wisely." Wilfrid replied, "Far be it from us to charge John with folly, for he literally observed the precepts of the Jewish law, whilst the church still Judaized in many points, and the apostles were not able at once to cast off all the observances of the law which had been instituted by God. In which way it is necessary that all who come to the faith should forsake the idols which were invented by devils, that they might not give scandal to the Jews that were among the Gentiles. For this reason it was that Paul circumcised Timothy, that he offered sacrifice in the temple, that he shaved his head with Aquila and Priscilla at Corinth; for no other advantage than to avoid giving scandal to the Jews. Hence it was that James said, to the same Paul, 'You see, brother, how many thousands of the Jews have believed; and they are all zealous for the law. And yet, at this time, the Gospel spreading throughout the world, it is needless, nay, it is not lawful, for the faithful either to be circumcised, or to offer up to God sacrifices of flesh.' So John, pursuant to the custom of the law, began the celebration of the feast of Easter, on the fourteenth day of the first month, in the evening, not regarding whether the same happened on a Saturday, or any other day. But when Peter preached at Rome, being mindful that our Lord arose from the dead, and gave the world the hopes of resurrection, on the first day after the Sabbath, he understood that Easter ought to be observed, so as always to stay till the rising of the moon on the fourteenth day of the first moon, in the evening, according to the custom and precepts of the law, even as John did. And when that came, if the Lord's day, then called the first day after the Sabbath, was the next day, he began that very evening to keep Easter, as we all do at this day. But if the Lord's day did not fall the next morning after the fourteenth moon, but on the sixteenth, or the seventeenth, or any other moon till the twenty-first, he waited for that, and on the Saturday before, in the evening, began to observe the holy solemnity of Easter. Thus it came to pass, that Easter Sunday was only kept from the fifteenth moon to the twenty-first. Nor does this evangelical and apostolic tradition abolish the law, but rather fulfil it; the command being to keep the passover from the fourteenth moon of the first month in the evening to the twenty-first moon of the same month in the evening; which observance all the successors of St. John in Asia, since his death, and all the church throughout the world, have since followed; and that this is the true Easter, and the only one to be kept by the faithful, was not newly decreed by the council of Nice, but only confirmed afresh; as the Church History informs us.

"Thus it appears, that you, Colman, neither follow the example of John, as you imagine, nor that of Peter, whose traditions you knowingly contradict; and that you neither agree with the law nor the Gospel in the keeping of your Easter. For John, keeping the Paschal time according to the decree of the Mosaic law, had no regard to the first day after the Sabbath, which you do not practise, who celebrate Easter only on the first day after the Sabbath. Peter kept Easter Sunday between the fifteenth and the twenty-first moon, which you do not, but keep Easter Sunday from the fourteenth to the twentieth moon; so that you often begin Easter on the thirteenth moon in the evening, whereof neither the law made any men-tion, nor did our Lord, the Author and Giver of the Gospel, on that day, but on the fourteenth, either eat the old passover in the evening, or deliver the sacraments of the New Testament, to be celebrated by the church, in memory of his passion. Besides, in your celebration of Easter, you utterly exclude the twenty-first moon, which the law ordered to be principally observed. Thus, as I said before, you agree neither with John nor Peter, nor with the law, nor the Gospel, in the celebration of the greatest festival.

"But as for you and your companions, you certainly sin, if, having heard the decrees of the Apostolic See, and of the universal church, and that the same is confirmed by holy writ, you refuse to follow them; for, though your fathers were holy, do you think that their small number, in a corner of the remotest island, is to be preferred before the universal church of Christ throughout the world? And if that Columba of yours (and, I may say, ours also, if he was Christ's servant), was a holy man and powerful in miracles, yet could he be preferred before the most blessed prince of the apostles, to whom our Lord said, 'Thou art Peter, and upon this rock I will build my church, and the gates of hell shall not prevail against it, and to thee I will give the keys of the kingdom of heaven?' "

When Wilfrid had spoken thus, the king said, "Is it true, Colman, that these words were spoken to Peter by our Lord?" He answered, "It is true, O king!" Then says he, "Can you show any such power given to your Columba?" Colman answered, "None." Then added the king, "Do you both agree that these words were principally directed to Peter, and that the keys of heaven were given to him by our Lord?" They both answered, "We do." Then the king concluded, "And I also say unto you, that he is the door-keeper, whom I will not contradict, but will, as far as I know and am able, in all things obey his decrees, lest, when I come to the gates of the kingdom of heaven, there should be none to open them, he being my adversary who is proved to have the keys." The king having said this, all present, both great and small, gave their assent, and renouncing the more imperfect institution, resolved to conform to that which they found to be better.

BOOK FOUR

A Brother on Whom the Gift of Writing Verses Was Bestowed by Heaven

THERE was a certain brother, particularly remarkable for the grace of God, who was wont to make pious and religious verses, so that whatever was interpreted to him out of Scripture, he soon after put the same into poetical expressions of much sweetness and humility, in English, which was his native language. By his verses the minds of many were often excited to despise the world, and to aspire to heaven. Others after him attempted, in the English nation, to compose religious poems, but none could ever compare with him, for he did not learn the art of poetry from men, but from God; for which reason he never could compose any trivial or vain poem, but only those which relate to religion suited his religious tongue; for having lived in a secular habit till he was well advanced in years, he had never learned anything of versifying; for which reason being sometimes at entertainments, when it was agreed for the sake of mirth that all present should sing in their turns, when he saw the instrument come towards him, he rose up from table and returned home.

Having done so at a certain time, and gone out of the house where the entertainment was, to the stable, where he had to take care of the horses that night, he there composed himself to rest at the proper time; a person appeared to him in his sleep, and saluting him by his name, said, "Caedmon, sing some song to me." He answered, "I cannot sing; for that was the reason why I left the entertainment, and retired to this place because I could not sing." The other who talked to him, replied, "However, you shall sing."—"What shall I sing?" rejoined he. "Sing the beginning of created beings," said the other. Hereupon he presently began to sing verses to the praise of God, which he had never heard, the purport whereof was thus:—We are now to praise the Maker of the heavenly kingdom, the power of the Creator and his counsel, the deeds of the Father of glory. How He, being the eternal God, became the author of all miracles, who first, as almighty preserver of the human race, created heaven for the sons of men as the roof of the house, and next the earth. This is the sense, but not the words in order as he sang them in his sleep; for verses, though never so well composed, cannot be literally translated out of one language into another, without losing much of their beauty and loftiness. Awaking from his sleep, he remembered all that he had sung in his dream, and soon added much more to the same effect in verse worthy of the Deity.

In the morning he came to the steward, his superior, and having acquainted him with the gift he had received, was conducted to the abbess, by whom he was ordered, in the presence of many learned men, to tell his dream, and repeat the verses, that they might all give their judgment what it was, and whence his verse proceeded. They all concluded, that heavenly grace had been conferred on him by our Lord. They expounded to him a passage in holy writ, either historical, or doctrinal, ordering him, if he could, to put the same into verse. Having undertaken it, he went away, and returning the next morning, gave it to them composed in most excellent verse; whereupon the abbess, embracing the grace of God in the man, instructed him to quit the secular habit, and take upon him the monastic life; which being accordingly done, she associated him to the rest of the brethren in her monastery, and ordered that he should be taught the whole series of sacred history. Thus Caedmon, keeping in mind all he heard, and as it were chewing the cud, converted the same into most harmonious verse; and sweetly repeating the same, made his masters in their turn his hearers. He sang the creation of the world, the origin of man, and all the history of Genesis: and made many verses on the departure of the children of Israel out of Egypt, and their entering into the land of promise, with many other histories from holy writ; the incarnation, passion, resurrection of our Lord, and his ascension into heaven; the coming of the Holy Ghost, and the preaching of the apostles; also the terror of future judgment, the horror of the pains of hell, and the delights of heaven; besides many more about the Divine benefits and judgments, by which he endeavoured to turn away all men from the love of vice, and to excite in them the love of, and application to, good actions; for he was a very religious man, humbly submissive to regular discipline, but full of zeal against those who behaved themselves otherwise; for which reason he ended his life happily.

For when the time of his departure drew near, he laboured for the space of fourteen days under a bodily infirmity which seemed to prepare the way, yet so moderate that he could talk and walk the whole time. In his neighbourhood was the house to which those that were sick, and like shortly to die, were carried. He desired the person that attended him, in the evening, as the night came on in which he was to depart this life, to make ready a place there for him to take his rest. This person, wondering why he should desire it, because there was as yet no sign of his dying soon, did what he had ordered. He accordingly went there, and conversing pleasantly in a joyful manner with the rest that were in the house before, when it was past midnight, he asked them, whether they had the Eucharist there? They answered, "What need of the Eucharist? for you are not likely to die, since you talk so merrily with us, as if you were in perfect health."—"However," said he, "bring me the Eucharist." Having received the same into his hand, he asked whether they were all in charity with him, and without any enmity or rancour? They answered that they were all in perfect charity, and free from anger; and in their turn asked him whether he was in the same mind towards them? He answered, "I am in charity, my children, with all the servants of God." Then strengthening himself with the heavenly viaticum, he prepared for the entrance into another life, and asked how near the time was when the brothers were to be awakened to sing the nocturnal praises of our Lord? They answered, "It is not far off." Then he said, "Well, let us wait that hour;" and signing himself with the sign of the cross, he laid his head on the pillow, and falling into a slumber, ended his life so in silence.

Thus it came to pass, that as he had served God with a simple and pure mind, and undisturbed devotion, so he now departed to his presence, leaving the world by a quiet death; and that tongue, which had composed so many holy words in praise of the Creator, uttered its last words whilst he was in the act of signing himself with the cross, and recommending himself into his hands, and by what has been here said, he seems to have had foreknowledge of his death.

BOOK FIVE

I. *Several Churches of the Scots Conformed to the Catholic Easter*

AT THIS TIME [A.D. 703] a great part of the Scots in Ireland, and some also of the Britons in Britain, through the goodness of God, conformed to the proper and ecclesiastical time of keeping Easter. Adamnan, priest and abbat of the monks that were in the isle of Hii, was sent ambassador by his nation to Alfrid, king of the English, where he made some stay, observing the canonical rites of the church, and was earnestly admonished by many, who were more learned than himself, not to presume to live contrary to the universal custom of the Church, either in relation to the observance of Easter, or any other decrees whatsoever, considering the small number of his followers, seated in so distant a corner of the world; in consequence of this he changed his mind, and readily preferred those things which he had seen and heard in the English churches, to the customs which he and his people had hitherto followed. For he was a good and wise man, and remarkably learned in Holy Scripture. Returning home, he endeavoured to bring his own people that were in the isle of Hii, or that were subject to that monastery, into the way of truth, which he had learned and embraced with all his heart; but in this he could not prevail. He then sailed over into Ireland, to preach to those people, and by modestly declaring the legal time of Easter, he reduced many of them, and almost all that were not under the dominion of those of Hii, to the Catholic unity, and taught them to keep the legal time of Easter.

Returning to his island, after having celebrated the canonical Easter in Ireland, he most earnestly inculcated the observance of the Catholic time of Easter in his monastery, yet without being able to prevail; and it so happened that he departed this life before the next year came round, the Divine goodness so ordaining it, that as he was a great lover of peace and unity, he should be taken away to everlasting life before he should be obliged, on the return of the time of Easter, to quarrel still more seriously with those that would not follow him in the truth.

This same person wrote a book about the holy places, most useful to many readers; his authority, from whom he procured his information, was Arculf, a French bishop, who had gone to Jerusalem for the sake of the holy places; and having seen all the Land of Promise, travelled to Damascus, Constantinople, Alexandria, and many islands, and returning home by sea, was by a violent storm forced upon the western coast of Britain. After many other accidents, he came to the aforesaid servant of Christ, Adamnan, who, finding him to be learned in the Scriptures, and acquainted with the holy places, entertained him zealously, and attentively gave ear to him, in so much that he presently committed to writing all that Arculf said he had seen remarkable in the holy places. Thus he composed a work beneficial to many, and particularly to those who, being far removed from those places where the patriarchs and apostles lived, know no more of them than what they learn by reading. Adamnan presented this book to King Alfrid, and through his bounty it came to be read by lesser persons.

II. *The Present State of the English Nation*

In the year of our Lord's incarnation 725, being the seventh year of Osric, king of the Northumbrians, who succeeded Coenred, Wictred, the son of Egbert, king of Kent, died on the 23rd of April, and left his three sons, Ethelbert, Eadbert, and Alric, heirs of that kingdom, which he had governed thirty-four years and a half. The next year died Tobias, bishop of the church of Rochester, a most learned man, disciple to those teachers of blessed memory, Theodore, the archbishop, and Abbat Hadrian, by which means, besides his erudition in ecclesiastical and general literature, he learned both the Greek and Latin tongues to such perfection, that they were as well known and familiar to him as his native language. He was buried in the porch of St. Paul the Apostle, which he had built within the church of St. Andrew for his own place of burial. After him Aldwulf took upon him the office of bishop, having been consecrated by Archbishop Bertwald.

In the year of our Lord's incarnation 729, two comets appeared about the sun, to the great terror of the beholders. One of them went before the rising sun in the morning, the other followed him when he set at night, as it were presaging much destruction to the east and west; one was the forerunner of the day, and the other of the night, to signify that mortals were threatened with calamities at both times. They carried their flaming tails towards the north, as it were ready to set the world on fire. They appeared in January, and continued nearly a fortnight. At which time a dreadful plague of Saracens ravaged France with miserable slaughter; but they not long after in that country received the punishment due to their wickedness. In which year the holy man of God, Egbert, departed to our Lord on Easter day; and immediately after Easter, that is, on the 9th of May, Osric, king of the Northumbrians, departed this life, after he had reigned eleven years, and appointed Ceolwulf, brother to Coenred, who had reigned before him, his successor; the beginning and progress of whose reign were so filled with commotions, that it cannot yet be known what is to be said concerning them, or what end they will have.

In the year of our Lord's incarnation 731, Archbishop Bertwald died of old age, on the 9th of January, having held his see thirty-seven years, six months and fourteen days. In his stead, the same year, Tatwine, of the province of the Mercians, was made archbishop, having been a priest in the monastery called Briudun. He was consecrated in the city of Canterbury by the venerable men, Daniel, bishop of Winchester, Ingwald of London, Aldwin of Lichfield, and Aldwulf of Rochester, on Sunday, the

10th of June, being a man renowned for religion and wisdom, and notably learned in Sacred Writ.

Thus at present, the bishops Tatwine and Aldwulf preside in the churches of Kent; Ingwald in the province of the East Saxons. In the province of the East Angles, Aldbert and Hadulac are bishops; in the province of the West Saxons, Daniel and Forthere are bishops; in the province of the Mercians, Aldwin. Among those people who live beyond the river Severn to the westward, Walstod is bishop; in the province of the Wiccians, Wilfrid; in the province of the Lindisfarnes, Cynebert presides: the bishopric of the Isle of Wight belongs to Daniel, bishop of Winchester. The province of the South Saxons, having now continued some years without a bishop, receives the episcopal ministry from the prelate of the West Saxons. All these provinces, and the others southward to the bank of the river Humber, with their kings, are subject to King Ethelbald.

But in the province of the Northumbrians, where King Ceolwulf reigns, four bishops now preside: Wilfrid in the church of York, Ethelwald in that of Lindisfarne, Acca in that of Hagulstad, Pechthelm in that which is called the White House, which, from the increased number of believers, has lately become an episcopal see, and has him for its first prelate. The Picts also at this time are at peace with the English nation, and rejoice in being united in peace and truth with the whole Catholic Church. The Scots that inhabit Britain, satisfied with their own territories, meditate no hostilities against the nation of the English. The Britons, though they, for the most part, through innate hatred, are adverse to the English nation, and wrongfully, and from wicked custom, oppose the appointed Easter of the whole Catholic Church; yet, from both the Divine and human power withstanding them, can in no way prevail as they desire; for though in part they are their own masters, yet elsewhere they are also brought under subjection to the English. Such being the peaceable and calm disposition of the times, many of the Northumbrians, as well of the nobility as private persons, laying aside their weapons, rather incline to dedicate both themselves and their children to the tonsure and monastic vows, than to study martial discipline. What will be the end hereof, the next age will show. This is for the present the state of all Britain; in the year since the coming of the English into Britain about 285, but in the 731st year of the incarnation of our Lord, in whose reign may the earth ever rejoice; may Britain exult in the profession of His faith; and may many islands be glad, and sing praises in honour of His holiness!

THE HISTORY OF ENGLAND FROM THE ACCESSION OF JAMES THE SECOND

by

THOMAS BABINGTON MACAULAY

CONTENTS

THOMAS BABINGTON MACAULAY

1800–1859

THOMAS BABINGTON MACAULAY was a child prodigy who remained a prodigy. Before he was eight years old he had written a *Compendium of Universal History* and a romance in three cantos, *The Battle of Cheviot*. His mind became a storehouse of readily accessible information—a fact which in part accounts for his brilliance as a conversationalist in later life. It has been remarked that it was as difficult for Macaulay to forget as for the ordinary man to remember. To pass the time while traveling he sometimes would run through a book he had read from beginning to end from memory. He once remarked that if every copy of *Pilgrim's Progress, Paradise Lost,* and *The History of Sir Charles Grandison* were destroyed he could reproduce them from memory.

From a private school Macaulay entered Trinity College, Cambridge, in 1818. In the course of his university career he carried off a number of prizes in literary and declamatory competitions. From his earliest years he seems to have possessed a special faculty for commanding attention. His first public speech, made in 1824 at an anti-slavery meeting, was prominently noticed by the *Edinburgh Review*. An essay on Milton, published the following year in the same review, established his literary reputation. His brilliance as a conversationalist brought him into contact with, and won him the admiration of, the most distinguished personages of the day.

However, the failure of his father's company, Babington and Macaulay, confronted the brilliant young man with the necessity for earning a living. In 1830 he entered Parliament representing the pocket borough of Calne, which was offered him by Lord Lansdowne. Macaulay came prominently to the fore in an eloquent support of the Reform Bill. His defense of the Government of India Bill won him a seat in the Supreme

Council of India created by the new act at a salary of ten thousand pounds a year. His Indian policy was governed by liberal principles—support of freedom of the press and equality of natives and Europeans before the law. He inaugurated a system of national education for India, and his draft became the basis of the Indian penal code. In 1838 Macaulay returned to England and re-entered Parliament. The following year he became a member of the Cabinet as Secretary for War.

In 1847 Macaulay retired from public life in order to devote his principal energies to the great historical work which long had occupied his thoughts. This was to have been a grandly conceived history of England from the accession of James II to Macaulay's own day. It was to be much more than a political history, for in addition to disclosing the progress of government Macaulay sought "to trace the progress of useful and ornamental arts, to describe the rise of religious sects and the change of literary taste, to portray the manners of successive generations." However, it became clear upon the appearance of the first volume in 1847 that Macaulay's treatment of his subject was so detailed that the projected work could not be completed in his lifetime. When Macaulay died twelve years later, in 1859, the five volumes completed covered but sixteen years of English history from 1685 to 1701.

Macaulay's *History of England* was written to appeal to a wide public. The author sought to make every sentence flow smoothly and to end every paragraph with a telling sentence. The attention and enjoyment of the reader were not to be checked by any necessity for pondering the meaning of a phrase or a sentence. In his narration he does not stop to weigh pros and cons, to debate the exact significance of an event. He is sure of himself and his confidence assures the reader. Macaulay was not a trained historian although widely read and possessed of a capacious memory. He heightens contrasts, simplifies and exaggerates character in the interest of literary and dramatic effect. But his work is readable, enjoyable. Many read Macaulay who had never previously read a history book. The general reader was not disturbed by exaggerations which facilitated his grasp of the whole. Despite its defects the *History of England* is a monument of erudition, painstaking research, and literary genius.

THE HISTORY OF ENGLAND FROM THE ACCESSION OF JAMES THE SECOND

I. THE RESTORATION OF THE MONARCHY UNDER CHARLES THE SECOND

THE history of England, during the seventeenth century, is the history of the transformation of a limited monarchy, constituted after the fashion of the middle ages, into a limited monarchy suited to that more advanced state of society in which the public charges can no longer be borne by the estates of the crown, and in which the public defence can no longer be entrusted to a feudal militia. The politicians who were at the head of the Long Parliament made, in 1642, a great effort to accomplish this change by transferring, directly and formally, to the Estates of the realm the choice of ministers, the command of the army, and the superintendence of the whole executive administration. This scheme was, perhaps, the best that could then be contrived: but it was completely disconcerted by the course which the civil war took. The Houses [of Parliament] triumphed, it is true; but not till after such a struggle as made it necessary for them to call into existence a power which they could not control, and which soon began to domineer over all orders and all parties. For a time, the evils inseparable from military government were, in some degree, mitigated by the wisdom and magnanimity of the great man [Oliver Cromwell] who held the supreme command. But, when the sword which he had wielded, with energy indeed, but with energy always guided by good sense and generally tempered by good nature, had passed to captains who possessed neither his abilities nor his virtues, it seemed too probable that order and liberty would perish in one ignominious ruin.

That ruin was happily averted. It has been too much the practice of writers zealous for freedom to represent the Restoration as a disastrous event, and to condemn the folly or baseness of that Convention which recalled the royal family without exacting new securities against maladministration. Those who hold this language do not comprehend the real nature of the crisis which followed the deposition of Richard Cromwell. England was in imminent danger of sinking under the tyranny of a succession of small men raised up and pulled down by military caprice. To deliver the country from the domination of the soldiers was the first object of every enlightened patriot: but it was an object which, while the soldiers were united, the most sanguine could scarcely expect to attain. On a sudden a gleam of hope appeared. General was opposed to general, army to army. On the use which might be made of one auspicious moment depended the future destiny of the nation. Our ancestors used that moment well. They forgot old injuries, waived petty scruples, adjourned to a more convenient season all dispute about the reforms which our institutions needed, and stood together, Cavaliers and Roundheads, Episcopalians and Presbyterians, in firm union, for the old laws of the land against military despotism. The exact partition of power among King, Lords, and Commons, might well be postponed till it had been decided whether England should be governed by King, Lords, and Commons, or by cuirassiers and pikemen. Had the statesmen of the Convention taken a different course, had they held long debates on the principles of government, had they drawn up a new constitution and sent it to Charles [the Second], had conferences been opened, had couriers been passing and repassing during some weeks between Westminster and the Netherlands, with projects and counterprojects, the coalition on which the public safety depended would have been dissolved: the Presbyterians and Royalists would certainly have quarrelled: the military factions might possibly have been reconciled: and the misjudging friends of liberty might long have regretted, under a rule worse than that of the worst Stuart, the golden opportunity which had been suffered to escape.

The old civil polity was, therefore, by the general consent of both the great parties, re-established. It was again exactly what it had been when Charles the First, eighteen years before, withdrew from his capital. All those acts of the Long Parliament which had received the royal assent were admitted to be still in full force. One fresh concession, a concession in which the Cavaliers were even more deeply interested than the Roundheads, was easily obtained from the restored King. The military tenure of land had been originally created as a means of national defence. But in the course of ages whatever was useful in the institution had disappeared; and nothing was left but ceremonies and grievances. A landed proprietor who held an estate under the crown by knight service—and it was thus that most of the soil of England was held—had to pay a large fine on coming to his property. He could not alienate one acre without purchasing a license. When he died, if his domains descended to an infant, the sovereign was guardian, and was not only entitled to great part of the rents during the minority, but could require the ward, under heavy penalties, to marry any person of suitable rank. The chief bait which attracted a needy sycophant to the court was the hope of obtaining, as the reward of servility and flattery, a royal letter to an heiress. These abuses had perished with the monarchy. That they should not revive with it was the wish of every landed gentleman in the kingdom. They were, therefore, solemnly abolished by statute; and no relic of the ancient tenures in chivalry was suffered to remain, except those honorary services which are still, at a coronation, rendered to the person of the sovereign by some lords of manors.

The troops were now to be disbanded. Fifty thousand men, accustomed to the profession of arms, were at once thrown on the world: and experience seemed to warrant the belief that this change would produce much misery and crime, that the discharged veterans would be seen begging in every street, or that they would be driven by hunger to pillage. But no such result followed. In a few months there remained not a trace indicating that the most formidable army in the world had just been absorbed into the mass of the community. The Royalists themselves confessed that, in every department of honest industry, the discarded warriors prospered beyond other men, that none was charged with any theft or robbery, that none was heard to ask an alms, and that, if a baker, a mason, or a waggoner attracted notice by his diligence and sobriety, he was in all probability one of Oliver's old soldiers.

The military tyranny had passed away; but it had left deep and enduring traces in the public mind. The name of a standing army was long held in abhorrence: and it is remarkable that this feeling was even stronger among the Cavaliers than among the Roundheads. It ought to be considered as a most fortunate circumstance that, when our country was, for the first and last time, ruled by the sword, the sword was in the hands, not of her legitimate princes, but of those rebels who slew the King and demolished the Church. Had a prince, with a title as good as that of Charles, commanded an army as good as that of Cromwell, there would have been little hope indeed for the liberties of England. Happily that instrument by which alone the monarchy could be made absolute became an object of peculiar horror and disgust to the monarchical party, and long continued to be inseparably associated in the imagination of Royalists and Prelatists with regicide and field preaching. A century after the death of Cromwell, the Tories still continued to clamour against every augmentation of the regular soldiery, and to sound the praise of a national militia. So late as the year 1786, a minister who enjoyed no common measure of their confidence found it impossible to overcome their aversion to his scheme of fortifying the coast: nor did they ever look with entire complacency on the standing army, till the French Revolution gave a new direction to their apprehensions.

The coalition which had restored the King terminated with the danger from which it had sprung; and two hostile parties again appeared ready for conflict. Both indeed were agreed as to the propriety of inflicting punishment on some unhappy men who were, at that moment, objects of almost universal hatred. Cromwell was no more; and those who had fled before him were forced to content themselves with the miserable satisfaction of digging up, hanging, quartering, and burning the remains of the greatest prince that has ever ruled England. Other objects of vengeance, few indeed, yet too many, were found among the republican chiefs. Soon, however, the conquerors, glutted with the blood of the regicides, turned against each other. The Roundheads, while admitting the virtues of the late King [Charles the First], and while condemning the sentence passed upon him by an illegal tribunal, yet maintained that his administration had been, in many things, unconstitutional, and that the Houses had taken arms against him from good motives and on strong grounds. The monarchy, these politicians conceived, had no worse enemy than the flatterer who exalted the prerogative above the law, who condemned all opposition to regal encroachments, and who reviled, not only Cromwell and Harrison, but Pym and Hampden, as traitors. If the King wished for a quiet and prosperous reign, he must confide in those who, though they had drawn the sword in defence of the invaded privileges of Parliament, had yet exposed themselves to the rage of the soldiers in order to save his father, and had taken the chief part in bringing back the royal family.

The feeling of the Cavaliers was widely different. During eighteen years they had, through all vicissitudes, been faithful to the crown. Having shared the distress of their prince, were they not to share his triumph? Was no distinction to be made between them and the disloyal subject who had fought against his rightful sovereign, who had adhered to Richard Cromwell, and who had never concurred in the restoration of the Stuarts, till it appeared that nothing else could save the nation from the tyranny of the army? Grant that such a man had, by his recent services, fairly earned his pardon. Yet were his services, rendered at the eleventh hour, to be put in comparison with the toils and sufferings of those who had borne the burden and heat of the day? Was he to be ranked with men who had no need of the royal clemency, with men who had, in every part of their lives, merited the royal gratitude? Above all, was he to be suffered to retain a fortune raised out of the substance of the ruined defenders of the throne? Was it not enough that his head and his patrimonial estate, a hundred times forfeited to justice, were secure, and that he shared, with the rest of the nation, in the blessings of that mild government of which he had long been the foe? Was it necessary that he should be rewarded for his treason at the expense of men whose only crime was the fidelity with which they had observed their oath of allegiance? And what interest had the King in gorging his old enemies with prey torn from his old friends? What confidence could be placed in men who had opposed their sovereign, made war on him, imprisoned him, and who, even now, instead of hanging down their heads in shame and contrition, vindicated all that they had done, and seemed to think that they had given an illustrious proof of loyalty by just stopping short of regicide? It was true that they had lately assisted to set up the throne: but it was not less true that they had previously pulled it down, and that they still avowed principles which might impel them to pull it down again. Undoubtedly it might be fit that marks of royal approbation should be bestowed on some converts who had been eminently useful: but policy, as well as justice and gratitude, enjoined the King to give the highest place in his regard to those who, from first to last, through good and evil, had stood by his house. On these grounds the Cavaliers very naturally demanded indemnity for all that they had suffered, and preference in the distribution of the favours of the crown. Some violent members of the party went further, and clamoured for large categories of proscription.

The political feud was, as usual, exasperated by a religious feud. The King found the Church in a singular state. A short time before the commencement of the civil war, his father had given a reluctant assent to a bill which deprived the Bishops of their seats in the House of Lords: but Episcopacy and the Liturgy had never been abolished by law. The Long Parliament, however, had passed ordinances which had made a complete revolution in Church government and in public worship. The new system was, in principle, scarcely less Erastian than that which it displaced. The Houses, guided chiefly by the counsels of the accomplished Selden, had determined to keep the spiritual power strictly subordinate to the temporal power. They had refused to declare that any form of ecclesiastical polity was of divine origin; and they had provided that, from all the Church courts, an appeal should lie in the last resort to Parliament. The authority of councils, rising one above another in regular gradation, was substituted for the authority of Bishops and Archbishops. The Liturgy gave place to the Presbyterian directory. But scarcely had the new regulations been framed, when the Independents rose to supreme influence in the state. The Independents had no disposition to enforce the ordinances touching classical, provincial, and national synods. Those ordinances, therefore, were never carried into full execution. The Presbyterian system was fully established nowhere but in Middlesex and Lancashire. In the other fifty counties, almost every parish seems to have been unconnected with the neighbouring parishes. In some districts, indeed, the ministers formed themselves into voluntary associations, for the purpose of mutual help and counsel; but these associations had no coercive power. The patrons of livings, being now checked by neither Bishop nor Presbytery, would have been at liberty to confide the cure of souls to the most scandalous of mankind, but for the arbitrary intervention of Oliver. He established, by his own authority, a board of commissioners, called Triers. Most of these persons were Independent divines; but a few Presbyterian ministers and a few laymen had seats. The certificate of the Triers stood in the place both of institution and of induction; and without such a certificate no person could hold a benefice. This was undoubtedly one of the most despotic acts ever done by any English ruler. Yet, as it was generally felt that, without some such precaution, the country would be overrun by ignorant and drunken reprobates, bearing the name and receiving the pay of ministers, some highly respectable persons, who were not in general friendly to Cromwell, allowed that, on this occasion, he had been a public benefactor. The presentees whom the Triers had approved took possession of the rectories, cultivated the glebe lands, collected the tithes, prayed without book or surplice, and administered the Eucharist to communicants seated at long tables.

Thus the ecclesiastical polity of the realm was in inextricable confusion. Episcopacy was the form of government prescribed by the old law which was still unrepealed. The form of government prescribed by parliamentary ordinance was Presbyterian. But neither the old law nor the parliamentary ordinance was practically in force. The Church actually established may be described as an irregular body made up of a few Presbyteries, and of many Independent congregations, which were all held down and held together by the authority of the government.

Of those who had been active in bringing back the King, many were zealous for synods and for the directory, and many were desirous to terminate by a compromise the religious dissensions which had long agitated England. Between the bigoted followers of Laud and the bigoted followers of Calvin there could be neither peace nor truce: but it did not seem impossible to effect an accommodation between the moderate Episcopalians of the school of Usher and the moderate Presbyterians of the school of Baxter. The moderate Episcopalians would admit that a Bishop might lawfully be assisted by a council. The moderate Presbyterians would not deny that each provincial assembly might lawfully have a permanent president, and that this president might lawfully be called a Bishop. There might be a revised Liturgy which should not exclude extemporaneous prayer, a baptismal service in which the sign of the cross might be used or omitted at discretion, a communion service at which the faithful might sit if their consciences forbade them to kneel. But to no such plan could the great body of the Cavaliers listen with patience. The religious members of that party were conscientiously attached to the whole system of their Church. She had been dear to their murdered King. She had consoled them in defeat and penury. Her service, so often whispered in an inner chamber during the season of trial, had such a charm for them that they were unwilling to part with a single response. Other Royalists, who made little pretence to piety, yet loved the Episcopal Church because she was the foe of their foes. They valued a prayer or a ceremony, not on account of the comfort which it conveyed to themselves, but on account of the vexation which it gave to the Roundheads, and were so far from being disposed to purchase union by concession that they objected to concession chiefly because it tended to produce union.

Such feelings, though blamable, were natural and not wholly inexcusable. The Puritans in the day of their power had undoubtedly given cruel provocation. They ought to have learned, if from nothing else, yet from their own discontents, from their own struggles, from their own victory, from the fall of that proud hierarchy by which they had been so heavily oppressed, that, in England, and in the seventeenth century, it was not in the power of the civil magistrate to drill the minds of men into conformity with his own system of theology. They proved, however, as intolerant and as meddling as ever Laud had been. They interdicted under heavy penalties the use of the Book of Common Prayer, not only in churches, but even in private houses. It was a crime in a child to read by the bedside of a sick parent one of those beautiful collects which had soothed the griefs of forty generations of Christians. Severe punishments were denounced against such as should presume to blame the Calvinistic mode of worship. Clergymen of respectable character were not only ejected from their benefices, by thousands, but were frequently exposed to the outrages of a fanatical rabble. Churches and sepulchres, fine works of art and curious remains of antiquity, were brutally defaced. The Parliament resolved that all pictures in the royal collection which contained representations of Jesus or of the Virgin Mother should be burned. Sculpture fared as ill as painting. Nymphs and Graces, the work of Ionian chisels, were delivered over to Puritan stonemasons to be made decent. Against the lighter vices the ruling faction waged war with a zeal little tempered by humanity or by common sense. Sharp laws were passed against betting. It was enacted that adultery should be punished with death. The illicit intercourse of the sexes, even where neither violence nor seduction was imputed, where no public scandal was given, where no conjugal right was violated, was made a misdemeanour. Public amusements, from the masques which were exhibited at the mansions of the great down to the wrestling matches and grinning matches on village greens, were vigorously attacked. One ordinance directed that all the Maypoles in England should forthwith be hewn down. Another proscribed all theatrical diversions. The playhouses were to be dismantled, the spectators fined, the actors whipped at the cart's tail. Rope-dancing, puppet shows, bowls, horse racing, were regarded with no friendly eye. But bearbaiting, then a favourite diversion of high and low, was the abomination which most strongly stirred the wrath of the austere sectaries. It is to be remarked that their antipathy to this sport had nothing in common with the feeling which has, in our own time, induced the legislature to interfere for the purpose of protecting beasts against the wanton cruelty of men. The Puritan hated bearbaiting, not because it gave pain to the bear, but because it gave pleasure to the spectators. Indeed, he generally contrived to enjoy the double pleasure of tormenting both spectators and bear.

The theology, the manners, the dialect of the Puritan were associated in the public mind with the darkest and meanest vices. As soon as the Restoration had made it safe to avow enmity to the party which had so long been predominant in the state, a general outcry against Puritanism rose from every corner of the kingdom, and was often swollen by the voices of those very dissemblers whose villany had brought disgrace on the Puritan name.

Thus the two great parties, which, after a long contest, had for a moment concurred in restoring monarchy, were, both in politics and in religion, again opposed to each other. The great body of the nation leaned to the Royalists.

The restored King was at this time more loved by the people than any of his predecessors had ever been. The calamities of his house, the heroic death of his father, his own long sufferings and romantic adventures, made him an object of tender interest. His return had delivered the country from an intolerable bondage. Recalled by the voice of both the contending factions, he was in a position which enabled him to arbitrate between them; and in some respects he was well qualified for the task. He had received from nature excellent parts and a happy temper. His education had been such as might have been expected to develope his understanding, and to form him to the practice of every public and private virtue. He had passed through all varieties of fortune, and had seen both sides of human nature. He had, while very young, been driven forth from a palace to a life of exile, penury, and danger. He had, at the age when the mind and body are in their highest perfection, and when the first effervescence of boyish passions should have subsided, been recalled from his wanderings to wear a crown. He had been taught by bitter experience how much baseness, perfidy, and ingratitude may lie hid under the obsequious demeanour of courtiers. He had found, on the other hand, in the huts of the poorest, true nobility of soul. When wealth was offered to any who would betray him, when death was denounced against all who should shelter him, cottagers and serving men had kept his secret truly, and had kissed his hand under his mean disguises with as much reverence as if he had been seated on his ancestral throne. From such a school it might have been expected that a young man who wanted neither abilities nor amiable qualities would have come forth a great and good King. Charles came forth from that school with social habits, with polite and engaging manners, and with some talent for lively conversation, addicted beyond measure to sensual indulgence, fond of sauntering and of frivolous amusements, incapable of self-denial and of exertion, without faith in human virtue or in human attachment, without desire of renown, and without sensibility to reproach. According to him, every person was to be bought: but some people haggled more about their price than others; and when this haggling was very obstinate and very skilful it was called by some fine name. The chief trick by which clever men kept up the price of their abilities was called integrity. The chief trick by which handsome women kept up the price of their beauty was called modesty. The love of God, the love of country, the love of family, the love of friends, were phrases of the same sort, delicate and convenient synonyms for the love of self. Thinking thus of mankind, Charles naturally cared very little what they thought of him. Honour and shame were scarcely more to him than light and darkness to the blind. His contempt of flattery has been highly commended, but seems, when viewed in connection with the rest of his character, to deserve no commendation. It is possible to be below flattery as well as above it. One who trusts nobody will not trust sycophants. One who does not value real glory will not value its counterfeit.

The motives which governed the political conduct of Charles the Second differed widely from those by which his predecessor and his successor were actuated. He was not a man to be imposed upon by the patriarchal theory of government and the doctrine of divine right. He was utterly without ambition. He detested business, and would sooner have abdicated his crown than have undergone the trouble of really directing the administration. Such was his aversion to toil, and such his ignorance of affairs, that the very clerks who attended him when he sate in council could not refrain from sneering at his frivolous remarks, and at his childish impatience. His favourite vices were precisely those to which the Puritans were least indulgent. He could not get through one day without the help of diversions which the Puritans regarded as sinful. As a man eminently well bred, and keenly sensible of the ridiculous, he was moved to contemptuous mirth by the Puritan oddities. He had indeed some reason to dislike the rigid sect. He had, at the age when the passions are most impetuous and when levity is most pardonable, spent some months in Scotland, a King in name, but in fact a state prisoner in the hands of austere Presbyterians. Not content with requiring him to conform to their worship and to subscribe their Covenant, they had watched all his motions, and lectured him on all his youthful follies. He had been compelled to give reluctant attendance at endless prayers and sermons, and might think himself fortunate when he was not insolently reminded from the pulpit of his own frailties, of his father's tyranny, and of his mother's idolatry. Indeed he had been so miserable during this part of his life that the defeat which made him again a wanderer might be regarded as a deliverance rather than as a calamity. Under the influence of such feelings as these Charles was desirous to depress the party which had resisted his father.

The King's brother, James Duke of York [later King James the Second], took the same side. Though a libertine, James was diligent, methodical, and fond of authority and business. His understanding was singularly slow and narrow, and his temper obstinate, harsh, and unforgiving. That such a prince should have looked with no good will on the free institutions of England, and on the party which was peculiarly zealous for those institutions, can excite no surprise. As yet the Duke professed himself a member of the Anglican Church: but he had already shown inclinations which had seriously alarmed good Protestants.

II. THE CORONATION OF JAMES THE SECOND

THE death of King Charles the Second took the nation by surprise. When all was over, James retired from the bedside to his closet, where, during a quarter of an hour, he remained alone. Meanwhile the Privy Councillors who were in the palace assembled. The new King came forth, and took his place at the head of the board. He commenced his administration, according to usage, by a speech to the Council. He expressed his regret for the loss which he had just sustained, and he promised to imitate the singular lenity which had distinguished the late reign. He was aware, he said, that he had been accused of a fondness for arbitrary power. But that was not the only falsehood which had been told of him. He was resolved to maintain the established government both in Church and State. The Church of England he knew to be eminently loyal. It should therefore always be his care to support and defend her. The laws of England, he also knew, were sufficient to make him as great a King as he could wish to be. He would not relinquish his own rights; but he would respect the rights of others. He had formerly risked his life in defence of his country, and he would still go as far as any man in support of her just liberties.

This speech was not, like modern speeches on similar occasions, carefully prepared by the advisers of the sovereign. It was the extemporaneous expression of the new King's feelings at a moment of great excitement. The members of the Council broke forth into clamours of delight and gratitude.

The King had been exhausted by long watching and by many violent emotions. He now retired to rest. The Privy Councillors, having respectfully accompanied him to his bedchamber, returned to their seats and issued orders for the ceremony of proclamation. The Guards were under arms; the heralds appeared in their gorgeous coats; and the pageant proceeded without any obstruction. Casks of wine were broken up in the streets, and all who passed were invited to drink to the health of the new sovereign. But, though an occasional shout was raised, the people were not in a joyous mood. Tears were seen in many eyes; and it was remarked that there was scarcely a housemaid in London who had not contrived to procure some fragment of black crape in honour of King Charles.

The King early put the loyalty of his Protestant friends to the proof. While he was a subject, he had been in the habit of hearing mass with closed doors in a small oratory which had been fitted up for his wife. He now ordered the doors to be thrown open, in order that all who came to pay their duty to him might see the ceremony. When the host was elevated there was a strange confusion in the antechamber. The Roman Catholics fell on their knees: the Protestants hurried out of the room. Soon a new pulpit was erected in the palace; and, during Lent, a series of sermons was preached there by Popish divines, to the great discomposure of zealous churchmen.

A more serious innovation followed. Passion week came; and the King determined to hear mass with the same pomp with which his predecessors had been surrounded when they repaired to the temples of the established religion. He announced his intention to the three members of the interior cabinet, and requested them to attend him. Sunderland, to whom all religions were the same, readily consented. Godolphin, as

Chamberlain of the Queen, had already been in the habit of giving her his hand when she repaired to her oratory, and felt no scruple about bowing himself officially in the house of Rimmon. But Rochester was greatly disturbed.

Within a week after this ceremony James made a far greater sacrifice of his own religious prejudices than he had yet called on any of his Protestant subjects to make. He was crowned on the twenty-third of April, the feast of the patron saint of the realm. The Abbey and the Hall were splendidly decorated. The presence of the Queen and of the peeresses gave to the solemnity a charm which had been wanting to the magnificent inauguration of the late King. Yet those who remembered that inauguration pronounced that there was a great falling off. The ancient usage was that, before a coronation, the sovereign, with all his heralds, judges, councillors, lords, and great dignitaries, should ride in state from the Tower to Westminster. Of these cavalcades the last and the most glorious was that which passed through the capital while the feelings excited by the Restoration were still in full vigour. Arches of triumph overhung the road. All Cornhill, Cheapside, Saint Paul's Church Yard, Fleet Street, and the Strand were lined with scaffolding. The whole city had thus been admitted to gaze on royalty in the most splendid and solemn form that royalty could wear. James ordered an estimate to be made of the cost of such a procession, and found that it would amount to about half as much as he proposed to expend in covering his wife with trinkets. He accordingly determined to be profuse where he ought to have been frugal, and niggardly where he might pardonably have been profuse. More than a hundred thousand pounds were laid out in dressing the Queen, and the procession from the Tower was omitted. The folly of this course is obvious. If pageantry be of any use in politics, it is of use as a means of striking the imagination of the multitude. It is surely the height of absurdity to shut out the populace from a show of which the main object is to make an impression on the populace. James would have shown a more judicious munificence and a more judicious parsimony, if he had traversed London from east to west with the accustomed pomp, and had ordered the robes of his wife to be somewhat less thickly set with pearls and diamonds.

James had ordered [Archbishop] Sancroft to abridge the ritual. The reason publicly assigned was that the day was too short for all that was to be done. But whoever examines the changes which were made will see that the real object was to remove some things highly offensive to the religious feelings of a zealous Roman Catholic. The Communion Service was not read. The ceremony of presenting the sovereign with a richly bound copy of the English Bible, and of exhorting him to prize above all earthly treasures a volume which he had been taught to regard as adulterated with false doctrine, was omitted. What remained, however, after all this curtailment, might well have raised scruples in the mind of a man who sincerely believed the Church of England to be a heretical society, within the pale of which salvation was not to be found. The King made an oblation on the altar. He appeared to join in the petitions of the Litany which was chaunted by the Bishops. He received from those false prophets the unction typical of a divine influence, and knelt with the semblance of devotion while they called down upon him that Holy Spirit of which they were, in his estimation, the malignant and obdurate foes. Such are the inconsistencies of human nature that this man, who, from a fanatical zeal for his religion, threw away three kingdoms, yet chose to commit what was little short of an act of apostasy, rather than forego the childish pleasure of being invested with the gewgaws symbolical of kingly power.

Francis Turner, Bishop of Ely, preached. He was one of those writers who still affected the obsolete style of Archbishop Williams and Bishop Andrews. The sermon was made up of quaint conceits, such as seventy years earlier might have been admired, but such as moved the scorn of a generation accustomed to the purer eloquence of Sprat, of South, and of Tillotson. King Solomon was King James. Adonijah was Monmouth. Joab was a Rye House conspirator; Shimei, a Whig libeller; Abiathar, an honest but misguided old Cavalier. One phrase in the Book of Chronicles was construed to mean that the King was above the Parliament, and another was cited to prove that he alone ought to command the militia. Towards the close of the discourse the orator very timidly alluded to the new and embarrassing position in which the Church stood with reference to the sovereign, and reminded his hearers that the Emperor Constantius Chlorus, though not himself a Christian, had held in honour those Christians who remained true to their religion, and had treated with scorn those who sought to earn his favour by apostasy. The service in the Abbey was followed by a stately banquet in the Hall, the banquet by brilliant fireworks, and the fireworks by much bad poetry.

This may be fixed upon as the moment at which the enthusiasm of the Tory party reached the zenith. Ever since the accession of the new King, addresses had been pouring in which expressed profound veneration for his person and office, and bitter detestation of the vanquished Whigs. The magistrates of Middlesex thanked God for having confounded the designs of those regicides and excluders who, not content with having murdered one blessed monarch, were bent on destroying the foundations of monarchy. The city of Gloucester execrated the bloodthirsty villains who had tried to deprive His Majesty of his just inheritance. The burgesses of Wigan assured their sovereign that they would defend him against all plotting Achitophels and rebellious Absaloms. The grand jury of Suffolk expressed a hope that the Parliament would proscribe all the excluders. Many corporations pledged themselves never to return to the House of Commons any person who had voted for taking away the birthright of James. Even the capital was profoundly obsequious. The lawyers and traders vied with each other in servility. Inns of Court and Inns of Chancery sent up fervent professions of attachment and submission. All the great commercial societies, the East India Company, the African Company, the Turkey Company, the Muscovy Company, the Hudson's Bay

Company, the Maryland Merchants, the Jamaica Merchants, the Merchant Adventurers, declared that they most cheerfully complied with the royal edict which required them still to pay custom. Bristol, the second city of the island, echoed the voice of London. But nowhere was the spirit of loyalty stronger than in the two Universities. Oxford declared that she would never swerve from those religious principles which bound her to obey the King without any restrictions or limitations. Cambridge condemned, in severe terms, the violence and treachery of those turbulent men who had maliciously endeavoured to turn the stream of succession out of the ancient channel.

Such addresses as these filled, during a considerable time, every number of the London Gazette. But it was not only by addressing that the Tories showed their zeal. The writs for the new Parliament had gone forth, and the country was agitated by the tumult of a general election. No election had ever taken place under circumstances so favourable to the court.

The general result of the elections exceeded the most sanguine expectations of the court. James found with delight that it would be unnecessary for him to expend a farthing in buying votes. He said that, with the exception of about forty members, the House of Commons was just such as he should himself have named. And this House of Commons it was in his power, as the law then stood, to keep to the end of his reign.

III. THE REBELLION OF MONMOUTH AND ARGYLE

CHARLES, while a wanderer on the Continent, had fallen in at the Hague with Lucy Walters, a Welsh girl of great beauty, but of weak understanding and dissolute manners. She became his mistress, and presented him with a son. A suspicious lover might have had his doubts; for the lady had several admirers, and was not supposed to be cruel to any. Charles, however, readily took her word, and poured forth on little James Croft, as the boy was then called, an overflowing fondness, such as seemed hardly to belong to that cool and careless nature. Soon after the Restoration, the young favourite, who had learned in France the exercises then considered necessary to a fine gentleman, made his appearance at Whitehall. He was lodged in the palace, attended by pages, and permitted to enjoy several distinctions which had till then been confined to princes of the blood royal. He was married, while still in tender youth, to Anne Scott, heiress of the noble house of Buccleuch. He took her name, and received with her hand possession of her ample domains. The estate which he acquired by this match was popularly estimated at not less than ten thousand pounds a year. Titles, and favours more substantial than titles, were lavished on him. He was made Duke of Monmouth in England, Duke of Buccleuch in Scotland, a Knight of the Garter, Master of the Horse, Commander of the first troop of Life Guards, Chief Justice of Eyre south of Trent, and

Chancellor of the University of Cambridge. While Monmouth was still a child, and while the Duke of York still passed for a Protestant, it was rumoured throughout the country, and even in circles which ought to have been well informed, that the King had made Lucy Walters his wife, and that, if every one had his right, her son would be Prince of Wales. Much was said of a certain black box which, according to the vulgar belief, contained the contract of marriage. When Monmouth had returned from the Low Countries with a high character for valour and conduct, and when the Duke of York was known to be a member of a church detested by the great majority of the nation, this idle story became important. For it there was not the slightest evidence. Against it there was the solemn asseveration of the King, made before his Council, and by his order communicated to his people. But the multitude, always fond of romantic adventures, drank in eagerly the tale of the secret espousals and the black box. When Monmouth arrived in London at midnight, the watchmen were ordered by the magistrates to proclaim the joyful event through the streets of the City: the people left their beds: bonfires were lighted: the windows were illuminated: the churches were opened; and a merry peal rose from all the steeples. When he travelled, he was everywhere received with not less pomp, and with far more enthusiasm, than had been displayed when Kings had made progresses through the realm.

It is a curious circumstance that, at two of the greatest conjunctures in our history, the chiefs of the Protestant party should have committed the same error, and should by that error have greatly endangered their country and their religion. At the death of Edward the Sixth they set up the Lady Jane, without any show of birthright, in opposition, not only to their enemy Mary, but also to Elizabeth, the true hope of England and of the Reformation. Thus the most respectable Protestants, with Elizabeth at their head, were forced to make common cause with the Papists. In the same manner, a hundred and thirty years later, a part of the opposition, by setting up Monmouth as a claimant of the crown, attacked the rights, not only of James, whom they justly regarded as an implacable foe of their faith and their liberties, but also of the Prince and Princess of Orange, who were eminently marked out, both by situation and by personal qualities, as the defenders of all free governments and of all reformed Churches.

The true policy of the Whigs was to submit with patience to adversity which was the natural consequence and the just punishment of their errors, to wait patiently for that turn of public feeling which must inevitably come, to observe the law, and to avail themselves of the protection, imperfect indeed, but by no means nugatory, which the law afforded to innocence. Unhappily they took a very different course. Unscrupulous and hotheaded chiefs of the party formed and discussed schemes of resistance, and were heard, if not with approbation, yet with the show of acquiescence, by much better men than themselves. The just indignation excited by the Rye House plot [which had had for its object the assassination of King Charles the Second and of the Duke of York] was extended for a time to the whole Whig body. Shaftesbury had fled to Holland. Monmouth had thought it prudent to go into voluntary exile.

Misgovernment, such as had never been known in the southern part of our island, had driven from Scotland to the Continent many fugitives, the intemperance of whose political and religious zeal was proportioned to the oppression which they had undergone. These men were not willing to follow an English leader. Even in destitution and exile they retained their punctilious national pride, and would not consent that their country should be, in their persons, degraded into a province. They had a captain of their own, Archibald, ninth Earl of Argyle, who, as chief of the great tribe of Campbell, was known among the population of the Highlands by the proud name of Mac Callum More.

Amsterdam was the place where the leading emigrants, Scotch and English, assembled. Argyle repaired thither from Friesland, Monmouth from Brabant. It soon appeared that the fugitives had scarcely anything in common except hatred of James and impatience to return from banishment. The Scots were jealous of the English, the English of the Scots.

At length all differences were compromised. It was determined that an attempt should be forthwith made on the western coast of Scotland, and that it should be promptly followed by a descent on England.

Argyle was to hold the nominal command in Scotland: but he was placed under the control of a Committee which reserved to itself all the most important parts of the military administration.

Monmouth was to command in England. His soft mind had taken an impress from the society which surrounded him. Ambitious hopes, which had seemed to be extinguished, had revived in his bosom. He remembered the affection with which he had been constantly greeted by the common people in town and country, and expected that they would now rise by hundreds of thousands to welcome him. He remembered the good will which the soldiers had always borne him, and flattered himself that they would come over to him by regiments.

The exiles were able to raise, partly from their own resources and partly from the contributions of well wishers in Holland, a sum sufficient for the two expeditions.

The last hours which Argyle passed on the coast of Holland were hours of great anxiety. But no effectual step was taken for the purpose of detaining him; and on the afternoon of the second of May [1685] he stood out to sea before a favourable breeze.

The voyage was prosperous. On the sixth the Orkneys were in sight. Argyle very unwisely anchored off Kirkwall. It was speedily known at Edinburgh that the rebel squadron had touched at the Orkneys. Troops were instantly put in motion.

The state of public feeling in Scotland was not such as the exiles, misled by the infatuation common in all ages to exiles, had supposed it to be. The government was, indeed, hateful and hated. But the malcontents were divided into parties which were almost as hostile to one another as to their rulers; nor was any of those parties eager to join the invaders.

Argyle resolved to make a bold push for Glasgow. But, as soon as this resolution was announced, the very men, who had, up to that moment, been urging him to hasten into the low country, took fright, argued, remonstrated, and, when argument and remonstrance proved vain, laid a scheme for seizing the boats, making their own escape, and leaving their General and his clansmen to conquer or perish unaided. This scheme failed; and the poltroons who had formed it were compelled to share with braver men the risks of the last venture.

During the march through the country which lies between Loch Long and Loch Lomond, the insurgents were constantly infested by parties of militia. Some skirmishes took place, in which the Earl had the advantage; but the bands which he repelled, falling back before him, spread the tidings of his approach, and, soon after he had crossed the river Leven, he found a strong body of regular and irregular troops prepared to encounter him. The hostile armies encamped at no great distance from each other. The Earl ventured to propose a night attack, and was overruled.

There was a chance, that by decamping secretly, and hastening all night across heaths and morasses, the Earl might gain many miles on the enemy, and might reach Glasgow without further obstruction. The watch fires were left burning; and the march began. And now disaster followed disaster fast. The guides mistook the track across the moors, and led the army into boggy ground. Military order could not be preserved by undisciplined and disheartened soldiers under a dark sky, and on a treacherous and uneven soil. Panic after panic spread through the broken ranks. Every sight and sound was thought to indicate the approach of pursuers. Some of the officers contributed to spread the terror which it was their duty to calm. The army had become a mob; and the mob melted fast away. Great numbers fled under cover of the night. Rumbold and some other brave men whom no danger could have scared lost their way, and were unable to rejoin the main body. When the day broke, only five hundred fugitives, wearied and dispirited, assembled at Kilpatrick.

All thought of prosecuting the war was at an end: and it was plain that the chiefs of the expedition would have sufficient difficulty in escaping with their lives. They fled in different directions. Argyle hoped to find a secure asylum under the roof of one of his old servants who lived near Kilpatrick. But this hope was disappointed, and he was forced to cross the Clyde. He assumed the dress of a peasant, and pretended to be the guide of Major Fullarton, whose courageous fidelity was proof to all danger. The only ford by which the travellers could cross was guarded by a party of militia. Some questions were asked. Fullarton tried to draw suspicion on himself, in order that his companion might escape unnoticed. But the minds of the questioners misgave them that the guide was not the rude clown that he seemed. They laid hands on him. He broke loose and sprang into the water, but was instantly chased. He stood at bay for a short time against five assailants. But he had no arms except his pocket pistols, and they were so wet in consequence of his plunge, that they would not go off. He was struck to the ground with a broadsword, and secured.

In Amsterdam the Admiralty suffered Monmouth to sail unmolested. The weather was bad: the voyage was long; and several English men of war were cruising in the Channel. But Monmouth escaped both the sea and the enemy.

On the morning of the eleventh of June the Helderenbergh, accompanied by two smaller vessels, appeared off the port of Lyme. That town is a small knot of steep and narrow alleys, lying on a coast wild, rocky, and beaten by a stormy sea.

The appearance of the three ships, foreign built and without colours, perplexed the inhabitants of Lyme; and the uneasiness increased when it was found that the Customhouse officers, who had gone on board according to usage, did not return. The town's people repaired to the cliffs, and gazed long and anxiously, but could find no solution of the mystery. At length seven boats put off from the largest of the strange vessels, and rowed to the shore. From these boats landed about eighty men, well armed and appointed. Among them were Monmouth, Grey, Fletcher, Ferguson, Wade, and Anthony Buyse, an officer who had been in the service of the Elector of Brandenburg.

Monmouth commanded silence, kneeled down on the shore, thanked God for having preserved the friends of liberty and pure religion from the perils of the sea, and implored the divine blessing on what was yet to be done by land. He then drew his sword and led his men over the cliffs into the town.

As soon as it was known under what leader and for what purpose the expedition came, the enthusiasm of the populace burst through all restraints. The little town was in an uproar with men running to and fro, and shouting "A Monmouth! a Monmouth! the Protestant religion!" Meanwhile the ensign of the adventurers, a blue flag, was set up in the market place. The military stores were deposited in the town hall; and a Declaration setting forth the objects of the expedition was read from the Cross.

On the evening on which the Duke landed, Gregory Alford, Mayor of Lyme, a zealous Tory, and a most bitter persecutor of Nonconformists, sent off his servants to give the alarm to the gentry of Somersetshire and Dorsetshire, and himself took horse for the West. Late at night he stopped at Honiton, and thence despatched a few hurried lines to London with the ill tidings.

The Court and the Parliament had been greatly moved by the news from the West. At five in the morning of Saturday the thirteenth of June, the King had received the letter which the Mayor of Lyme had despatched from Honiton. The Privy Council was instantly called together. Orders were given that the strength of every company of infantry and of every troop of cavalry should be increased. Commissions were issued for the levying of new regiments. Alford's communication was laid before the Lords; and its substance was communicated to the Commons by a message. The Commons examined the couriers who had arrived from the West, and instantly ordered a bill to be brought in for attainting Monmouth of high treason. Addresses were voted assuring the King that both his peers and his people were determined to stand by him with life and fortune against all his enemies. At the next meeting of the Houses they ordered the declaration of the rebels to be burned by the hangman, and passed the bill of attainder through all its stages. That bill received the royal assent on the same day; and a reward of five thousand pounds was promised for the apprehension of Monmouth.

While the Parliament was devising sharp laws against Monmouth and his partisans, he found at Taunton a reception which might well encourage him to hope that his enterprise would have a prosperous issue. The children of the men who, forty years before, had manned the ramparts of Taunton against the Royalists, now welcomed Monmouth with transports of joy and affection. Every door and window was adorned with wreaths of flowers. No man appeared in the streets without wearing in his hat a green bough, the badge of the popular cause. Damsels of the best families in the town wove colours for the insurgents. One flag in particular was embroidered gorgeously with emblems of royal dignity, and was offered to Monmouth by a train of young girls. He received the gift with the winning courtesy which distinguished him. The lady who headed the procession presented him also with a small Bible of great price. He took it with a show of reverence. "I come," he said, "to defend the truths contained in this book, and to seal them, if it must be so, with my blood."

But, while Monmouth enjoyed the applause of the multitude, he could not but perceive, with concern and apprehension, that the higher classes were, with scarcely an exception, hostile to his undertaking, and that no rising had taken place except in the counties where he had himself appeared. The Duke had put himself into a false position by declining the royal title. Had he declared himself sovereign of England, his cause would have worn a show of legality. Monmouth talked in private with dissentients, assured them that he saw no other way of obtaining the support of any portion of the aristocracy [than by proclaiming his sovereignty], and succeeded in extorting their reluctant consent. On the morning of the twentieth of June he was proclaimed in the market place of Taunton. His followers repeated his new title with affectionate delight. But, as some confusion might have arisen if he had been called King James the Second, they commonly used the strange appellation of King Monmouth; and by this name their unhappy favourite was often mentioned in the western counties.

On the day following that on which Monmouth had assumed the regal title he marched from Taunton to Bridgewater. His own spirits, it was remarked, were not high. The acclamations of the devoted thousands who surrounded him wherever he turned could not dispel the gloom which sate on his brow. A small body guard of forty young men, well armed and mounted at their own charge, attended Monmouth. The people of Bridgewater, who were enriched by a thriving coast trade, furnished him with a small sum of money.

All this time the forces of the government were fast assembling. On the west of the rebel army Albemarle still kept together a large body of Devonshire militia. On the east the trainbands of Wiltshire had mustered under the command of Thomas Herbert, Earl of Pembroke. On the north east, Henry Somerset, Duke of Beaufort, was in arms.

And now the time for the great hazard drew near. The night was not ill suited for such an enterprise. The moon was indeed at the full, and the northern streamers were shining brilliantly. But the marsh fog lay so thick on Sedgemoor that no object could be discerned there at the distance of fifty paces.

The clock struck eleven; and the Duke with his body guard rode out. He was not in the frame of mind which befits one who is about to strike a decisive blow. The very children who pressed to see him pass observed, and long remembered, that his look was sad and full of evil augury. His army marched by a circuitous path, near six miles in length, towards the royal encampment on Sedgemoor. Part of the route is to this day called War Lane. The foot were led by Monmouth himself.

At about one in the morning of Monday the sixth of July, the rebels were on the open moor. But between them and the enemy lay three broad rhines filled with water and soft mud. Two of these, called the Black Ditch and the Langmoor Rhine, Monmouth knew that he must pass.

The wains which carried the ammunition remained at the entrance of the moor. The horse and foot, in a long narrow column, passed the Black Ditch by a causeway. There was a similar causeway across the Langmoor Rhine: but the guide, in the fog, missed his way. There was some delay and some tumult before the error could be rectified. At length the passage was effected: but, in the confusion, a pistol went off. Some men of the Horse Guards, who were on watch, heard the report, and perceived that a great multitude was advancing through the mist.

"For whom are you?" called out an officer of the Foot Guards. "For the King," replied a voice from the ranks of the rebel cavalry. "For which King?" was then demanded. The answer was a shout of "King Monmouth," mingled with the war cry, which forty years before had been inscribed on the colours of the parliamentary regiments, "God with us."

A few minutes after the Duke's horse had dispersed themselves over the moor, his infantry came up running fast. The royal troops instantly fired such a volley of musketry as sent the rebel horse flying in all directions.

Monmouth was startled by finding that a broad and profound trench lay between him and the camp which he had hoped to surprise. The insurgents halted on the edge of the rhine, and fired. Part of the royal infantry on the opposite bank returned the fire. During three quarters of an hour the roar of the musketry was incessant. The Somersetshire peasants behaved themselves as if they had been veteran soldiers, save only that they levelled their pieces too high.

But now the other divisions of the royal army were in motion. The Life Guards and Blues came pricking fast from Weston Zoyland. Fugitives spread a panic among their comrades in the rear, who had charge of the ammunition. The waggoners drove off at full speed, and never stopped till they were many miles from the field of battle. Monmouth had hitherto done his part like a stout and able warrior. He had been seen on foot, pike in hand, encouraging his infantry by voice and by example. But he was too well acquainted with military affairs not to know that all was over. His men had lost the advantage which surprise and darkness had given them. They were deserted by the horse and by the ammunition waggons. The King's forces were now united and in good order. The day was about to break. The event of a conflict on an open plain, by broad sunlight, could not be doubtful. Yet Monmouth should have felt that it was not for him to fly, while thousands whom affection for him had hurried to destruction were still fighting manfully in his cause. But vain hopes and the intense love of life prevailed. He saw that if he tarried the royal cavalry would soon intercept his retreat. He mounted and rode from the field.

Yet his foot, though deserted, made a gallant stand. The Life Guards attacked them on the right, the Blues on the left: but the Somersetshire clowns, with their scythes and the butt ends of their muskets, faced the royal horse like old soldiers. Sarsfield, a brave Irish officer, whose name afterwards obtained a melancholy celebrity, charged on a flank. His men were beaten back. He was himself struck to the ground, and lay for a time as one dead. But the struggle of the hardy rustics could not last. Their powder and ball were spent. Cries were heard of "Ammunition! for God's sake ammunition!" But no ammunition was at hand. And now the King's artillery came up. It had been posted half a mile off, on the high road from Weston Zoyland to Bridgewater. So defective were then the appointments of an English army that there would have been much difficulty in dragging the great guns to the place where the battle was raging, had not the Bishop of Winchester offered his coach horses and traces for the purpose. This interference of a Christian prelate in a matter of blood has, with strange inconsistency, been condemned by some Whig writers who can see nothing criminal in the conduct of the numerous Puritan ministers then in arms against the government. Even when the guns had arrived, there was such a want of gunners that a sergeant was forced to take on himself the management of several pieces. The cannon, however, though ill served, brought the engagement to a speedy close. The pikes of the rebel battalions began to shake; the ranks broke; the King's cavalry charged again, and bore down everything before them; the King's infantry came pouring across the ditch. Even in that extremity the Mendip miners stood bravely to their arms, and sold their lives dearly.

But the rout was in a few minutes complete. Three hundred of the soldiers had been killed or wounded. Of the rebels more than a thousand lay dead on the moor.

IV. JEFFREYS AND THE "BLOODY ASSIZES"

THE great offices of state had become vacant by the demise of the crown; and it was necessary for James to determine how they should be filled. Few of the members of the late cabinet had any reason to accept his favour. The Lord Keeper Guildford could hardly be said to belong to either of the parties into which the court was divided. He could by no means be called a friend of liberty; and yet he had so great a reverence for the letter of the law that he was not a serviceable tool of arbitrary power. He was accordingly designated by the vehement Tories as a Trimmer, and was to James an object of aversion with which contempt was largely mingled.

The Great Seal was left in Guildford's custody: but a marked indignity was at the same time offered to him. It was determined that another lawyer of more vigour and audacity should be called to assist in the administration. The person selected was Sir George Jeffreys, Chief Justice of the Court of King's Bench. The depravity of this man has passed into a proverb.

His enemies could not deny that he possessed some of the qualities of a great judge. His legal knowledge, indeed, was merely such as he had picked up in practice of no very high kind. But he had one of those happily constituted intellects which, across labyrinths of sophistry, and through masses of immaterial facts, go straight to the true point. Of his intellect, however, he seldom had the full use. Even in civil causes his malevolent and despotic temper perpetually disordered his judgment. To enter his court was to enter the den of a wild beast, which none could tame, and which was as likely to be roused to rage by caresses as by attacks.

Early in September [1685] Jeffreys, accompanied by four other judges, set out on that circuit of which the memory will last as long as our race and language. The officers who commanded the troops in the districts through which his course lay had orders to furnish him with whatever military aid he might require.

At Winchester the Chief Justice first opened his commission. Hampshire had not been the theatre of war; but many of the vanquished rebels had, like their leader, fled thither. Two of them, John Hickes, a Nonconformist divine, and Richard Nelthorpe, a lawyer who had been outlawed for his share in the Rye House Plot, had sought refuge at the house of Alice, widow of John Lisle. John Lisle had sate in the Long Parliament and in the High Court of Justice, had been a Commissioner of the Great Seal in the days of the Commonwealth, and had been created a lord by Cromwell. The titles given by the Protector had not been recognised by any government which had ruled England since the downfall of his house; but they appear to have been often used in conversation even by Royalists. John Lisle's widow was therefore commonly known as the Lady Alice. She was related to many respectable, and to some noble, families; and she was generally esteemed even by the Tory gentlemen of her county. For it was well known to them that she had deeply regretted some violent acts in which her husband had borne a part, that she had shed bitter tears for Charles the First, and that she had protected and relieved many Cavaliers in their distress. The same womanly kindness, which had led her to befriend the Royalists in their time of trouble, would not suffer her to refuse a meal and a hiding place to the wretched men who now intreated her to protect them. She took them into her house, set meat and drink before them, and showed them where they might take rest. The next morning her dwelling was surrounded by soldiers. Strict search was made. Hickes was found concealed in the malthouse, and Nelthorpe in the chimney. If Lady Alice knew her guests to have been concerned in the insurrection, she was undoubtedly guilty of what in strictness is a capital crime. For the law of principal and accessory, as respects high treason, then was, and is to this day, in a state disgraceful to English jurisprudence. In cases of felony, a distinction, founded on justice and reason, is made between the principal and the accessory after the fact. He who conceals from justice one whom he knows to be a murderer, though liable to punishment, is not liable to the punishment of murder; but he who shelters one whom he knows to be a traitor is, according to all our jurists, guilty of high treason. It is unnecessary to point out the absurdity and cruelty of a law which includes under the same definition, and visits with the same penalty, offences lying at the opposite extremes of the scale of guilt. The feeling which makes the most loyal subject shrink from the thought of giving up to a shameful death the rebel who, vanquished, hunted down, and in mortal agony, begs for a morsel of bread and a cup of water, may be a weakness: but it is surely a weakness very nearly allied to virtue, a weakness which, constituted as human beings are, we can hardly eradicate from the mind without eradicating many noble and benevolent sentiments. A wise and good ruler may not think it right to sanction this weakness; but he will generally connive at it, or punish it very tenderly. In no case will he treat it as a crime of the blackest dye. Whether Flora Macdonald was justified in concealing the attainted heir of the Stuarts, whether a brave soldier of our own time was justified in assisting the escape of Lavalette, are questions on which casuists may differ: but to class such actions with the crimes of Guy Faux and Fieschi is an outrage to humanity and common sense. Such, however, is the classification of our law. It is evident that nothing but a lenient administration could make such a state of the law endurable. And it is just to say that, during many generations, no English government, save one, has treated with rigour persons guilty merely of harbouring defeated and flying insurgents. To women especially has been granted, by a kind of tacit prescription, the right of indulging, in the midst of havoc and vengeance, that compassion which is the most endearing of all their charms. Since the beginning of the great civil war, numerous rebels, some of them far more important than Hickes or Nelthorpe, have been protected against the severity of victorious governments by female adroitness and generosity. But no English ruler who has been thus baffled, the savage and implacable James alone excepted, has had the barbarity even to think of putting a lady to a cruel and shameful death for so venial and amiable a transgression.

Odious as the law was, it was strained for the purpose of destroying Alice Lisle. She could not, according to the doctrine laid down by the highest authority, be convicted till after the conviction of the rebels whom she had harboured. She was, however, sent to the bar before either Hickes or Nelthorpe had been tried. It was no easy matter in such a case to obtain a verdict for the crown. The witnesses prevaricated. The jury, consisting of the principal gentlemen of Hampshire, shrank from the thought of sending a fellow creature to the stake for conduct which seemed deserving rather of praise than of blame. Jeffreys was beside himself with fury. This was the first case of treason on the circuit; and there seemed to be a strong probability that his prey would escape him. He stormed, cursed, and swore in language which no well-bred man would have used at a race or a cockfight. One witness named Dunne, partly from concern for Lady Alice, and partly from fright at the threats and maledictions of the Chief Justice, entirely lost his head, and at last stood silent. "Oh how hard the truth is," said Jeffreys, "to come out of a lying Presbyterian knave." The witness, after a pause of some minutes, stammered a few unmeaning words. "Was there ever," exclaimed the judge, with an oath, "was there ever such a villain on the face of the earth? Dost thou believe that there is a God? Dost thou believe in hell fire? Of all the witnesses that I ever met with I never saw thy fellow." Still the poor man, scared out of his senses, remained mute; and again Jeffreys burst forth. "I hope, gentlemen of the jury, that you take notice of the horrible carriage of this fellow. How can one help abhorring both these men and their religion? A Turk is a saint to such a fellow as this. A Pagan would be ashamed of such villainy. Oh blessed Jesus! What a generation of vipers do we live among!" "I cannot tell what to say, my Lord," faltered Dunne. The judge again broke forth into a volley of oaths. "Was there ever," he cried, "such an impudent rascal? Hold the candle to him that we may see his brazen face. You, gentlemen, that are of counsel for the crown, see that an information for perjury be preferred against this fellow." After the witnesses had been thus handled, the Lady Alice was called on for her defence. She began by saying, what may possibly have been true, that, though she knew Hickes to be in trouble when she took him in, she did not know or suspect that he had been concerned in the rebellion. He was a divine, a man of peace. It had, therefore, never occurred to her that he could have borne arms against the government;

and she had supposed that he wished to conceal himself because warrants were out against him for field preaching. The Chief Justice began to storm. "But I will tell you. There is not one of those lying, snivelling, canting Presbyterians but, one way or another, had a hand in the rebellion. Presbytery has all manner of villainy in it. Nothing but Presbytery could have made Dunne such a rogue. Show me a Presbyterian; and I'll show thee a lying knave." He summed up in the same style, declaimed during an hour against Whigs and Dissenters, and reminded the jury that the prisoner's husband had borne a part in the death of Charles the First, a fact which was not proved by any testimony, and which, if it had been proved, would have been utterly irrelevant to the issue. The jury retired, and remained long in consultation. The judge grew impatient. He could not conceive, he said, how, in so plain a case, they should even have left the box. He sent a messenger to tell them that, if they did not instantly return, he would adjourn the court and lock them up all night. Thus put to the torture, they came, but came to say that they doubted whether the charge had been made out. Jeffreys expostulated with them vehemently, and, after another consultation, they gave a reluctant verdict of Guilty.

On the following morning sentence was pronounced. Jeffreys gave directions that Alice Lisle should be burned alive that very afternoon. This excess of barbarity moved the pity and indignation even of the class which was most devoted to the crown. The clergy of Winchester Cathedral remonstrated with the Chief Justice, who, brutal as he was, was not mad enough to risk a quarrel on such a subject with a body so much respected by the Tory party. He consented to put off the execution five days. During that time the friends of the prisoner besought James to show her mercy. Ladies of high rank interceded for her. Feversham, who, it is said, had been bribed to take the compassionate side, spoke in her favour. Clarendon, the King's brother in law, pleaded her cause. But all was vain. The utmost that could be obtained was that her sentence should be commuted from burning to beheading. She was put to death on a scaffold in the market place of Winchester, and underwent her fate with serene courage.

In Hampshire Alice Lisle was the only victim: but, on the day following her execution, Jeffreys reached Dorchester, the principal town of the county in which Monmouth had landed, and the judicial massacre began.

The court was hung, by order of the Chief Justice, with scarlet; and this innovation seemed to the multitude to indicate a bloody purpose. It was also rumoured that, when the clergyman who preached the assize sermon inforced the duty of mercy, the ferocious mouth of the Judge was distorted by an ominous grin. These things made men augur ill of what was to follow.

More than three hundred prisoners were to be tried. The work seemed heavy; but Jeffreys had a contrivance for making it light. He let it be understood that the only chance of obtaining pardon or respite was to plead guilty. Twenty-nine persons, who put themselves on their country and were convicted, were ordered to be tied up without delay. The remaining prisoners pleaded guilty by scores. Two hundred and ninety-two received sentence of death. The whole number hanged in Dorchester amounted to seventy-four.

From Dorchester Jeffreys proceeded to Exeter. The civil war had barely grazed the frontier of Devonshire. Here, therefore, comparatively few persons were capitally punished. Somersetshire, the chief seat of the rebellion, had been reserved for the last and most fearful vengeance. In this county two hundred and thirty-three prisoners were in a few days hanged, drawn, and quartered. At every spot where two roads met, on every market place, on the green of every large village which had furnished Monmouth with soldiers, ironed corpses clattering in the wind, or heads and quarters stuck on poles, poisoned the air, and made the traveller sick with horror. In many parishes the peasantry could not assemble in the house of God without seeing the ghastly face of a neighbour grinning at them over the porch. The Chief Justice was all himself. His spirits rose higher and higher as the work went on. He laughed, shouted, joked, and swore in such a way that many thought him drunk from morning to night. But in him it was not easy to distinguish the madness produced by evil passions from the madness produced by brandy. A prisoner affirmed that the witnesses who appeared against him were not entitled to credit. One of them, he said, was a Papist, and another a prostitute. "Thou impudent rebel," exclaimed the judge, "to reflect on the King's evidence! I see thee, villain, I see thee already with the halter round thy neck." Another produced testimony that he was a good Protestant. "Protestant!" said Jeffreys; "you mean Presbyterian. I'll hold you a wager of it. I can smell a Presbyterian forty miles." One wretched man moved the pity even of bitter Tories. "My Lord," they said, "this poor creature is on the parish." "Do not trouble yourselves," said the Judge, "I will ease the parish of the burden." It was not only on the prisoners that his fury broke forth. Gentlemen and noblemen of high consideration and stainless loyalty, who ventured to bring to his notice any extenuating circumstance, were almost sure to receive what he called, in the coarse dialect which he had learned in the pothouses of Whitechapel, a lick with the rough side of his tongue. Lord Stawell, a Tory peer, who could not conceal his horror at the remorseless manner in which his poor neighbours were butchered, was punished by having a corpse suspended in chains at his park gate. In such spectacles originated many tales of terror, which were long told over the cider by the Christmas fires of the farmers of Somersetshire.

Jeffreys boasted that he had hanged more traitors than all his predecessors together since the Conquest. It is certain that the number of persons whom he executed in one month, and in one shire, very much exceeded the number of all the political offenders who have been executed in our island since the Revolution. The rebellions of 1715 and 1745 were of longer duration, of wider extent, and of more formidable aspect than that which was put down at Sedgemoor. It has not been generally thought that, either after the rebellion of 1715, or after the rebellion of 1745, the

House of Hanover erred on the side of clemency. Yet all the executions of 1715 and 1745 added together will appear to have been few indeed when compared with those which disgraced the Bloody Assizes. The number of the rebels whom Jeffreys hanged on this circuit was three hundred and twenty.

At a later period, when all men of all parties spoke with horror of the Bloody Assizes, the wicked Judge and the wicked King attempted to vindicate themselves by throwing the blame on each other. Jeffreys, in the Tower, protested that, in his utmost cruelty, he had not gone beyond his master's express orders, nay, that he had fallen short of them. James, at Saint Germain's, would willingly have had it believed that his own inclinations had been on the side of clemency, and that unmerited obloquy had been brought on him by the violence of his minister. But neither of these hard-hearted men must be absolved at the expense of the other. The plea set up for James can be proved under his own hand to be false in fact. The plea of Jeffreys, even if it be true in fact, is utterly worthless.

V. KING JAMES ALIENATES HIS SUBJECTS

JAMES was now at the height of power and prosperity. Both in England and in Scotland he had vanquished his enemies, and had punished them with a severity which had indeed excited their bitterest hatred, but had, at the same time, effectually quelled their courage. The Whig party seemed extinct. The name of Whig was never used except as a term of reproach. The Parliament was devoted to the King; and it was in his power to keep that Parliament to the end of his reign. The Church was louder than ever in professions of attachment to him, and had, during the late insurrection, acted up to those professions. The Judges were his tools; and if they ceased to be so, it was in his power to remove them. The corporations were filled with his creatures. His revenues far exceeded those of his predecessors. His pride rose high. Visions of dominion and glory rose before him. He already saw himself, in imagination, the umpire of Europe, the champion of many states oppressed by one too powerful monarchy [that of Lewis the Fourteenth]. So early as the month of June [1685] he had assured the United Provinces [of Holland] that, as soon as the affairs of England were settled, he would show the world how little he feared France. In conformity with these assurances, he, within a month after the battle of Sedgemoor, concluded with the States General [of Holland] a defensive treaty. It was regarded, both at the Hague and at Versailles, as a most significant circumstance that Halifax, who was the constant and mortal enemy of French ascendency, and who had scarcely ever before been consulted on any grave affair since the beginning of the reign, took the lead on this occasion, and seemed to have the royal ear. It was a circumstance not less significant that no previous communication was made to Barillon [the French Ambassador]. Both he and his master were taken by surprise. Lewis was much troubled, and expressed great, and not unreasonable, anxiety as to the ulterior designs of the prince who had lately been his pensioner and vassal. There were strong rumours that William of Orange was busied in organizing a great confederacy, which was to include both branches of the House of Austria, the United Provinces, the kingdom of Sweden, and the electorate of Brandenburg. It now seemed that this confederacy would have at its head the King and Parliament of England.

One of his objects was to obtain a repeal of the Habeas Corpus Act, which he hated, as it was natural that a tyrant should hate the most stringent curb that ever legislation imposed on tyranny. This feeling remained deeply fixed in his mind to the last, and appears in the instructions which he drew up, in exile, for the guidance of his son. But the Habeas Corpus Act, though passed during the ascendency of the Whigs, was not more dear to the Whigs than to the Tories. It is indeed not wonderful that this great law should be highly prized by all Englishmen without distinction of party: for it is a law which, not by circuitous, but by direct operation, adds to the security and happiness of every inhabitant of the realm.

James had yet another design, odious to the party which had set him on the throne and which had upheld him there. He wished to form a great standing army. He had taken advantage of the late insurrection to make large additions to the military force which his brother had left. The bodies now designated as the first six regiments of dragoon guards, the third and fourth regiments of dragoons, and the nine regiments of infantry of the line, from the seventh to the fifteenth inclusive, had just been raised. The effect of these augmentations, and of the recall of the garrison of Tangier, was that the number of regular troops in England had, in a few months, been increased from six thousand to near twenty thousand. No English King had ever, in time of peace, had such a force at his command. Yet even with this force James was not content. He often repeated that no confidence could be placed in the fidelity of the trainbands, that they sympathised with all the passions of the class to which they belonged, that, at Sedgemoor, there had been more militia men in the rebel army than in the royal encampment, and that, if the throne had been defended only by the array of the counties, Monmouth would have marched in triumph from Lyme to London.

The revenue, large as it was when compared with that of former Kings, barely sufficed to meet this new charge. A great part of the produce of the new taxes was absorbed by the naval expenditure. At the close of the late reign the whole cost of the army, the Tangier regiments included, had been under three hundred thousand pounds a year. Six hundred thousand pounds a year would not now suffice. If any further augmentation were made, it would be necessary to demand a supply from Parliament; and it was not likely that Parliament would be in a complying mood. The very name of standing army was hateful to the whole nation, and to no part of the nation more hateful than to the Cavalier gentlemen who filled the Lower House. In their minds a standing army was inseparably associated with the Rump, with the Protector, with the spoliation of the Church, with the purgation of the Universities, with the abolition of the peerage, with the murder of the King, with the sullen reign of the Saints, with cant and asceticism, with fines and sequestrations, with the insults which Major Generals, sprung from the dregs of the people, had offered to the oldest and most honourable families of the kingdom. There was, moreover, scarcely a baronet or a squire in the Parliament who did not owe part of his importance in his own county to his rank in the militia. If that national force were set aside, the gentry of England must lose much of their dignity and influence. It was therefore probable that the King would find it more difficult to obtain funds for the support of his army than even to obtain the repeal of the Habeas Corpus Act.

But both the designs which have been mentioned were subordinate to one great design on which the King's whole soul was bent, but which was abhorred by those Tory gentlemen who were ready to shed their blood for his rights, abhorred by that Church which had never, during three generations of civil discord, wavered in fidelity to his house, abhorred even by that army on which, in the last extremity, he must rely.

His religion was still under proscription. Many rigorous laws against Roman Catholics appeared on the Statute Book, and had, within no long time, been rigorously executed. The Test Act excluded from civil and military office all who dissented from the Church of England; and, by a subsequent Act, passed when the fictions of [Titus] Oates had driven the nation wild, it had been provided that no person should sit in either House of Parliament without solemnly abjuring the doctrine of transubstantiation. That the King should wish to obtain for the Church to which he belonged a complete toleration was natural and right; nor is there any reason to doubt that, by a little patience, prudence, and justice, such a toleration might have been obtained.

The extreme antipathy and dread with which the English people regarded his religion was not to be ascribed solely or chiefly to theological animosity. That salvation might be found in the Church of Rome, nay, that some members of that Church had been among the brightest examples of Christian virtue, was admitted by all divines of the Anglican communion and by the most illustrious Nonconformists. It is notorious that the penal laws against Popery were strenuously defended by many who thought Arianism, Quakerism, and Judaism more dangerous, in a spiritual point of view, than Popery, and who yet showed no disposition to enact similar laws against Arians, Quakers, or Jews.

It is easy to explain why the Roman Catholic was treated with less indulgence than was shown to men who renounced the doctrine of the Nicene fathers, and even to men who had not been admitted by baptism within the Christian pale. There was among the English a strong conviction that the Roman Catholic, where the interests of his religion were concerned, thought himself free from all the ordinary rules of morality, nay, that he thought it meritorious to violate those rules if, by so doing, he could avert injury or reproach from the Church of which he was a member.

It is evident that, in such circumstances, the greatest service which an English Roman Catholic could render to his brethren in the faith was to convince the public that, whatever some rash men might, in times of violent excitement, have written or done, his Church did not hold that any end could sanctify means inconsistent with morality. And this great service it was in the power of James to render. He was King. He was more powerful than any English King had been within the memory of the oldest man. It depended on him whether the reproach which lay on his religion should be taken away or should be made permanent.

Had he conformed to the laws, had he fulfilled his promises, had he abstained from employing any unrighteous methods for the propagation of his own theological tenets, had he suspended the operation of the penal statutes by a large exercise of his unquestionable prerogative of mercy, but, at the same time, carefully abstained from violating the civil or ecclesiastical constitution of the realm, the feeling of his people must have undergone a rapid change. But such reasoning had no effect on the slow understanding and imperious temper of James. In his eagerness to remove the disabilities under which the professors of his religion lay, he took a course which convinced the most enlightened and tolerant Protestants of his time that those disabilities were essential to the safety of the state. To his policy the English Roman Catholics owed three years of lawless and insolent triumph, and a hundred and forty years of subjection and degradation.

Many members of his Church held commissions in the newly raised regiments. This breach of the law for a time passed uncensured: for men were not disposed to note every irregularity which was committed by a King suddenly called upon to defend his crown and his life against rebels. But the danger was now over. The insurgents had been vanquished and punished. Their unsuccessful attempt had strengthened the government which they had hoped to overthrow. Yet still James continued to grant commissions to unqualified persons; and speedily it was announced that he was determined to be no longer bound by the Test Act, that he hoped to induce the Parliament to repeal that Act, but that, if the Parliament proved refractory, he would not the less have his own way.

As soon as this was known, a deep murmur, the forerunner of a tempest, gave him warning that the spirit before which his grandfather, his father, and his brother had been compelled to recede, though dormant, was not extinct. Opposition appeared first in the cabinet. Halifax did not attempt to conceal his disgust and alarm. At the Council board he courageously gave utterance to those feelings which, as it soon appeared, pervaded the whole nation.

Some of those who were about the King advised him not, on the eve of the meeting of Parliament, to drive the most eloquent and accomplished statesman of the age into opposition. The king was peremptory. Halifax was informed that his services were no longer needed; and his name was struck out of the Council Book.

His dismission produced a great sensation not only in England, but also at Paris, at Vienna, and at the Hague: for it was well known, that he had always laboured to counteract the influence exercised by the court of Versailles on English affairs.

It soon became clear that Halifax would have many followers. A portion of the Tories, with their older leader, Danby, at their head, began to hold Whiggish language. Even the prelates hinted that there was a point at which the loyalty due to the prince must yield to higher considerations. The discontent of the chiefs of the army was still more extraordinary and still more formidable. Already began to appear the first symptoms of that feeling which, three years later, impelled so many officers of high rank to desert the royal standard. Factions were fast taking new forms. Old allies were separating. Old enemies were uniting. Discontent was spreading fast through all the ranks of the party lately dominant. A hope, still indeed faint and indefinite, of victory and revenge, animated the party which had lately seemed to be extinct. Amidst such circumstances the eventful and troubled year 1685 terminated, and the year 1686 began.

From his predecessors James had inherited two prerogatives, of which the limits had never been defined with strict accuracy, and which, if exerted without any limit, would of themselves have sufficed to overturn the whole polity of the State and of the Church. These were the dispensing power and the ecclesiastical supremacy. By means of the dispensing power the King purposed to admit Roman Catholics, not merely to civil and military, but to spiritual, offices. By means of the ecclesiastical supremacy he hoped to make the Anglican clergy his instruments for the destruction of their own religion.

No course was too bold for James. The Deanery of Christchurch became vacant. That office was, both in dignity and in emolument, one of the highest in the University of Oxford. The Dean was charged with the government of a greater number of youths of high connections and of great hopes than could then be found in any other college. He was also the head of a Cathedral. In both characters it was necessary that he should be a member of the Church of England. Nevertheless John Massey, who was notoriously a member of the Church of Rome, and who had not one single recommendation, except that he was a member of the Church of Rome, was appointed by virtue of the dispensing power; and soon within the walls of Christchurch an altar was decked, at which mass was daily celebrated.

Yet even this was a small evil compared with that which Protestants had good ground to apprehend. It seemed but too probable that the whole government of the Anglican Church would shortly pass into the hands of her deadly enemies. Three important sees had lately become vacant, that of York, that of Chester, and that of Oxford. The Bishopric of Oxford was given to Samuel Parker, a parasite, whose religion, if he had any religion, was that of Rome, and who called himself a Protestant only because he was encumbered with a wife. The Bishopric of Chester, vacant by the death of John Pearson, a great name both in philology and in divinity, was bestowed on Thomas Cartwright, a still viler sycophant than Parker. The Archbishopric of York remained several years vacant. As no good reason could be found for leaving so important a place unfilled, men suspected that the nomination was delayed only till the King could venture to place the mitre on the head of an avowed Papist.

The celebration of the Roman Catholic worship had long been pro- hibited by Act of Parliament. During several generations no Roman Catholic clergyman had dared to exhibit himself in any public place with the badges of his office. Against the regular clergy, and against the rest- less and subtle Jesuits by name, had been enacted a succession of rigorous statutes. Every Jesuit who set foot in this country was liable to be hanged, drawn, and quartered. A reward was offered for his detection. He was not allowed to take advantage of the general rule, that men are not bound to accuse themselves. Whoever was suspected of being a Jesuit might be interrogated, and, if he refused to answer, might be sent to prison for life. These laws, though they had not, except when there was supposed to be some peculiar danger, been strictly executed, and though they had never prevented Jesuits from resorting to England, had made disguise necessary. But all disguise was now thrown off. Injudicious members of the King's Church, encouraged by him, took a pride in defying statutes which were still of undoubted validity, and feelings which had a stronger hold of the national mind than at any former period. Roman Catholic chapels rose all over the country. Cowls, girdles of ropes, and strings of beads constantly appeared in the streets, and astonished a population, the oldest of whom had never seen a conventual garb except on the stage. A convent rose at Clerkenwell on the site of the ancient cloister of Saint John. The Franciscans occupied a mansion in Lincoln's Inn Fields. The Carmelites were quartered in the City. A society of Benedictine monks was lodged in Saint James's Palace. In the Savoy a spacious house, includ- ing a church and a school, was built for the Jesuits. The skill and care with which those fathers had, during several generations, conducted the education of youth, had drawn forth reluctant praises from the wisest Protestants. Bacon had pronounced the mode of instruction followed in the Jesuit colleges to be the best yet known in the world, and had warmly expressed his regret that so admirable a system of intellectual and moral discipline should be subservient to the interests of a corrupt religion. It was not improbable that the new academy in the Savoy might, under royal patronage, prove a formidable rival to the great foundations of Eton, Westminster, and Winchester. Indeed, soon after the school was opened, the classes consisted of four hundred boys, about one half of whom were

Protestants. The Protestant pupils were not required to attend mass: but there could be no doubt that the influence of able preceptors, devoted to the Roman Catholic Church, and versed in all the arts which win the confidence and affection of youth, would make many converts.

These things produced great excitement among the populace, which is always more moved by what impresses the senses than by what is addressed to the reason. Thousands of rude and ignorant men, to whom the dispensing power and the Ecclesiastical Commission were words without a meaning, saw with dismay and indignation a Jesuit college rising on the banks of the Thames, friars in hoods and gowns walking in the Strand, and crowds of devotees pressing in at the doors of temples where homage was paid to graven images. Riots broke out in several parts of the country. At Coventry and Worcester the Roman Catholic worship was violently interrupted. At Bristol the rabble, countenanced, it was said, by the magistrates, exhibited a profane and indecent pageant, in which the Virgin Mary was represented by a buffoon, and in which a mock host was carried in procession. The garrison was called out to disperse the mob. The mob, then and ever since one of the fiercest in the kingdom, resisted. Blows were exchanged, and serious hurts inflicted. The agitation was great in the capital, and greater in the City, properly so called, than at Westminster. For the people of Westminster had been accustomed to see among them the private chapels of Roman Catholic Ambassadors: but the City had not, within living memory, been poluted by any idolatrous exhibition. Now, however, the resident of the Elector Palatine, encouraged by the King, fitted up a chapel in Lime Street. The heads of the corporation, though men selected for office on account of their known Toryism, protested against this proceeding, which, as they said, the ablest gentlemen of the long robe regarded as illegal. The Lord Mayor was ordered to appear before the Privy Council. "Take heed what you do," said the King. "Obey me; and do not trouble yourself either about gentlemen of the long robe or gentlemen of the short robe." The Chancellor took up the word, and reprimanded the unfortunate magistrate with the genuine eloquence of the Old Bailey bar. The chapel was opened. All the neighbourhood was soon in commotion. Great crowds assembled in Cheapside to attack the new mass house. The priests were insulted. A crucifix was taken out of the building and set up on the parish pump. The Lord Mayor came to quell the tumult, but was received with cries of "No wooden gods." The trainbands were ordered to disperse the crowd: but they shared in the popular feeling; and murmurs were heard from the ranks, "We cannot in conscience fight for Popery."

VI. THE SEVEN BISHOPS AND THE ROYAL HEIR

On the eighteenth of March [1687] King James informed the Privy Council that he had determined to prorogue the Parliament till the end of November, and to grant, by his own authority, entire liberty of conscience to all his subjects. On the fourth of April appeared the memorable Declaration of Indulgence.

In this Declaration the King avowed that it was his earnest wish to see his people members of that Church to which he himself belonged. But, since that could not be, he announced his intention to protect them in the free exercise of their religion. He repeated all those phrases which, eight years before, when he was himself an oppressed man, had been familiar to his lips, but which he had ceased to use from the day on which a turn of fortune had put it into his power to be an oppressor. He had long been convinced, he said, that conscience was not to be forced, that persecution was unfavourable to population and to trade, and that it never attained the ends which persecutors had in view. He repeated his promise, already often repeated and often violated, that he would protect the Established Church in the enjoyment of her legal rights. He then proceeded to annul, by his own sole authority, a long series of statutes. He suspended all penal laws against all classes of Noncomformists. He authorised both Roman Catholics and Protestant Dissenters to perform their worship publicly. He forbade his subjects, on pain of his highest displeasure, to molest any religious assembly. He also abrogated all those acts which imposed any religious test as a qualification for any civil or military office.

On the twenty-seventh of April 1688, the King put forth a second Declaration of Indulgence. In this paper he recited at length the Declaration of the preceding April. His past life, he said, ought to have convinced his people that he was not a person who could easily be induced to depart from any resolution which he had formed. But, as designing men had attempted to persuade the world that he might be prevailed on to give way in this matter, he thought it necessary to proclaim that his purpose was immutably fixed, that he was resolved to employ those only who were prepared to concur in his design, and that he had, in pursuance of that resolution, dismissed many of his disobedient servants from civil and military employments. He announced that he meant to hold a Parliament in November at the latest; and he exhorted his subjects to choose representatives who would assist him in the great work which he had undertaken.

This Declaration at first produced little sensation. It contained nothing new; and men wondered that the King should think it worth while to publish a solemn manifesto merely for the purpose of telling them that he had not changed his mind. Perhaps James was nettled by the indifference with which the announcement of his fixed resolution was received by the public, and thought that his dignity and authority would suffer unless he without delay did something novel and striking. On the fourth of May, accordingly, he made an Order in Council that his Declaration of the preceding week should be read, on two successive Sundays at the time of divine service, by the officiating ministers of all the churches and chapels of the kingdom. In London and in the suburbs the reading was to take place on the twentieth and twenty-seventh of May, in other parts of England on the third and tenth of June. The Bishops were directed to distribute copies of the Declaration through their respective dioceses.

When it is considered that the clergy of the Established Church, with scarcely an exception, regarded the Indulgence as a violation of the laws of the realm, as a breach of the plighted faith of the King, and as a fatal blow levelled at the interest and dignity of their own profession, it will scarcely admit of doubt that the Order in Council was intended to be felt by them as a cruel affront. It was popularly believed that [Father] Petre [Jesuit leader] had avowed this intention in a coarse metaphor borrowed from the rhetoric of the East. He would, he said, make them eat dirt, the vilest and most loathsome of all dirt. But, tyrannical and malignant as the mandate was, would the Anglican priesthood refuse to obey? The King's temper was arbitrary and severe. The proceedings of the Ecclesiastical Commission were as summary as those of a court martial. Whoever ventured to resist might in a week be ejected from his parsonage, deprived of his whole income, pronounced incapable of holding any other spiritual preferment, and left to beg from door to door.

The London clergy, then universally acknowledged to be the flower of their profession, held a meeting. Fifteen Doctors of Divinity were present. A resolution by which all present pledged themselves to one another not to read the Declaration was then drawn up. The paper was sent round the city, and was speedily subscribed by eighty-five incumbents.

On the eighteenth [of May] a meeting of prelates and of other eminent divines was held at Lambeth. Tillotson, Tenison, Stillingfleet, Patrick, and Sherlock, were present. Prayers were solemnly read before the consultation began. After long deliberation, a petition embodying the general sense was written by the Archbishop with his own hand. It was not drawn up with much felicity of style. Indeed, the cumbrous and inelegant structure of the sentences brought on Sancroft some raillery, which he bore with less patience than he showed under much heavier trials. But in substance nothing could be more skilfully framed than this memorable document. All disloyalty, all intolerance, was earnestly disclaimed. The King was assured that the Church still was, as she had ever been, faithful to the throne. He was assured also that the Bishops would, in proper place and time, as Lords of Parliament and members of the Upper House of Convocation, show that they by no means wanted tenderness for the conscientious scruples of Dissenters. But Parliament had, both in the late and in the present reign, pronounced that the sovereign was not constitutionally competent to dispense with statutes in matters ecclesiastical. The Declaration was therefore illegal; and the petitioners could not, in prudence, honour, or conscience, be parties to the solemn publication of an illegal Declaration in the house of God, and during the time of divine service.

This paper was signed by the Archbishop and by six of his suffragans,

Lloyd of St. Asaph, Turner of Ely, Lake of Chichester, Ken of Bath and Wells, White of Peterborough, and Trelawney of Bristol. The Bishop of London, being under suspension, did not sign.

In the City and Liberties of London were about a hundred parish churches. In only four of these was the Order in Council obeyed.

Another week of anxiety and agitation passed away. Sunday came again. Again the churches of the capital were thronged by hundreds of thousands. The Declaration was read nowhere except at the very few places where it had been read the week before.

Even the King stood aghast for a moment at the violence of the tempest which he had raised. What step was he next to take? He must either advance or recede: and it was impossible to advance without peril, or to recede without humiliation. At one moment he determined to put forth a second order enjoining the clergy in high and angry terms to publish his Declaration, and menacing every one who should be refractory with instant suspension. This order was drawn up and sent to the press, then recalled, then a second time sent to the press, then recalled a second time. A different plan was suggested by some of those who were for rigorous measures.

On the twenty-seventh of May it was notified to the Bishops that on the eighth of June they must appear before the King in Council.

On the evening of the eighth of June the seven prelates, furnished by the ablest lawyers in England with full advice, repaired to the palace, and were called into the Council chamber. The King was so absurd as to think himself personally affronted because they chose, on a legal question, to be guided by legal advice. "You believe everybody," he said, "rather than me." He was indeed mortified and alarmed. For he had gone so far that, if they persisted, he had no choice left but to send them to prison; and, though he by no means foresaw all the consequences of such a step, he foresaw probably enough to disturb him. They were resolute. A warrant was therefore made out directing the Lieutenant of the Tower to keep them in safe custody, and a barge was manned to convey them down the river.

It was known all over London that the Bishops were before the Council. The public anxiety was intense. A great multitude filled the courts of Whitehall and all the neighbouring streets. Many people were in the habit of refreshing themselves at the close of a summer day with the cool air of the Thames. But on this evening the whole river was alive with wherries. When the Seven came forth under a guard, the emotions of the people broke through all restraint. Thousands fell on their knees and prayed aloud for the men who had, with the Christian courage of Ridley and Latimer, confronted a tyrant inflamed by all the bigotry of Mary. Many dashed into the stream, and, up to their waists in ooze and water, cried to the holy fathers to bless them. All down the river, from Whitehall to London Bridge, the royal barge passed between lines of boats, from which arose a shout of "God bless your Lordships."

Scarcely had the gates of the Tower been closed on the prisoners when an event took place which increased the public excitement. It had been announced that the Queen [was *enceinte*. She] did not expect to be delivered till July. But, on the day after the Bishops had appeared before the Council, it was observed that the King seemed to be anxious about her state. In the evening, however, she sate playing cards at Whitehall till near midnight. Then she was carried in a sedan to Saint James's Palace, where apartments had been very hastily fitted up for her reception. Soon messengers were running about in all directions to summon physicians and priests, Lords of the Council, and Ladies of the Bedchamber. In a few hours many public functionaries and women of rank were assembled in the Queen's room. There, on the morning of Sunday, the tenth of June, a day long kept sacred by the too faithful adherents of a bad cause, was born the most unfortunate of princes, destined to seventy-seven years of exile and wandering, of vain projects, of honours more galling than insults, and of hopes such as make the heart sick.

The calamities of the poor child had begun before his birth. The nation over which, according to the ordinary course of succession, he would have reigned, was fully persuaded that his mother was not really pregnant. By whatever evidence the fact of his birth had been proved, a considerable number of people would probably have persisted in maintaining that the Jesuits had practised some skilful sleight of hand: and the evidence, partly from accident, partly from gross mismanagement, was open to some objections. Many persons of both sexes were in the royal bedchamber when the child first saw the light; but none of them enjoyed any large measure of public confidence. Of the Privy Councillors present half were Roman Catholics; and those who called themselves Protestants were generally regarded as traitors to their country and their God. Many of the women in attendance were French, Italian, and Portuguese. Of the English ladies some were Papists, and some were the wives of Papists. Some persons who were peculiarly entitled to be present, and whose testimony would have satisfied all minds accessible to reason, were absent; and for their absence the King was held responsible. The Princess Anne was, of all the inhabitants of the island, the most deeply interested in the event. Her sex and her experience qualified her to act as the guardian of her sister's birthright and her own. She had conceived strong suspicions which were daily confirmed by circumstances trifling or imaginary. She fancied that the Queen carefully shunned her scrutiny, and ascribed to guilt a reserve which was perhaps the effect of delicacy. In this temper Anne had determined to be present and vigilant when the critical day should arrive. But she had not thought it necessary to be at her post a month before that day, and had, in compliance, it was said, with her father's advice, gone to drink the Bath waters. Sancroft, whose great place made it his duty to attend, and on whose probity the nation placed entire reliance, had a few hours before been sent to the Tower by James. The Dutch Ambassador might be regarded as the representative of William, who, as first prince of the blood and consort of the King's eldest daughter, had a deep interest in what was passing. He was not invited to be present.

Posterity has fully acquitted the King of the fraud which his people imputed to him. But it is impossible to acquit him of folly and perverseness such as explain and excuse the error of his contemporaries. He was perfectly aware of the suspicions which were abroad. He ought to have known that those suspicions would not be dispelled by the evidence of members of the Church of Rome, or of persons who, though they might call themselves members of the Church of England, had shown themselves ready to sacrifice the interests of the Church of England in order to obtain his favour. That he was taken by surprise is true. But he had twelve hours to make his arrangements. He found no difficulty in crowding St. James's Palace with bigots and sycophants on whose word the nation placed no reliance. It would have been quite as easy to procure the attendance of some eminent persons whose attachment to the Prince and to the established religion was unquestionable.

The cry of the whole nation was that an imposture had been practised. Papists had, during some months, been predicting, from the pulpit and through the press, in prose and verse, in English and Latin, that a Prince of Wales would be given to the prayers of the Church; and they had now accomplished their own prophecy. Every witness who could not be corrupted or deceived had been studiously excluded. Anne had been tricked into visiting Bath. The Primate had, on the very day preceding that which had been fixed for the villainy, been sent to prison in defiance of the rules of law and of the privileges of peerage. Not a single man or woman who had the smallest interest in detecting the fraud had been suffered to be present. The Queen had been removed suddenly and at the dead of night to St. James's Palace, because that building, less commodious for honest purposes than Whitehall, had some rooms and passages well suited for the purpose of the Jesuits.

The demeanour of the seven prelates meanwhile strengthened the interest which their situation excited. On the evening of the Black Friday, as it was called, on which they were committed, they reached their prison just at the hour of divine service. They instantly hastened to the chapel. It chanced that in the second lesson were these words: "In all things approving ourselves as the ministers of God, in much patience, in afflictions, in distresses, in stripes, in imprisonments." All zealous Churchmen were delighted by this coincidence, and remembered how much comfort a similar coincidence had given, near forty years before, to Charles the First at the time of his death.

Before the day of trial the agitation had spread to the farthest corners of the island. From Scotland the Bishops received letters assuring them of the sympathy of the Presbyterians of that country, so long and so bitterly hostile to prelacy. The people of Cornwall, a fierce, bold, and athletic race, among whom there was a stronger provincial feeling than in any other part of the realm, were greatly moved by the danger of Trelawney, whom they reverenced less as a ruler of the Church than as the head of an honourable house, and the heir through twenty descents of ancestors who had been of great note before the Normans had set foot on English ground. All over the county the peasants chanted a ballad of which the burden is still remembered:

"And shall Trelawney die, and shall Trelawney die?
Then thirty thousand Cornish boys will know the reason why."

On the twenty-ninth of June, Westminster Hall, Old and New Palace Yard, and all the neighbouring streets to a great distance were thronged with people. Such an auditory had never before and has never since been assembled in the Court of King's Bench. Thirty-five temporal peers of the realm were counted in the crowd.

All the four Judges of the Court were on the bench. The jury was sworn; it consisted of persons of highly respectable station. The foreman was Sir Roger Langley, a baronet of old and honourable family. With him were joined a knight and ten esquires, several of whom are known to have been men of large possessions. There were some Nonconformists in the number; for the Bishops had wisely resolved not to show any distrust of the Protestant Dissenters.

The crown lawyers undertook to prove that the Bishops had published a libel in the county of Middlesex. The difficulties were great. The delivery of the petition to the King was undoubtedly, in the eye of the law, a publication. But how was this delivery to be proved? No person had been present at the audience in the royal closet, except the King and the defendants. The King could not well be sworn. It was therefore only by the admissions of the defendants that the fact of publication could be established. Blathwayt [Clerk of the Privy Council] was examined, but in vain. He well remembered, he said, that the Bishops owned their hands; but he did not remember that they owned the paper which lay on the table of the Privy Council to be the same paper which they had delivered to the King, or that they were even interrogated on that point. Several other official men who had been in attendance on the Council were called, and among them Samuel Pepys, Secretary of the Admiralty; but none of them could remember that anything was said about the delivery. It was to no purpose that Williams [one of the crown lawyers] put leading questions till the counsel on the other side declared that such twisting, such wiredrawing, was never seen in a court of justice, and till Wright himself [one of the presiding Judges] was forced to admit that the Solicitor's mode of examination was contrary to all rule. As witness after witness answered in the negative, roars of laughter and shouts of triumph, which the Judges did not even attempt to silence, shook the hall.

At length Wright proceeded to sum up the evidence. His language showed that the awe in which he stood of the government was tempered by the awe with which the audience, so numerous, so splendid, and so strongly excited, had impressed him. He said that he would give no opinion on the question of the dispensing power, that it was not necessary for him to do so, that he could not agree with much of the Solicitor's speech, that it was the right of the subject to petition, but that the particular petition before the Court was improperly worded, and was, in the contemplation of law, a libel.

It was dark before the jury retired to consider of their verdict. The night was a night of intense anxiety.

At ten [the next morning] the Court again met. The crowd was greater than ever. The jury appeared in their box; and there was a breathless stillness.

Sir Samuel Astry spoke. "Do you find the defendants, or any of them, guilty of the misdemeanour whereof they are impeached, or not guilty?" Sir Roger Langley answered, "Not guilty." As the words passed his lips, benches and galleries raised a shout. In a moment ten thousand persons, who crowded the great hall, replied with a still louder shout, which made the old oaken roof crack; and in another moment the innumerable throng without set up a third huzza, which was heard at Temple Bar. The boats which covered the Thames gave an answering cheer. A peal of gunpowder was heard on the water, and another, and another; and so, in a few moments, the glad tidings went flying past the Savoy and the Friars to London Bridge, and to the forest of masts below. As the news spread, streets and squares, market places and coffeehouses, broke forth into acclamations. Yet were the acclamations less strange than the weeping. For the feelings of men had been wound up to such a point that at length the stern English nature, so little used to outward signs of emotion, gave way, and thousands sobbed aloud for very joy.

VII. THE APPEAL TO WILLIAM

THE acquittal of the Bishops was not the only event which makes the thirtieth of June 1688 a great epoch in history. On that day, while the bells of a hundred churches were ringing, while multitudes were busied, from Hyde Park to Mile End, in piling faggots and dressing Popes for the rejoicings of the night, was despatched from London to the Hague an instrument scarcely less important to the liberties of England than the Great Charter.

The prosecution of the Bishops, and the birth of the Prince of Wales, had produced a great revolution in the feelings of many Tories. At the very moment at which their Church was suffering the last excess of injury and insult, they were compelled to renounce the hope of peaceful deliverance. Hitherto they had flattered themselves that the trial to which their loyalty was subjected would, though severe, be temporary, and that their wrongs would shortly be redressed without any violation of the ordinary rule of succession. A very different prospect was now before them. As far as they could look forward they saw only misgovernment, such as that of the last three years, extending through ages. The cradle of the heir apparent of the crown was surrounded by Jesuits. Deadly hatred of that Church of which he would one day be the head would be studiously instilled into his infant mind, would be the guiding principle of his life, and would be bequeathed by him to his posterity. This vista of calamities had no end. It stretched beyond the life of the youngest man living, beyond the eighteenth century. None could say how many generations of Protestant Englishmen might have to bear oppression, such as, even when it had been believed to be short, had been found almost insupportable. Was there then no remedy? One remedy there was, quick, sharp, and decisive, a remedy which the Whigs had been but too ready to employ, but which had always been regarded by the Tories as, in all cases, unlawful.

In May, before the birth of the Prince of Wales, and while it was still uncertain whether the Declaration would or would not be read in the churches, Edward Russell had repaired to the Hague. He had strongly represented to the Prince of Orange the state of the public mind, and had advised his Highness to appear in England at the head of a strong body of troops, and to call the people to arms.

William had seen, at a glance, the whole importance of the crisis. "Now or never," he exclaimed in Latin.

During June the meetings of those who were in the secret were frequent. At length, on the last day of the month, the day on which the Bishops were pronounced not guilty, the decisive step was taken. A formal invitation, transcribed by [Henry] Sidney [the Earl of Romney] but drawn up by some person more skilled than Sidney, in the art of composition, was despatched to the Hague. In this paper William was assured that nineteen twentieths of the English people were desirous of a change, and would willingly join to effect it, if only they could obtain the help of such a force from abroad as might secure those who should rise in arms from the danger of being dispersed and slaughtered before they could form themselves into anything like military order. If his Highness would appear in the island at the head of some troops, tens of thousands would hasten to his standard.

The conspirators implored the Prince to come among them with as little delay as possible. They pledged their honour that they would join him; and they undertook to secure the co-operation of as large a number of persons as could safely be trusted with so momentous and perilous a secret. On one point they thought it their duty to remonstrate with his Highness. He had not taken advantage of the opinion which the great body of the English people had formed respecting the late birth. He had, on the contrary, sent congratulations to Whitehall, and had thus seemed to acknowledge that the child who was called Prince of Wales was rightful heir of the throne. This was a grave error, and had damped the zeal of many. Not one person in a thousand doubted that the boy was suppositititious; and the Prince would be wanting to his own interests if the suspicious circumstances which had attended the Queen's confinement were not put prominently forward among his reasons for taking arms.

This paper was signed in cipher by the seven chiefs of the conspiracy, Shrewsbury, Devonshire, Danby, Lumley, Compton, Russell and Sidney. [Arthur] Herbert [former Master of the Robes and Rear Admiral of England] undertook to be their messenger. His errand was one of no ordinary peril. He assumed the garb of a common sailor, and in this disguise reached the Dutch coast in safety, on the Friday after the trial of the Bishops. He instantly hastened to the Prince. Bentinck and Dykvelt were summoned, and several days were passed in deliberation. The first result of this deliberation was that the prayer for the Prince of Wales ceased to be read in the Princess's chapel.

From his wife William had no opposition to apprehend. Her understanding had been completely subjugated by his; and, what is more extraordinary, he had won her entire affection. He was to her in the place of the parents whom she had lost by death and by estrangement, of the children who had been denied to her prayers, and of the country from which she was banished. His empire over her heart was divided only with her God. To her father [James the Second] she had probably never been attached: she had quitted him young: many years had elapsed since she had seen him; and no part of his conduct to her, since her marriage, had indicated tenderness on his part, or had been calculated to call forth tenderness on hers. He had done all in his power to disturb her domestic happiness, and had established a system of spying, eavesdropping, and talebearing under her roof. He had a far greater revenue than any of his predecessors had ever possessed, and regularly allowed to her younger sister forty thousand pounds a year: but the heiress presumptive of his throne had never received from him the smallest pecuniary assistance, and was scarcely able to make that appearance which became her high rank among European princesses. She had ventured to intercede with him on behalf of her old friend and preceptor Compton, who, for refusing to commit an act of flagitious injustice, had been suspended from his episcopal functions; but she had been ungraciously repulsed. From the day on which it had become clear that she and her husband were determined not to be parties to the subversion of the English constitution, one chief object of the politics of James had been to injure them both. It was now believed by the great body of his people, and by many persons high in rank and distinguished by abilities, that he had introduced a supposititious Prince of Wales into the royal family, in order to deprive her of a magnificent inheritance; and there is no reason to doubt that she partook of the prevailing suspicion. That she should love such a father was impossible. Her religious principles, indeed, were so strict that she would probably have tried to perform what she considered as her duty, even to a father whom she did not love. On the present occasion, however, she judged that the claim of James to her obedience ought to yield to a claim more sacred. And indeed all divines and publicists agree in this, that, when the daughter of a prince of one country is married to a prince of another country, she is bound to forget her own people and her father's house, and, in the event of a rupture between her husband and her parents, to side with her husband. This is the undoubted rule even when the husband is in the wrong; and to Mary the enterprise which William meditated appeared not only just, but holy.

VIII.　THE ARRIVAL OF WILLIAM AND MARY

And now William [who had arrived in London] thought that the time had come when he ought to explain himself. He accordingly sent for Halifax, Danby, Shrewsbury, and some other political leaders of great note, and, with that air of stoical apathy under which he had, from a boy, been in the habit of concealing his strongest emotions, addressed to them a few deeply meditated and weighty words.

He had hitherto, he said, remained silent; he had used neither solicitation nor menace: he had not even suffered a hint of his opinions or wishes to get abroad: but a crisis had now arrived at which it was necessary for him to declare his intentions. He had no right and no wish to dictate to the Convention. All that he claimed was the privilege of declining any office which he felt that he could not hold with honour to himself and with benefit to the public.

A strong party was for a Regency. It was for the Houses to determine whether such an arrangement would be for the interest of the nation. He had a decided opinion on that point; and he thought it right to say distinctly that he would not be Regent.

Another party was for placing the Princess on the throne, and for giving to him, during her life, the title of King, and such a share in the administration as she might be pleased to allow him. He could not stoop to such a post. He esteemed the Princess as much as it was possible for man to esteem woman: but not even from her would he accept a subordinate and a precarious place in the government. He was so made that he could not submit to be tied to the apron strings even of the best of wives. He did not desire to take any part in English affairs; but, if he did consent to take a part, there was one part only which he could usefully or honorably take. If the Estates offered him the crown for life, he would accept it. If not, he should, without repining, return to his native country. He concluded by saying that he thought it reasonable that the Lady Anne and her posterity should be preferred in the succession to any children whom he might have by any other wife than the Lady Mary.

The meeting broke up; and what the Prince had said was in a few hours known all over London. That he must be King was now clear. The only question was whether he should hold the regal dignity alone or conjointly with the Princess. Halifax and a few other politicians, who saw in a strong light the danger of dividing the supreme executive authority, thought it desirable that, during William's life, Mary should be only Queen Consort and a subject. But this arrangement, though much might doubtless be said for it in argument, shocked the general feeling even of those Englishmen who were most attached to the Prince. His wife had given an unprecedented proof of conjugal submission and affection; and the very least return that could be made to her would be to bestow on her the dignity of Queen Regent.

The time arrived for the free conference between the Houses. The managers for the Lords, in their robes, took their seats along one side of the table in the Painted Chamber: but the crowd of members of the House of Commons on the other side was so great that the gentlemen who were to argue the question in vain tried to get through. It was not without much difficulty and long delay that the Serjeant at Arms was able to clear a passage.

At length the discussion began. After a colloquy of several hours the disputants separated. The Lords assembled in their own house. It was well understood that they were about to yield, and that the conference had been a mere form. When the question was put whether King James had abdicated the government, only three lords said Not Content. On the question whether the throne was vacant, a division was demanded. The Contents were sixty-two; the Not Contents forty-seven. It was immediately proposed and carried, without a division, that the Prince and Princess of Orange should be declared King and Queen of England.

It was now known to whom the crown would be given. On what conditions it should be given, still remained to be decided. The Commons had appointed a committee to consider what steps it might be advisable to take, in order to secure law and liberty against the aggressions of future sovereigns; and the committee had made a report. This report recommended, first, that those great principles of the constitution which had been violated by the dethroned King should be solemnly asserted, and, secondly, that many new laws should be enacted, for the purpose of curbing the prerogative and purifying the administration of justice. Most of the suggestions of the committee were excellent; but it was utterly impossible that the Houses could, in a month, or even in a year, deal properly with matters so numerous, so various, and so important.

Some orators vehemently said that too much time had already been lost, and that the government ought to be settled without the delay of a day. Society was unquiet; trade was languishing; the English colony in Ireland was in imminent danger of perishing; a foreign war was impending.

On these grounds the Commons wisely determined to postpone all reforms till the ancient constitution of the kingdom should have been restored in all its parts, and forthwith to fill the throne without imposing on William and Mary any other obligation than that of governing according to the existing laws of England. In order that the questions which had been in dispute between the Stuarts and the nation might never again be stirred, it was determined that the instrument by which the Prince and Princess of Orange were called to the throne, and by which the order of succession was settled, should set forth, in the most distinct and solemn manner, the fundamental principles of the constitution. This instrument, known by the name of the Declaration of Right, began by recapitulating the crimes and errors which had made a revolution necessary. James had invaded the province of the legislature; had treated modest petitioning as a crime; had oppressed the Church by means of an illegal tribunal; had, without the consent of Parliament, levied taxes and maintained a standing army in time of peace; had violated the freedom of election, and perverted the course of justice. Proceedings which could lawfully be questioned only in Parliament had been made the subjects of prosecution in the King's Bench. Partial and corrupt juries had been returned; excessive bail had been required from prisoners; excessive fines had been imposed; barbarous and unusual punishments had been inflicted; the estates of accused persons had been granted away before conviction. He, by whose authority these things had been done, had abdicated the government. The Prince of Orange, whom God had made the glorious instrument of delivering the nation from superstition and tyranny, had invited the Estates of the Realm to meet and to take counsel together for the securing of religion, of law, and of freedom. The Lords and Commons, having deliberated, had resolved that they would first, after the example of their ancestors, assert the ancient rights and liberties of England. Therefore it was declared that the dispensing power, lately assumed and exercised, had no legal existence; that, without grant of Parliament, no money could be exacted by the sovereign from the subject; that, without consent of Parliament, no standing army could be kept up in time of peace. The right of subjects to petition, the right of electors to choose representatives freely, the right of Parliaments to freedom of debate, the right of the nation to a pure and merciful administration of justice according to the spirit of its own mild laws, were solemnly affirmed. All these things the Convention claimed, in the name of the whole nation, as the undoubted inheritance of Englishmen. Having thus vindicated the principles of the constitution, the Lords and Commons, in the entire confidence that the deliverer would hold sacred the laws and liberties which he had saved, resolved that William and Mary, Prince and Princess of Orange, should be declared King and Queen of England for their joint and separate lives, and that, during their joint lives, the administration of the government should be in the Prince alone. After them the crown was settled on the posterity of Mary, then on Anne and her posterity, and then on the posterity of William.

By this time the wind had ceased to blow from the west. The ship in which the Princess of Orange had embarked lay off Margate on the eleventh of February, and, on the following morning, anchored at Greenwich. She was received with many signs of joy and affection.

On the morning of Wednesday, the thirteenth of February [1689], the court of Whitehall and all the neighbouring streets were filled with gazers. The magnificent Banqueting House, the masterpiece of Inigo, embellished by masterpieces of Rubens, had been prepared for a great ceremony. The walls were lined by the yeomen of the guard. Near the northern door, on the right hand, a large number of Peers had assembled. On the left were the Commons with their Speaker, attended by the mace. The southern door opened: and the Prince and Princess of Orange, side by side, entered, and took their place under the canopy of state.

Both houses approached bowing low. William and Mary advanced a few steps. Halifax on the right, and Powle on the left, stood forth; and Halifax spoke. The Convention, he said, had agreed to a resolution which he prayed Their Highnesses to hear. They signified their assent; and the clerk of the House of Lords read, in a loud voice, the Declaration of Right. When he had concluded, Halifax, in the name of all the Estates of the Realm, requested the Prince and Princess to accept the crown.

William, in his own name and in that of his wife, answered that the crown was, in their estimation, the more valuable because it was presented to them as a token of the confidence of the nation. "We thankfully accept," he said, "what you have offered us." Then he assured them that the laws of England should be the rules of his conduct, that it should be his study to promote the welfare of the kingdom, and that he should constantly recur to the advice of the Houses, and should be disposed to trust their judgment rather than his own. These words were received with a shout of joy which was heard in the streets below, and was instantly answered by huzzas from many thousands of voices. The Lords and Commons then reverently retired from the Banqueting House and went in procession to the great gate of Whitehall, where the heralds and pursuivants were waiting in their gorgeous tabards. All the space as far as Charing Cross was one sea of heads. The kettle drums struck up; the trumpets pealed; and Garter King at arms, in a loud voice, proclaimed the Prince and Princess of Orange King and Queen of England, charged all Englishmen to pay, from that moment, faith and true allegiance to the new sovereigns, and besought God, who had already wrought so signal a deliverance for our Church and nation, to bless William and Mary with a long and happy reign.

Thus was consummated the English Revolution. When we compare it with those revolutions which have, during the last sixty years, overthrown so many ancient governments, we cannot but be struck by its peculiar character. Why that character was so peculiar is sufficiently obvious, and yet seems not to have been always understood either by eulogists or by censors.

The continental revolutions of the eighteenth and nineteenth centuries took place in countries where all trace of the limited monarchy of the middle ages had long been effaced. The right of the prince to make laws and to levy money had, during many generations, been undisputed. His throne was guarded by a great regular army. His administration could not, without extreme peril, be blamed even in the mildest terms. His subjects held their personal liberty by no other tenure than his pleasure. Not a single institution was left which had, within the memory of the oldest man, afforded efficient protection to the subject against the utmost excess of tyranny. Those great councils which had once curbed the regal power had sunk into oblivion. Their composition and their privileges were known only to antiquaries. We cannot wonder, therefore, that, when men who had been thus ruled succeeded in wresting supreme power from a government which they had long in secret hated, they should have been impatient to demolish and unable to construct, that they should have been fascinated by every specious novelty, that they should have proscribed every title, ceremony, and phrase associated with the old system, and that, turning away with disgust from their own national precedents and traditions, they should have sought for principles of government in the writings of theorists, or aped, with ignorant and ungraceful affectation, the patriots of Athens and Rome. As little can we wonder that the violent action of the revolutionary spirit should have been followed by reaction equally violent, and that confusion should speedily have engendered despotism sterner than that from which it had sprung.

Had we been in the same situation; had Strafford succeeded in his favourite scheme of Thorough; had he formed an army as numerous and as well disciplined as that which, a few years later, was formed by Cromwell; had a series of judicial decisions, similar to that which was pronounced by the Exchequer Chamber in the case of shipmoney, transferred to the crown the right of taxing the people; had the Star Chamber and the High Commission continued to fine, mutilate, and imprison every man who dared to raise his voice against the government; had the press been as completely enslaved here as at Vienna or at Naples; had our Kings gradually drawn to themselves the whole legislative power; had six generations of Englishmen passed away without a single session of Parliament; and had we then at length risen up in some moment of wild excitement against our masters, what an outbreak would that have been! With what a crash, heard and felt to the farthest ends of the world, would the whole vast fabric of society have fallen! How many thousands of exiles, once the most prosperous and the most refined members of this great community, would have begged their bread in continental cities, or have sheltered their heads under huts of bark in the uncleared forests of America! How often should we have seen the pavement of London piled up in barricades, the houses dinted with bullets, the gutters foaming with blood! How many times should we have rushed wildly from extreme to extreme, sought refuge from anarchy in despotism, and been again driven by despotism into anarchy! How many years of blood and confusion would it have cost us to learn the very rudiments of political science! How many childish theories would have duped us! How many rude and ill poised constitutions should we have set up, only to see them tumble down! Happy would it have been for us if a sharp discipline of half a century had sufficed to educate us into a capacity of enjoying true freedom.

These calamities our Revolution averted. It was a revolution strictly defensive, and had prescription and legitimacy on its side. Here, and here only, a limited monarchy of the thirteenth century had come down unimpaired to the seventeenth century. Our parliamentary institutions were in full vigour. The main principles of our government were excellent. They were not, indeed, formally and exactly set forth in a single written instrument; but they were to be found scattered over our ancient and noble statutes; and, what was of far greater moment, they had been engraven on the hearts of Englishmen during four hundred years. That, without the consent of the representatives of the nation, no legislative act could be passed, no tax imposed, no regular soldiery kept up, that no man could be imprisoned, even for a day, by the arbitrary will of the sovereign, that no tool of power could plead the royal command as a justification for violating any right of the humblest subject, were held, both by Whigs and Tories, to be fundamental laws of the realm.

As our Revolution was a vindication of ancient rights, so it was conducted with strict attention to ancient formalities. In almost every word and act may be discerned a profound reverence for the past. The Estates of the Realm deliberated in the old halls and according to the old rules. Powle [Speaker of the House of Commons] was conducted to his chair with the accustomed forms. The Serjeant with his mace brought up the messengers of the Lords to the table of the Commons; and the three obeisances were duly made. The conference was held with all the antique ceremonial. On one side of the table, in the Painted Chamber, the managers of the Lords sate covered and robed in ermine and gold. The managers of the Commons stood bareheaded on the other side. The speeches present an almost ludicrous contrast to the revolutionary oratory of every other country. Both the English parties agreed in treating with solemn respect the ancient constitutional traditions of the state. The only question was, in what sense those traditions were to be understood. The assertors of liberty said not a word about the natural equality of men and the inalienable sovereignty of the people, about Harmodius or Timoleon, Brutus the elder or Brutus the younger. When they were told that, by the English law, the crown, at the moment of a demise, must descend to the next heir, they answered that, by the English law, a living man could have no heir. When they were told that there was no precedent for declaring the throne vacant, they produced from among the records in the Tower a roll of parchment, near three hundred years old, on which, in quaint characters and barbarous Latin, it was recorded that the Estates of the Realm had declared vacant the throne of a perfidious and tyrannical Plantagenet. When at length the dispute had been accommodated, the new sovereigns were proclaimed with the old pageantry. All the fantastic pomp of heraldry was there, Clarencieux and Norroy, Portcullis and Rouge Dragon, the trumpets, the banners, the grotesque coats embroidered with lions and lilies. The title of King of France, assumed by the conqueror of

Cressy, was not omitted in the royal style. To us, who have lived in the year 1848, it may seem almost an abuse of terms to call a proceeding, conducted with so much deliberation, with so much sobriety, and with such minute attention to prescriptive etiquette, by the terrible name of Revolution.

And yet this revolution, of all revolutions the least violent, has been of all revolutions the most beneficent. It finally decided the great question whether the popular element which had, ever since the age of Fitzwalter and De Montfort, been found in the English polity, should be destroyed by the monarchical element, or should be suffered to develope itself freely, and to become dominant. The strife between the two principles had been long, fierce, and doubtful. It had lasted through four reigns. It had produced seditions, impeachments, rebellions, battles, sieges, proscriptions, judicial massacres. Sometimes liberty, sometimes royalty, had seemed to be on the point of perishing. During many years one half of the energy of England had been employed in counteracting the other half. The executive power and the legislative power had so effectually impeded each other that the state had been of no account in Europe. The King at Arms, who proclaimed William and Mary before Whitehall Gate, did in truth announce that this great struggle was over; that there was entire union between the throne and the Parliament; that England, long dependent and degraded, was again a power of the first rank; that the ancient laws by which the prerogative was bounded would henceforth be held as sacred as the prerogative itself, and would be followed out to all their consequences; that the executive administration would be conducted in conformity with the sense of the representatives of the nation; and that no reform, which the two Houses should, after mature deliberation, propose, would be obstinately withstood by the sovereign. The Declaration of Right, though it made nothing law which had not been law before, contained the germ of the law which gave religious freedom to the Dissenter, of the law which secured the independence of the Judges, of the law which limited the duration of Parliaments, of the law which placed the liberty of the press under the protection of juries, of the law which prohibited the slave trade, of the law which abolished the sacramental test, of the law which relieved the Roman Catholics from civil disabilities, of the law which reformed the representative system, of every good law which has been passed during a hundred and sixty years, of every good law which may hereafter, in the course of ages, be found necessary to promote the public weal, and to satisfy the demands of public opinion.

The highest eulogy which can be pronounced on the revolution of 1688 is this, that it was our last revolution. Several generations have now passed away since any wise and patriotic Englishman has meditated resistance to the established government. In all honest and reflecting minds there is a conviction, daily strengthened by experience, that the means of effecting every improvement which the constitution requires may be found within the constitution itself.

HISTORY OF THE
UNITED STATES OF AMERICA

by

GEORGE BANCROFT

CONTENTS

History of the United States of America

GEORGE BANCROFT

1800–1891

THE family of George Bancroft, American historian and states-man, had been in America since 1632. His father was a Revo-lutionary soldier, clergyman, and author of a popular life of George Washington. Bancroft received a thorough education at Phillips Academy (Exeter), Harvard, Heidelberg, Göttingen, and Berlin. Indeed, he so distinguished himself at Harvard that upon the recommendation of Edward Everett a group of Harvard men raised a fund which supported the young scholar during four years of study and travel abroad. Bancroft returned from Germany in 1822 and, after a brief experience of tutoring at Harvard, founded the Round Hill School at Northampton, Massachusetts.

Although sensitive, high-strung, and impulsive, Bancroft possessed abundant energy, ambition, and a hard core of common sense, qualities which made him equal to most practical exigencies. The modern European texts which he translated into English for use at Round Hill were soon adopted by other American schools, bringing him profit and some reputation. His offer to write for the *North American Review,* then edited by the historian Jared Sparks, was accepted and he contributed frequently to that publication as well as to the *American Quarterly.*

Although Bancroft's family were Whig, his political sympathies soon led him to become an active member of the Democratic party. While still a teacher in his own school, he was elected to the state legislature but declined to serve. Again in 1831 he declined the nomination of the Massachusetts Democrats for the post of Secretary of State. However, President Van Buren appointed him Collector of the Port of Boston, an office which he administered with efficiency.

In 1844 Bancroft was defeated as Democratic candidate for governor. But the following year he was appointed a member of Polk's Cabinet as Secretary of the Navy, serving also for a month as Acting Secretary of War. The national reputation which brought him these appointments was due to the great popularity of the first volumes of his *History of the United States,* published in 1834, 1837, and 1840. The work was enthusiastically received in England also and was immediately translated into Danish, Italian, German, and French. Bancroft's brief term as Secretary of the Navy is remembered chiefly because of his founding of the Naval Academy at Annapolis.

In 1846 Bancroft resigned his Cabinet post to become minister to London. There his historical interests provided a basis for friendships with Macaulay and Hallam, while his residence in England enabled him to accumulate a wealth of basic materials for the continuation of his American history. Bancroft returned to America in 1849 and settled in New York, where, partly as a consequence of the change in the political scene, he retired to private life, devoting his principal energies to the history. Volumes IV and V appeared in 1852, Volume VI in 1854, Volume VII in 1858, Volume VIII in 1860, and Volume IX in 1866. Then, in 1867, he accepted the Berlin ministry, which he held until his resignation in 1874. From that year until his death in 1891, Bancroft was engaged in the completion, extension, and revision of his *History of the United States.*

This history, the writing of which was spread over a long lifetime, is an epic work; in grandeur of concept it recalls Gibbon. But Bancroft reveals none of the slightly cynical detachment of the product of the era of "enlightenment." He is passionately involved with his subject; he is unashamedly a partisan and patriot. For him the progress of humankind was an unassailable fact, and the study of his country's history disclosed its fulfillment of a providential destiny, a role of major importance in the larger history of human progress. This was not a subject toward which one assumed an attitude of disinterest.

In the view of later critics of the work, its deficiencies are due to some of the very qualities which established Bancroft's immediate popularity. The rhetorical flights and patches of transparently artificial "writing" of the earlier volumes were modified in the final revision. Pages of philosophical reflection still interrupt the narrative. And Bancroft's frankly partisan treatment of the American Revolution diminishes its worth in the eyes of a generation capable of studying the event with more detachment than was possible in his day. Nevertheless, despite changing tastes and standards of historical scholarship, Bancroft's *History of the United States* remains a monumental achievement of continuing interest and influence.

HISTORY OF THE UNITED STATES OF AMERICA

I. AMERICA CLAIMS LEGISLATIVE INDEPENDENCE OF ENGLAND

1748

IN THE year of our Lord one thousand seven hundred and forty-eight, Montesquieu, wisest in his age of the reflecting statesmen of France, apprises the cultivated world that England has founded distant colonies more to extend her commerce than her sovereignty; and "as we love to establish elsewhere that which we find established at home, she will give to the people of her colonies the form of her own government, and, this government carrying with itself prosperity, a great people will form itself in the forests that she sent them forth to inhabit." The hereditary dynasties of Europe, all unconscious of the rapid growth of the power of the people, which was soon to bring them under its new and prevailing influence, were negotiating treaties among themselves to close their wars of personal ambition. The great maritime powers, weary of hopes of conquest, desired repose. To restore possessions as they had been, or were to have been, was accepted as the condition of peace, and guarantees were devised to keep them safe against vicissitude. But the eternal flow of resistance never rests, bearing the human race onward through continuous change. Principles grow into life in the public mind, and, following each other as they are bidden and without a pause, gain the mastery over events.

The hour of revolution was at hand, promising freedom to conscience and dominion to intelligence. History, escaping from the dictates of authority and the jars of insulated interests, enters upon new and unthought-of domains of culture and equality, the happier society where power springs freshly from ever-renewed consent; the life and activity of a connected world.

For Europe, the crisis foreboded the struggles of generations. The faith and affection which once bound together the separate classes of its civil hierarchy had lost their vigor. In the impending chaos of states, the ancient forms of society, after convulsive agonies, were doomed to be broken in pieces. The voice of reform, as it passed over the desolation, would inspire animation afresh; but conflict of the classes whose power was crushed with the oppressed who knew not that they were redeemed, might awaken wild and insatiable desires. In America, the influences of time were moulded by the creative force of reason, sentiment, and nature; its political edifice rose in lovely proportions, as if to the melodies of the lyre. Calmly, and without crime, humanity was to make for itself a new existence.

A few men of Anglo-Saxon descent, scholars, farmers, planters, and mechanics, with their wives and children, had crossed the Atlantic, in search of freedom and fortune. They brought the civilization which the past had bequeathed to Great Britain; they were followed by the slave-ship and the African; their prosperity invited emigrants from every nationality of central and western Europe; the mercantile system to which they were subjected prevailed in the councils of all metropolitan states, and extended its restrictions to every continent that allured to conquest, commerce, or colonization. The accomplishment of their independence would assert the freedom of the oceans as commercial highways, and vindicate power in the commonwealth for the self-directing judgment of its people.

The authors of the American revolution avowed for their object the welfare of mankind, and believed that they were in the service of their own and of all future generations. Their faith was just; for the world of mankind does not exist in fragments, nor can a country have an insulated existence. All men are brothers; and all are bondsmen for one another. All nations, too, are brothers; and each is responsible for that federative humanity which puts the ban of exclusion on none. New principles of government could not assert themselves in one hemisphere without affecting the other. The very idea of the progress of an individual people, in its relation to universal history, springs from the acknowledged unity of the race.

From the dawn of social being there has appeared a tendency toward commerce and intercourse between the scattered inhabitants of the earth. That mankind have ever earnestly desired this connection appears from their willing homage to the adventurer, and to every people who greatly enlarge the boundaries of the world, as known to civilization.

When civilization intrenched herself within the beautiful promontory of Italy, and Rome led the van of European reform, the same movement continued, with still vaster results; for, though the military republic gave dominion to property, and extended her own influence by the sword, yet, heaping up conquests, adding island to continent, absorbing nationalities, offering a shrine to strange gods, and citizenship to every vanquished people, she extended over a larger empire the benefits of fixed principles of law, and prepared the way for a universal religion.

To have asserted clearly the unity of mankind was the distinctive character of the Christian religion. No more were the nations to be severed by the worship of exclusive deities. They were taught that all men are of one blood; that for all there is but one divine nature and but one moral law; and the renovating faith which made known the singleness of the race, embodied its aspirations, and guided its advancement. The tribes of Northern Europe, emerging freshly from the wild nurseries of nations, opened new regions to culture, commerce, and refinement. The beams of the majestic temple, which antiquity had reared to its many gods, were already falling in; roving invaders, taking to their hearts the regenerating creed, became its intrepid messengers, and bore its symbols even to Iceland and Siberia.

Still nearer was the period of the connected world, when an enthusiast reformer, glowing with selfish ambition and angry at the hollow forms of idolatry, rose up in the deserts of Arabia, and founded a system of social equality dependent neither on birth nor race nor country.

In due time appeared the mariner from Genoa. To Columbus God gave the keys that unlock the barriers of the ocean; so that he filled Christendom with his glory. As he went forth toward the West, ploughing a wave which no European keel had entered, it was his high purpose not merely to open new paths to islands or to continents, but to bring together the ends of the earth, and join all nations in commerce and spiritual life.

While the world of mankind is accomplishing its nearer connection, it is advancing in the power of its intelligence. The possession of reason is the engagement for that progress of which history keeps the record. The faculties of each individual mind are limited in their development; the reason of the whole strives for perfection, has been restlessly forming itself from the first moment of human existence, and has never met bounds to its capacity for improvement. The generations of men are not like the leaves on the trees, which fall and renew themselves without melioration or change; individuals disappear like the foliage and the flowers; the existence of our kind is continuous, and its ages are recriprocally dependent. Were it not so, there would be no great truths inspiring action, no laws regulating human achievements: the movement of the living world would be as the ebb and flow of the ocean; and the mind would no more be touched by the visible agency of Providence in human affairs. In the lower creation, instinct may more nearly be always equal to itself; yet even there the beaver builds his hut, the bee his cell, with a gradual acquisition of inherited thought and increase of skill. By a more marked prerogative, as Pascal has written, "not only each man advances daily in the sciences, but all men unitedly make a never ceasing progress in them, as the universe grows older; so that the whole succession of human beings, during the course of so many ages, ought to be considered as one identical man, who subsists always, and who learns without end."

It is this idea of continuity which gives vitality to history. No period of time has a separate being; no public opinion can escape the influence of previous intelligence. We are cheered by rays from former centuries, and live in the sunny reflection of all their light.

From the intelligence that had been slowly ripening in the mind of cultivated humanity sprung the American revolution, which organized social union through the establishment of personal freedom, and emancipated the nations from all authority not flowing from themselves. In the old civilization of Europe, power moved from a superior to inferiors and subjects; a priesthood transmitted a common faith, from which it would tolerate no dissent; the government esteemed itself, by compact or by divine right, invested with sovereignty, dispensing protection and demanding allegiance. But a new principle, far mightier than the church and state of the middle ages, was forcing itself into activity. Successions of increasing culture had conquered for mankind the idea of the freedom of the individual; the creative, but long latent, energy that resides in the collective reason was next to be revealed. From this the state was to emerge, like the fabled spirit of beauty and love out of the foam of the ever troubled ocean. It was the office of America to substitute for hereditary privilege the natural equality of man; for the irresponsible authority of a sovereign, a government emanating from the concord of opinion; and, as she moved forward in her high career, the multitudes of every clime gazed toward her example with hopes of untold happiness, and all the nations of the earth learned the way to be renewed.

The American revolution, essaying to unfold the principles which organized its events, and bound to keep faith with the ashes of its heroes, was most radical in its character, yet achieved with such benign tranquillity that even conservatism hesitated to censure. A civil war armed men of the same ancestry against each other, yet for the advancement of the principles of everlasting peace and universal brotherhood. A new plebeian democracy took its place by the side of the proudest empires. Religion was disenthralled from civil institutions; thought obtained for itself free utterance by speech and by the press; industry was commissioned to follow the bent of its own genius; the system of commercial restrictions between states was reprobated and shattered; and the oceans were enfranchised for every peaceful keel. International law was humanized and softened; and a new, milder, and more just maritime code was concerted and enforced. The trade in slaves was branded and restrained. The language of Bacon and Milton, of Chatham and Washington, became so diffused that, in every zone, and almost in every longitude, childhood lisps the English as its mother tongue. The equality of all men was declared, personal freedom secured in its complete individuality, and common consent recognised as the only just origin of fundamental laws: so that in thirteen separate states, with ample territory for creating more, the inhabitants of each formed their own political institutions. By the side of the principle of the freedom of the individual and the freedom of the separate states, the noblest work of human intellect was consummated in a federal union; and that union put away every motive to its destruction by insuring to each successive generation the right to amend its constitution according to the increasing intelligence of the living people.

II. THE DAY-STAR OF THE AMERICAN UNION

April–July 1765

THIS is the moment when the power of the British oligarchy, under the revolution of 1688, was at its culminating point. The ministry esteemed the supreme power of parliament established firmly and forever. The colonists could not export the chief products of their industry—neither sugar, nor tobacco, nor cotton, nor indigo, nor ginger; nor fustic, nor other dyeing woods; nor molasses, nor rice, with some exceptions; nor beaver, nor peltry of any kind; nor copper ore, nor pitch, nor tar, nor turpentine, nor masts, nor yards, nor bowsprits, nor coffee, nor pimento, nor cocoanuts, nor whale-fins, nor raw silk, nor hides, nor skins, nor pot and pearl ashes—to any place but Great Britain, not even to Ireland. No foreign ship might enter a colonial harbor. Salt might be imported from any place into New England, New York, Pennsylvania, and Quebec; wines might be imported from the Madeiras and the Azores, but were to pay a duty in American ports for the British exchequer; and victuals, horses, and servants might be brought from Ireland. In all other respects, Great Britain was not only the sole market for the products of America, but the only storehouse for its supplies.

Lest the colonists should multiply their flocks of sheep and weave their own cloth, they might not use a ship, nor a boat, nor a carriage, nor even a pack-horse, to carry wool, or any manufacture of which wool forms a part, across the line of one province to another. They could not land wool from the nearest islands, nor ferry it across a river, nor even ship it to England. A British sailor, finding himself in want of clothes in their harbors, might not buy there more than forty shillings worth of woollens.

Where was there a house in the colonies that did not possess and cherish the English Bible? And yet to print that Bible in British America would have been a piracy; and the Bible, though printed in German and in a native savage dialect, was never printed there in English till the land became free.

That the country, which was the home of the beaver, might not manufacture its own hats, no man in the plantations could be a hatter or a journeyman at that trade unless he had served an apprenticeship of seven years. No hatter might employ a negro or more than two apprentices. No American hat might be sent from one plantation to another, or be loaded upon any horse, cart, or carriage for conveyance.

America abounded in iron ores of the best quality, as well as in wood and coal; slitting-mills, steel furnaces, and plating forges, to work with a tilt hammer, were prohibited in the colonies as "nuisances."

While free labor was debarred of its natural rights, the slave-trade was encouraged with unrelenting eagerness; and in the year that had just expired, from Liverpool alone seventy-nine ships had borne from Africa to the West Indies and the continent more than fifteen thousand three hundred negroes, two thirds as many as the first colonists of Massachusetts.

And now, in addition to colonial restrictions and the burdens attached to them, the British parliament had enacted a new system of taxes on America for the relief of the British exchequer. A duty was to be collected on foreign sugar, molasses, indigo, coffee, Madeira wine, imported directly into any of the plantations in America; also a duty on Portuguese and Spanish wines, on eastern silks, on eastern calicoes, on foreign linen cloth, on French lawn, though imported directly from Great Britain; on British colonial coffee shipped from one plantation to another. Nor was henceforward any part of the old subsidy to be drawn back on the export of foreign goods of Europe or the East Indies, and on the export of white calicoes and muslins a still higher duty was to be exacted and retained. And stamp duties were to be paid throughout all the British American colonies on and after the first day of the coming November.

These laws were to be enforced, not by the regular authorities only, but by naval and military officers, irresponsible to the civil power in the colonies. The penalties and forfeitures for breach of the revenue laws were to be decided in courts of vice-admiralty, without the interposition of a jury, by a single judge, who had no support whatever but from his share in the profits of his own condemnations.

But, if the British parliament can tax America, it may tax Ireland and India, and hold the wealth of the East and of the West at the service of its own oligarchy. As the relation of the government to its outlying dominions would become one of power and not of right, it could not but employ its accumulated resources to make itself the master of the ocean and the oppressor of mankind. "This system, if it is suffered to prevail," said Oxenbridge Thacher, of Boston, "will extinguish the flame of liberty all over the world."

Massachusetts had been led to rely on the inviolability of English freedom and on the equity of parliament; and, when the blow fell, "the people looked upon their liberties as gone." "Tears," said Otis, "relieve me a moment;" and, repelling the imputation "that the continent of America was about to become insurgent," "it is the duty of all," he added, "humbly and silently to acquiesce in all the decisions of the supreme legislature. Nine hundred and ninety-nine in a thousand of the colonists will never once entertain a thought but of submission to our sovereign, and to the authority of parliament in all possible contingencies." "They undoubtedly have the right to levy internal taxes on the colonies." "From my soul, I detest and abhor the thought of making a question of jurisdiction."

Hutchinson was only "waiting to know what more parliament would do toward raising the sums which the colonies were to pay," and which as yet were not half provided for. As chief justice, he charged "the jurors and people" of the several counties to obey. Nor did the result seem doubtful. There could be no danger but from union; and "no two colonies," said he, "think alike; there is no uniformity of measures; the bundle of sticks thus separated will be easily broken." "The stamp act," he assured the ministry, five weeks after the news of its passage, "is received among us with as much decency as could be expected; it leaves no room for evasion, and will execute itself."

In Boston, at the annual election of representatives in May, men called to mind the noble sentiments which had been interwoven into the remonstrances of New York, and were imbittered at the thought that their legislature had been cajoled by Hutchinson into forbearing to claim exemption from taxation as a right. While the patriots censured the acquiescence of Otis, as a surrender of their liberties, the friends of government jeered at him as a Massaniello and a madman.

At first the planters of Virginia foreboded universal ruin from the stamp act; but soon they resolved that the act should recoil on England: articles of luxury of English manufacture were banished; and threadbare coats came into fashion. A large provincial debt enforced the policy of thrift. The legislature of Virginia was then assembled, and the electors of Louisa county had just filled a vacancy in their representation by making choice of Patrick Henry, though he had resided among them scarcely a year. Devoted to their interest, he never flattered the people, and was never forsaken by them. As he took his place, not yet acquainted with the forms of business in the house or with its members, he saw the time for the enforcement of the stamp-tax drawing near, while all the other colonies, through timid hesitation or the want of opportunity, remained silent; and cautious loyalty hushed the experienced statesmen of his own. Many of the assembly had made the approaching close of the session an excuse for returning home; but Patrick Henry, a burgess of but a few days, unadvised and unassisted, in an auspicious moment, of which the recollection cheered him to his latest day, came forward in the committee of the whole house; and while Thomas Jefferson, a young collegian, from the mountain frontier, stood outside of the closed hall, eager to catch the first tidings of resistance, and George Washington, there is no cause to doubt, was in his place as a member, he maintained by resolutions that the inhabitants of Virginia inherited from the first adventurers and settlers of that dominion equal franchises with the people of Great Britain; that royal charters had declared this equality; that taxation by themselves, or by persons chosen by themselves to represent them, was the distinguishing characteristic of British freedom and of the constitution; that the people of that most ancient colony had uninterruptedly enjoyed the right of being thus governed by their own laws respecting their internal polity and taxation; that this right had never been forfeited, nor given up, and had been constantly recognised by the king and people of Great Britain.

It followed from these resolutions, and Patrick Henry so expressed it in a fifth supplementary one, that the general assembly of the whole colony have the sole right and power to lay taxes on the inhabitants of the colony, and that any attempt to vest such power in any other persons whatever tended to destroy British as well as American freedom. It was still further set forth, yet not by Henry, in two resolutions, which, though they were not officially produced, equally embodied the mind of the younger part of the assembly, that the inhabitants of Virginia were not bound to yield obedience to any law designed to impose taxation upon them other than the laws of their own general assembly; and that any one who should, either by speaking or writing, maintain the contrary, should be deemed an enemy to the colony.

A stormy debate arose, and many threats were uttered. Robinson, the speaker, already a defaulter, Peyton Randolph, the king's attorney, and the frank, honest, and independent George Wythe, a lover of classic learning, accustomed to guide the house by his strong understanding and single-minded integrity, exerted all their powers to moderate the tone of "the hot and virulent resolutions;" while John Randolph, the best lawyer in the colony, "singly" resisted the whole proceeding. But, on the other side, George Johnston, of Fairfax, reasoned with solidity and firmness; and Henry flamed with impassioned zeal. Lifted beyond himself, "Tarquin," he cried, "and Caesar, had each his Brutus; Charles I., his Cromwell; and George III."—"Treason!" shouted the speaker; "treason! treason!" was echoed round the house; while Henry, fixing his eye on the first who interrupted him, continued without faltering, "may profit by their example!"

This is the "way the fire began." "Virginia rang the alarum bell for the continent."

At the opening of the legislature of Massachusetts, Oliver, who had been appointed stamp distributor, was, on the joint ballot of both branches, re-elected councillor by a majority of but three out of about one hundred and twenty votes. More than half the representatives voted against him.

On the day on which the resolves of Virginia were adopted, a message from Governor Bernard informed the new legislature of Massachusetts that "the general settlement of the American provinces, though it might necessarily produce some regulations disagreeable from their novelty, had been long ago proposed, and would now be prosecuted to its utmost completion; that submission to the decrees of the supreme legislature, to which all other powers in the British empire were subordinate, was the duty and the interest of the colonies; that this supreme legislature, the parliament of Great Britain, was happily the sanctuary of liberty and justice; and that the prince who presided over it realized the idea of a patriot king."

Contrary to usage, the house made no reply; but, on the sixth of June, James Otis advised the calling of an American congress, which should consist of committees from each of the thirteen colonies, to be appointed respectively by the delegates of the people, without regard to the other branches of the legislature. Such an assembly had never existed; and the purpose of deliberating upon the acts of parliament was equally novel. The tories sneered at the proposal as visionary and impracticable; but the representatives of Massachusetts shared the creative instinct of Otis. Assuring unanimity by even refusing to consider the question of their exclusive right to originate measures of internal taxation, they sent letters to every assembly on the continent, proposing that committees of the several assemblies should meet at New York, on the first Tuesday of the following October, "to consult together" and "consider of a united representation to implore relief." They elected Otis and two others of their own members for their delegates.

Before the proceedings in Virginia and Massachusetts were known in New York, where the reprint of the stamp act was hawked about the streets as the "folly of England and the ruin of America," a freeman of that town, discussing the policy of Grenville, and the arguments on which it rested, demonstrated that they were leading alike to the reform of the British parliament and the independence of America.

"It is not the tax," said he, "it is the unconstitutional manner of imposing it, that is the great subject of uneasiness to the colonies. The minister admitted in parliament that they had in the fullest sense the right to be taxed only by their own consent, given by their representatives; and grounds his pretence of the right to tax them entirely upon this, that they are virtually represented in parliament.

"The great fundamental principles of a government should be common to all its parts and members, else the whole will be endangered. If, then, the interest of the mother country and her colonies cannot be made to coincide, if the same constitution may not take place in both, if the welfare of the mother country necessarily requires of the colonies a sacrifice of their right of making their own laws and disposing of their own property by representatives of their own choosing, then the connection between them ought to cease; and sooner or later it must inevitably cease."

These words embodied the sober judgment of New York. They were caught up by the impatient colonies, were reprinted in nearly all their newspapers, were approved of by their most learned and judicious statesmen, and even formed part of the instructions of South Carolina to its agent in England.

Thus revolution proceeded. Virginia marshalled resistance, Massachusetts entreated union, New York pointed to independence.

"There is not silver enough in the colonies to pay for the stamps," computed patriot financiers, "and the trade by which we could get more is prohibited." "And yet," declared the merchants of New York, "we have a natural right to every freedom of trade of the English." "To tax us, and bind our commerce and restrain manufactures," reasoned even the most patient, "is to bid us make brick without straw." "The northern colonies will be absolutely restricted from using any articles of clothing of their own fabric," predicted one colony to another. And men laughed as they added: "Catching a mouse within his majesty's colonies with a trap of our own making will be deemed, in the ministerial cant, an infamous, atrocious, and nefarious crime." "A colonist," murmured a Boston man, "cannot make a horseshoe or a hobnail but some ironmonger of Britain shall bawl that he is robbed by the 'American republican.'" "They are even stupid enough," it was said in Rhode Island, "to judge it criminal for us to become our own manufacturers."

"We will eat no lamb," promised the multitude, seeking to retaliate; "we will wear no mourning at funerals." "We will none of us import British goods," said the traders in the towns. The inhabitants of North Carolina set up looms for weaving their own clothes, and South Carolina was ready to follow the example. "The people," wrote Lieutenant-Governor Sharpe, of Maryland, "will go on upon manufactures." "We will have homespun markets of linens and woollens," passed from mouth to mouth, till it found its way across the Atlantic, and alarmed the king in council; "the ladies of the first fortune shall set the example of wearing homespun." "It will be accounted a virtue in them to wear a garment of their own spinning." "A little attention to manufactures will make us ample amends for the distresses of the present day, and render us a great, rich, and happy people."

Thus opinion was echoed from mind to mind, as the sun's rays beam from many clouds, all differing in tints, but every one taking its hue from the same fire. In the midst of the gloom, light broke forth from the excitement of a whole people. Associations were formed in Virginia, as well as in New England, to resist the stamp act by all lawful means. Hope began to rise that American rights and liberties might safely be trusted "to the watchfulness of a united continent."

The insolence of the royal officers provoked to insulated acts of resistance. The people of Rhode Island, angry with the commander of a ship-of-war who had boarded their vessels and impressed their seamen, seized his boat, and burned it on Newport common. Men of New England, "of a superior sort," had obtained of the government of New Hampshire a warrant for land down the western slope of the Green Mountains, on a branch of the Hoosic, twenty miles east of the Hudson river. They formed already a community of sixty-seven families, in as many houses, with an ordained minister, their own municipal officers, three several public schools, their meeting-house among the primeval forests of beech and maple; in a word, they enjoyed the flourishing state which springs from rural industry, intelligence, and piety. They called their village Bennington. The royal officers at New York disposed anew of that town, as well as of others near it, so that the king was known to the settlers near the Green Mountains chiefly by his agents, who had knowingly sold his lands twice over. In this way Bennington was made a battleground for independence.

But there was no present relief for America unless union could be perfected. Union was the hope of Otis—union that "should knit and work into the very blood and bones of the original system every region, as fast as settled." Yet how comprehensive and how daring the idea! The traditions of the board of trade branded it as "mutinous." Massachusetts had proceeded timidly, naming for its delegates to the proposed congress the patriot Otis, with two others who were "friends to government."

Virginia was ready to convince the world that her people were firm and unanimous in the cause of liberty, but its newly elected assembly was not suffered by Fauquier to come together. New Jersey received the circular letter of Massachusetts on the twentieth of June, the last day of the session of its legislature. The speaker, a friend to the British government, at first inclined to urge sending delegates to the proposed congress; but, on some "advice" from the governor, changed his mind, and the house, in the hurry preceding the adjournment, rather from uncertainty than the want of good-will, unanimously declined the invitation. The assembly of New Hampshire seemed to approve, but did not adopt it. "Nothing will be done in consequence of this intended congress," wrote Bernard, in July; and he seized the opportunity to press "more and more" upon the government at home "the necessity of taking into their hands the appointment of the American civil list," as well as changing the council of the province. Even the liberal governor of Maryland reported "that the resentment of the colonists would probably die out; and that, in spite of the violent outcries of the lawyers, the stamp act would be carried into execution."

But, far away toward the lands of the sun, the assembly of South Carolina was in session; and, on the twenty-fifth of July, debated the circular from Massachusetts. Many objections were made to the legality, the expediency, and most of all to the efficiency of the proposed measure; and many eloquent words were uttered, especially by the youthful John Rutledge, when the subject, on the deliberate resolve of a small majority, was referred to a committee, of which Christopher Gadsden was the chairman. He was a man of deep and clear convictions; thoroughly sincere; of an unbending will and a sturdy, impetuous integrity, which drove those about him, like a mountain torrent dashing on an over-shot wheel, though sometimes clogging with back-water from its own violence. He possessed not only that courage which defies danger, but that persistence which neither peril nor imprisonment nor the threat of death can shake. Full of religious faith, and at the same time inquisitive and tolerant, methodical, yet lavish of his fortune for public ends, he had in his nature nothing vacillating or low, and knew not how to hesitate or feign. After two legislatures had held back, South Carolina, by "his achievement," pronounced for union. "Our state," he used to say, "was the first, though at the extreme end, and one of the weakest, as well internally as externally, to listen to the call of our northern brethren in their distresses. Massachusetts sounded the trumpet, but to Carolina is it owing that it was attended to. Had it not been for South Carolina, no congress would then have happened. She was all alive, and felt at every pore." And when we count up those who, above others, contributed to the great result of union, we are to name the inspired "madman," James Otis, and the unwavering lover of his country, Christopher Gadsden.

Otis now seemed to himself to hear the prophetic song of the "Sibyls" chanting the springtime of a "new empire."

III. THE BOSTON "MASSACRE"

January–March 1770

THE Massachusetts assembly was to meet on the tenth of January, and distant members were on their journey, when [Thomas] Hutchinson, [Governor of Massachusetts] suddenly prorogued it to the middle of March. The spirit of non-importation had not abated; yet, as tea had advanced one hundred per cent, Hutchinson, who was himself a very large importer of it, could no longer restrain his covetousness. His two eldest sons, therefore, who were his agents, violating their engagement, broke open the lock, of which they had given the key to the committee of merchants, and secretly made sales. "Do they imagine," asked Samuel Adams, "they can still weary the patience of an injured country with impunity?"

The liberty pole raised by the people of New York in the Park stood safely for nearly three years. The soldiery, in February, resolved to cut it down, and, after three repulses, succeeded. The people, assembling in the fields to the number of three thousand, and, without planning retaliation, expressed abhorrence of the soldiers, as enemies to the constitution and to the peace of the city. The soldiers replied by an insulting placard; and, on two successive days, engaged in an affray with the citizens, in which the latter had the advantage. The newspapers loudly celebrated the victory; and the Sons of Liberty, purchasing a piece of land near the junction of Broadway and the high road to Boston, erected a pole, strongly guarded by iron bands and bars, and inscribed "Liberty and Property."

The men of Boston emulously applauded the spirit of the "Yorkers" [and established their own "Liberty Tree"]. Hatred of the parliament's taxes spread into every social circle. One week three hundred wives of Boston, the next a hundred and ten more, with one hundred and twenty-six of the young and unmarried of their sex, renounced the use of tea till the revenue acts should be repealed. How could the troops interfere?

Everybody knew that it was against the law for them to fire without the authority of a civil magistrate; and the more they paraded with their muskets and twelve rounds of ball, the more they were despised, as men who desired to terrify and had no power to harm. Hutchinson was taunted with wishing to destroy town-meetings, through which he himself had risen; and the press, calling to mind his days of shopkeeping, jeered him as in former days a notorious smuggler.

Theophilus Lillie, who had begun to sell contrary to the agreement, found a post planted before his door, with a hand pointed toward his house in derision. Richardson, an informer, asked a countryman to break the post down by driving the wheel of his cart against it. A crowd of boys chased Richardson to his own house and threw stones. Provoked but not endangered, he fired among them, and killed a boy of eleven years old, the son of a poor German. At his funeral, five hundred children walked in front of the bier; six of his schoolfellows held the pall; and men of all ranks moved in procession from Liberty Tree to the town-house, and thence to the "burying-place."

The evening of the fifth [of March] came on. The young moon was shining in a cloudless winter sky, and its light was increased by a new-fallen snow. Parties of soldiers were driving about the streets, making a parade of valor, challenging resistance, and striking the inhabitants indiscriminately with sticks or sheathed cutlasses.

A band, which poured out from Murray's barracks in Brattle street, armed with clubs, cutlasses, and bayonets, provoked resistance, and a fray ensued. Ensign Maul, at the gate of the barrack yard, cried to the soldiers: "Turn out, and I will stand by you; kill them; stick them; knock them down; run your bayonets through them." One soldier after another levelled a firelock, and threatened to "make a lane" through the crowd. Just before nine, as an officer crossed King street, now State street, a barber's lad cried after him: "There goes a mean fellow who hath not paid my master for dressing his hair;" on which the sentinel, stationed at the westerly end of the custom house, on the corner of King street and Exchange lane, left his post, and with his musket gave the boy a stroke on the head that made him stagger and cry for pain.

The street soon became clear, and nobody troubled the sentry, when a party of soldiers issued violently from the main guard, their arms glittering in the moonlight, and passed on, hallooing: "Where are they? where are they? Let them come." Presently twelve or fifteen more, uttering the same cries, rushed from the south into King street, and so by way of Cornhill, toward Murray's barracks. "Pray, soldiers, spare my life," cried a boy of twelve, whom they met. "No, no, I'll kill you all," answered one of them, and with his cutlass knocked him down. They abused and insulted several persons at their doors and others in the street, "running about like madmen in a fury," crying, "Fire!" which seemed their watchword, and "Where are they? knock them down." Their outrageous behavior occasioned the ringing of the bell at the head of King street.

The citizens, whom the alarm set in motion, came out with canes and clubs, and, partly by the courage of Crispus Attucks, a mulatto of nearly fifty years old, and some others, partly by the interference of well-disposed officers, the fray at the barracks was soon over. Of the citizens, the prudent shouted, "Home! home!" others, it was said, called out, "Huzza for the main guard! there is the nest;" but the main guard was not molested the whole evening.

A body of soldiers came up Royal Exchange lane, crying, "Where are the cowards?" and, brandishing their arms, passed through King street. From ten to twenty boys came after them, asking, "Where are they? where are they?" "There is the soldier who knocked me down," said the barber's boy, and they began pushing one another toward the sentinel. He loaded and primed his musket. "The lobster is going to fire," cried a boy. Waving his piece about, the sentinel pulled the trigger. "If you fire, you must die for it," said Henry Knox, who was passing by. "I don't care," replied the sentry; "if they touch me, I'll fire." "Fire!" shouted the boys, for they were persuaded he could not do it without leave from a civil officer, and a young fellow spoke out, "We will knock him down for snapping," while they whistled through their fingers and huzzaed. "Stand off!" said the sentry, and shouted aloud, "Turn out, main guard!" "They are killing the sentinel," reported a servant from the custom-house, running to the main guard. "Turn out! why don't you turn out?" cried Preston, who was captain of the day, to the guard. "He appeared in a great flutter of spirits," and "spoke to them roughly." A party of six, two of whom, Kilroi and Montgomery, had been worsted at the rope-walk, formed with a corporal in front and Preston following. With bayonets fixed, they "rushed through the people" upon the trot, cursing them, and pushing them as they went along. They found about ten persons round the sentry, while about fifty or sixty came down with them. "For God's sake," said Knox, holding Preston by the coat, "take your men back again; if they fire, your life must answer for the consequences." "I know what I am about," said he hastily, and much agitated. None pressed on them or provoked them, till they began loading, when a party of about twelve in number, with sticks in their hands, moved from the middle of the street where they had been standing, gave three cheers, and passed along the front of the soldiers, whose muskets some of them struck as they went by. "You are cowardly rascals," they said, "for bringing arms against naked men." "Lay aside your guns, and we are ready for you." "Are the soldiers loaded?" inquired Palmes of Preston. "Yes," he answered, "with powder and ball." "Are they going to fire upon the inhabitants?" asked Theodore Bliss. "They cannot, without my orders," replied Preston; while "the town-born" called out, "Come on, you rascals, you bloody backs, you lobster scoundrels, fire, if you dare. We know you dare not." Just then Montgomery received a blow from a stick which had hit his musket, and the word "Fire!" being given by Preston, he stepped a little on one side, and shot Attucks, who at the time was quietly leaning on a long stick. The people immediately began to move off. "Don't fire!" said Langford, the watchman, to Kilroi, looking him full in the face; but yet he did so, and Samuel Gray, who was standing next Langford, with his hands in his bosom, fell lifeless. The rest fired slowly and in succession on the people, who were dispersing. One aimed deliberately at a boy, who was running in a zigzag line for safety. Montgomery then pushed at Palmes to stab him; on which the latter knocked his gun out of his hand, and, levelling a blow at him, hit Preston. Three persons were killed, among them Attucks the mulatto; eight were wounded, two of them mortally. Of the eleven, not more than one had had any share in the disturbance.

When the men returned to take up the dead, the infuriated soldiers prepared to fire again, but were checked by Preston, while the twenty-ninth regiment appeared under arms in King street. "This is our time," cried soldiers of the fourteenth, and dogs were never seen more greedy for their prey.

The bells rung in all the churches; the town drums beat. "To arms! to arms!" was the cry. All the sons of Boston came forth, nearly distracted by the sight of the dead bodies, and of the blood, which ran plentifully in the street, and was imprinted in all directions by foot-tracks on the snow. "Our hearts," says Warren, "beat to arms, almost resolved by one stroke to avenge the death of our slaughtered brethren;" but, self-possessed, they demanded justice according to the law.

IV. THE BOSTON TEA-PARTY

August–December 1773

THE East India company, who were now by act of parliament authorized to export tea to America duty free in England, were warned by Americans that their adventure would end in loss; but their scruples were overruled by Lord North, who answered peremptorily: "It is to no purpose making objections, for the king will have it so. The king means to try the question with America."

The time was short, the danger to Boston imminent, resistance at all hazards was the purpose of its committee of correspondence; violent resistance might become necessary, and to undertake it without a certainty of union would only bring ruin on the town and on the cause.

The issue was to be tried at Boston. The governor himself, under the name of his sons, was selected as one of those to whom the tea-ships for that port were consigned; the moment for the decision was hastening on. In the night, between the first and second of November, a knock was heard at the door of each of the consignees commissioned by the East India company, and a summons left for them to appear without fail at Liberty Tree on the following Wednesday, at noon, to resign their commission; printed notices were posted up, desiring the freemen of Boston and the neighboring towns to meet at the same time and place as witnesses.

On the appointed day, a large flag was hung out on the pole at Liberty Tree; the bells in the meeting-houses were rung from eleven till noon. Adams, Hancock, and Phillips, three of the four representatives of the town of Boston, the selectmen, and William Cooper, the town clerk, with about five hundred more, gathered round the spot. As the consignees did not make their appearance, the assembly, appointing Molineux, Warren, and others a committee, marched into State street to the warehouse of Richard Clarke, where all the consignees were assembled. Molineux presented himself for a parley.

"From whom are you a committee?" asked Clarke. "From the whole people." "Who are the committee?" "I am one," replied Molineux; and he named all the rest. "And what is your request?" Molineux read a paper, requiring the consignee to promise not to sell the teas, but to return them to London in the same bottoms in which they were shipped. "Will you comply?" "I shall have nothing to do with you," answered Clarke, roughly and peremptorily.

On the twenty-second, the committees of Dorchester, Roxbury, Brookline, and Cambridge met the Boston committee by invitation at the selectmen's chamber in Faneuil Hall. Their question was: "Whether it be the mind of this committee to use their joint influence to prevent the landing and sale of the teas exported from the East India company?" And it passed in the affirmative unanimously.

The next day, the town of Charlestown assembled, and showed such a spirit that ever after its committee was added to those who assumed the executive direction.

The combination was hardly finished when, on Sunday, the twenty-eighth of November, the ship Dartmouth appeared in Boston harbor, with one hundred and fourteen chests of the East India company's tea. To keep the sabbath strictly was the New England usage. But hours were precious; let the tea be entered, and it would be beyond the power of the consignee to send it back. The selectmen held one meeting by day, and another in the evening; but they sought in vain for the consignees, who had taken sanctuary in the castle.

The committee of correspondence was more efficient. Meeting on Sunday, they obtained from the Quaker Rotch, who owned the Dartmouth, a promise not to enter his ship till Tuesday; and they authorized Samuel Adams to invite the committees of the five surrounding towns— Dorchester, Roxbury, Brookline, Cambridge, and Charlestown, with their townsmen and those of Boston—to hold a mass meeting the next morning. Faneuil Hall could not contain the people that poured in.

Thursday, the sixteenth of December 1773, dawned upon Boston, a day by far the most momentous in its annals. The inhabitants of the town must count the cost, and know well if they dare defy the wrath of

Great Britain, and if they love exile and poverty and death rather than submission. At ten o'clock the men of Boston, with at least two thousand from the country, assembled in the Old South meeting-house. A report was made that Rotch had been denied a clearance from the collector. "Then," said they to him, "protest immediately against the custom-house, and apply to the governor for his pass, so that your vessel may this very day proceed on her voyage for London."

The governor had stolen away to his country-seat at Milton. Bidding Rotch make all haste, the meeting adjourned to three in the afternoon. At that hour Rotch had not returned. It was incidentally voted, as other towns had already done, to abstain totally from the use of tea; and every town was advised to appoint its committee of inspection, to prevent the detested tea from being brought within any of them. Then, since the governor might refuse his pass, the question recurred, "whether it be the sense and determination of this body to abide by their former resolutions with respect to the not suffering the tea to be landed." On this question Samuel Adams and Young addressed the meeting, which was become far the most numerous ever held in Boston. Among them was Josiah Quincy, a patriot of fervid feeling, passionately devoted to liberty; still young, but wasting with hectic fever. He knew that for him life was ebbing. The work of vindicating American freedom must be done soon, or he will be no party to the achievement. He rises, but it is to restrain; and, being truly brave and truly resolved, he speaks the language of moderation: "Shouts and hosannas will not terminate the trials of this day, nor popular resolves, harangues, and acclamations vanquish our foes. We must be grossly ignorant of the value of the prize for which we contend, of the power combined against us, of the inveterate malice and insatiable revenge which actuate our enemies, public and private, abroad and in our bosom, if we hope that we shall end this controversy without the sharpest conflicts. Let us consider the issue before we advance to those measures which must bring on the most trying and terrible struggle this country ever saw." "The hand is to the plough," said others, "there must be no looking back;" and the thousands who were present voted unanimously that the tea should not be landed.

It had been dark for more than an hour. A delay of a few hours would place the tea under the protection of the admiral at the castle. The church in which they met was dimly lighted by candles, when, at a quarter before six, Rotch appeared, and related that the governor would not grant him a pass, because his ship was not properly cleared. As soon as he had finished his report, loud shouts were uttered; then Samuel Adams rose and gave the word: "This meeting can do nothing more to save the country." On the instant a cry was heard at the porch; the war-whoop resounded; a body of men, forty or fifty in number, clad in blankets as Indians, each holding a hatchet, passed by the door; and encouraged by Samuel Adams, Hancock, and others, and increased on the way to near two hundred, marched two by two to Griffin's Wharf, posted guards to prevent the intrusion of spies, took possession of the three tea-ships, and, in about three hours, three hundred and forty chests of tea, being the whole quantity that had been imported, were emptied into the bay, without the least injury to other property. "All things were conducted with great order, decency, and perfect submission to government." The people who looked on were so still that the noise of breaking open the tea-chests was plainly heard. After the work was done, the town became as quiet as if it had been holy time. That very night the men from the country took home the great news to their villages.

The next morning the committee of correspondence appointed Samuel Adams and four others to draw up a declaration of what had been done. They sent Paul Revere as express with the information to New York and Philadelphia.

The joy that sparkled in the eyes and animated the countenances and the hearts of the patriots, as they met one another, is unimaginable. The governor, meantime, was consulting his books and his lawyers to make out that the resolves of the meeting were treasonable. Threats were muttered of arrests, of executions, of transporting the accused to England; while the committee of correspondence pledged themselves to support and vindicate each other and all persons who had shared in their effort. The country was united with the town, and the colonies with one another, more firmly than ever. The Philadelphians unanimously approved what Boston had done. New York, all impatient at the winds which had driven its tea-ship off the coast, was resolved on following the example.

In South Carolina, the ship, with two hundred and fifty-seven chests of tea, arrived on the second of December; the spirit of opposition ran very high; but the consignees were persuaded to resign: so that, though the collector after the twentieth day seized the dutiable article, there was no one to vend it or to pay the duty, and it perished in the cellars where it was stored.

Late on Saturday, the twenty-fifth, news reached Philadelphia that its tea-ship was at Chester. It was met four miles below the town, where it came to anchor. On Monday, at an hour's notice, men, said to number five thousand, collected in a town-meeting; at their instance, the consignee who came as passenger resigned; and the captain agreed to take his ship and cargo directly back to London, and to sail the very next day. The Quakers, though they did not appear openly, gave every private encouragement. "The ministry had chosen the most effectual measures to unite the colonies. The Boston committee were already in close correspondence with the other New England colonies, with New York and Pennsylvania. Old jealousies were removed, and perfect harmony subsisted between all." "The heart of the king was hardened like that of Pharaoh;" and none believed he would relent. Union, therefore, was the cry—a union which should reach "from Florida to the icy plains" of Canada. "No time is to be lost," said the "Boston Gazette"; "a congress or a meeting of the American states is indispensable, and what the people wills shall be effected." Samuel Adams had led his native town to offer itself cheerfully as a sacrifice for the liberties of mankind.

V. THE FIRST AMERICAN CONGRESS

June–October 1774

SAMUEL ADAMS received a summons to come and guide the debates [of the Boston general assembly], but a higher duty kept him at Salem. He had on one evening secretly consulted four or five of his colleagues; on another, a larger number; on the third, so many as thirty; and on the morning of Friday, the seventeenth of June, confident of having the control of the house, one hundred and twenty-nine being present, he locked the door, and proposed a continental congress, to meet on the first day of September at Philadelphia, where there was no army to interrupt its sessions. Bowdoin, Samuel Adams, John Adams, Cushing, and Robert Treat Paine were chosen delegates. To defray their expenses, a tax of five hundred pounds was apportioned on the province. Domestic manufactures were encouraged, and it was strongly recommended to discontinue the use of all goods imported from the East Indies and Great Britain until the grievances of America should be radically redressed.

In the midst of these proceedings the governor sent his secretary with a message for dissolving the assembly; but he knocked at its door in vain, and could only read the proclamation to the crowd on the stairs.

George III. ranked "New York next to Boston in opposition to government." There was no place where a congress was more desired, and none where the determinations of the congress were more sure to be observed. After being severed from Holland, its mother country, New York had no attachment to any European state. All agreed in the necessity of resisting the pretensions of England; but differences arose as to the persons to be intrusted with the direction of that resistance, and as to the imminence and extent of the danger. On the fourth of July 1774, it was carried in the committee of fifty-one that delegates should be selected to serve in the general congress.

From New Hampshire, the members of its convention brought with them money, contributed by the several towns to defray the expenses of a representation in congress. The inhabitants of that province solemnized their action by keeping a day of fasting and public prayer. Massachusetts did the same; and [the English Colonel] Gage, who looked with stupid indifference on the spectacle of thirteen colonies organizing themselves as one people, on occasion of the fast issued a proclamation against "hypocrisy and sedition."

By the fifth of September, Gage had ordered ground to be broken for fortifications on the Neck, which formed the only entrance by land into Boston. In the evening the selectmen remonstrated, but with no effect.

The next day the convention of Suffolk county, which it had been agreed between Samuel Adams and Warren should send a memorial to the general congress, met in Dedham. Every town and district was represented, and their grand business was referred to a committee, of which Warren was the chairman.

An approval of the resistance of the people was embodied in the careful and elaborate report which Warren on the ninth presented to the adjourned Suffolk convention. "On the wisdom and on the exertions of this important day," such were its words, "is suspended the fate of the New World and of unborn millions." The resolutions which followed declared that the sovereign who breaks his compact with his people forfeits their allegiance. By their duty to God, their country, themselves, and posterity, they pledged the county to maintain their civil and religious liberties, and to transmit them entire to future generations. They rejected as unconstitutional the regulating act of parliament and all the officers appointed under its authority. They enjoined the mandamus councillors to resign their places within eleven days. Attributing to the British commander-in-chief hostile intentions, they directed the collectors of taxes to pay over no money to the treasurer whom he recognised. The governor and council had formerly appointed all military officers; now that the legal council was no longer consulted, they advised the towns to elect for themselves officers of their militia from such as were inflexible friends to the rights of the people. For purposes of provincial government they advised a provincial congress, while they promised respect and submission to the continental congress.

New England had surmounted its greatest difficulties; its enemies placed their hopes on the supposed timidity of the general congress.

At Philadelphia the South Carolinians greeted the delegates of Massachusetts as the heralds of freedom, and the Virginians equalled or surpassed their colleagues in resoluteness and spirit; but, while there was great diversity of opinions respecting the proper modes of resisting the aggressions of the mother country, all united in desiring "the union of Great Britain and the colonies on a constitutional foundation."

On Monday, the fifth of September, Galloway, the speaker of the Pennsylvania assembly, would have had congress use the state-house as the place for their deliberations, but the carpenters of Philadelphia offered their plain but spacious hall; and, from respect for the mechanics, it was accepted by a great majority. The names of the members were then called over; and Patrick Henry, Washington, Richard Henry Lee, Samuel Adams, John Adams, Jay, Gadsden, John Rutledge of South Carolina, the aged Hopkins of Rhode Island, and others, representing eleven colonies, answered to the call. Peyton Randolph, late speaker of the assembly of Virginia, was nominated for the chair by Lynch of South Carolina, and was unanimously chosen. The body named itself "the congress," and its chairman "the president." Jay and Duane would have selected a secretary from among themselves; but, on the motion of Lynch, Charles Thomson was appointed. Colonies differing in religious opinions, in commercial interests, and in everything dependent on climate and labor, in usages and manners swayed by reciprocal prejudices, and frequently quarrelling with each other respecting boundaries, found themselves united in one representative body.

VI. LEXINGTON AND CONCORD

April 19, 1775

GAGE, who had under his command about three thousand effective men, was informed by his spies of military stores, pitiful in their amount, collected by provincial committees at Worcester and Concord; and he resolved on striking a blow, as the king desired. On the afternoon of the day on which the provincial congress of Massachusetts adjourned he took the light infantry and grenadiers off duty, and secretly prepared an expedition to destroy the colony's stores at Concord. The attempt had for several weeks been expected; and signals were concerted to announce the first movement of troops for the country. Samuel Adams and Hancock, who had not yet left Lexington for Philadelphia, received a timely message from Warren, and, in consequence, the committee of safety removed a part of the public stores and secreted the cannon.

On Tuesday, the eighteenth of April, ten or more British sergeants in disguise dispersed themselves through Cambridge and farther west to intercept all communication. In the following night the grenadiers and light infantry, not less than eight hundred in number, the flower of the army at Boston, commanded by Lieutenant-Colonel Smith, crossed in the boats of the transport ships from the foot of the common to East Cambridge. There they received a day's provisions; and near midnight, after wading through wet marshes that are now covered by a stately city, they took the road through West Cambridge to Concord.

Gage directed that no one else should leave the town; but Warren had, at ten o'clock, despatched William Dawes through Roxbury, and Paul Revere by way of Charlestown, to Lexington.

Revere stopped only to engage a friend to raise the concerted signals, and two friends rowed him across Charles river five minutes before the sentinels received the order to prevent it. All was still, as suited the hour. The Somerset man-of-war was winding with the young flood; the waning moon just peered above a clear horizon; while, from a couple of lanterns in the tower of the North church, the beacon streamed to the neighboring towns as fast as light could travel.

A little beyond Charlestown neck, Revere was intercepted by two British officers on horseback; but, being well mounted, he turned suddenly, and escaped by the road to Medford. Of that town, he waked the captain of the minute-men, and continued to rouse almost every house on the way to Lexington. The troops had not advanced far when the firing of guns and ringing of bells announced that their expedition had been heralded; and Smith sent back for a re-enforcement.

In the earliest moments of the nineteenth of April the message from Warren reached Adams and Hancock, who at once divined the object of the expedition. Revere, therefore, and Dawes, joined by Samuel Prescott, "a high Son of Liberty" from Concord, rode forward, calling up the inhabitants as they passed along, till in Lincoln they fell upon a party of British officers. Revere and Dawes were seized and taken back to Lexington, where they were released; but Prescott leaped over a low stone wall, and galloped on for Concord.

There, at about two hours after midnight, a peal from the bell of the meeting-house brought together the inhabitants of the place, young and old, with their firelocks, ready to make good the resolute words of their town debates. Among the most alert was William Emerson, the minister, with gun in hand, his powder-horn and pouch of balls slung over his shoulder. By his sermons and his prayers his flock learned to hold the defence of their liberties a part of their covenant with God; his presence with arms strengthened their sense of duty.

From daybreak to sunrise, the summons ran from house to house through Acton. Express messengers and the call of minute-men spread widely the alarm. How children trembled as they were scared out of sleep by the cries! how women, with heaving breasts, bravely seconded their husbands! how the countrymen, forced suddenly to arm, without guides or counsellors, took instant counsel of their courage! The mighty chorus of voices rose from the scattered farm-houses, and, as it were, from the ashes of the dead. Come forth, champions of liberty; now free your country; protect your sons and daughters, your wives and homesteads; rescue the houses of the God of your fathers, the franchises handed down from your ancestors. Now all is at stake; the battle is for all.

Lexington, in 1775, may have had seven hundred inhabitants; their minister was the learned and fervent Jonas Clark, the bold inditer of patriotic state papers, that may yet be read on their town records. In December 1772, they had instructed their representative to demand "a radical and lasting redress of their grievances, for not through their neglect should the people be enslaved." A year later, they spurned the use of tea. In 1774, at various town-meetings, they voted "to increase their stock of ammunition," "to encourage military discipline, and to put themselves in a posture of defence against their enemies." In December they distributed to "the train band and alarm list" arms and ammunition, and resolved to "supply the training soldiers with bayonets."

At two in the morning, under the eye of the minister, and of Hancock and Adams, Lexington common was alive with the minute-men; and not with them only, but with the old men, who were exempts, except in case of immediate danger to the town. The roll was called, and, of militia and alarm men, about one hundred and thirty answered to their names. The captain, John Parker, ordered every one to load with powder and ball, but to take care not to be the first to fire. Messengers, sent to look for the British regulars, reported that there were no signs of their approach. A watch was therefore set, and the company dismissed with orders to come together at beat of drum. Some went to their own homes; some to the tavern, near the south-east corner of the common. Samuel Adams and Hancock, whose seizure was believed to be intended, were persuaded to retire toward Woburn.

The last stars were vanishing from night, when the foremost party, led by Pitcairn, a major of marines, was discovered, advancing quickly and in silence. Alarm guns were fired, and the drums beat, not a call to village husbandmen only, but the reveille to humanity. Less than seventy, perhaps less than sixty, obeyed the summons, and, in sight of half as many boys and unarmed men, were paraded in two ranks, a few rods north of the meeting-house.

How often in that building had they, with renewed professions of their faith, looked up to God as the stay of their fathers and the protector of their privileges! How often on that green, hard by the burial-place of their forefathers, had they pledged themselves to each other to combat manfully for their birthright inheritance of liberty! There they now stood side by side, under the provincial banner, with arms in their hands, silent and fearless, willing to shed their blood for their rights, scrupulous not to begin civil war. The ground on which they trod was the altar of freedom, and they were to furnish the victims.

The British van, hearing the drum and the alarm guns, halted to load; the remaining companies came up; and, at half an hour before sunrise, the advance party hurried forward at double quick time, almost upon a run, closely followed by the grenadiers. Pitcairn rode in front, and, when within five or six rods of the minute-men, cried out: "Disperse, ye villains! ye rebels, disperse! lay down your arms! why don't you lay down your arms and disperse?" The main part of the countrymen stood motionless in the ranks, witnesses against aggression; too few to resist, too brave to fly. At this, Pitcairn discharged a pistol, and with a loud voice cried, "Fire!" The order was followed first by a few guns, which did no execution, and then by a close and deadly discharge of musketry.

In the disparity of numbers, Parker ordered his men to disperse. Then, and not till then, did a few of them, on their own impulse, return the British fire. These random shots of fugitives or dying men did no harm, except that Pitcairn's horse was perhaps grazed, and a private of the tenth light infantry was touched slightly in the leg.

Jonas Parker, the strongest and best wrestler in Lexington, had promised never to run from British troops; and he kept his vow. A wound brought him on his knees. Having discharged his gun, he was preparing to load it again, when he was stabbed by a bayonet, and lay on the post which he took at the morning's drum-beat. So fell Isaac Muzzey, and so

died the aged Robert Munroe, who in 1758 had been an ensign at Louis-
burg. Jonathan Harrington, junior, was struck in front of his own house
on the north of the common. His wife was at the window as he fell. With
blood gushing from his breast, he rose in her sight, tottered, fell again,
then crawled on hands and knees toward his dwelling; she ran to meet
him, but only reached him as he expired on their threshold. Caleb Harrington, who had gone into the meeting-house for powder, was shot as
he came out. Samuel Hadley and John Brown were pursued, and killed
after they had left the green. Asahel Porter, of Woburn, who had been
taken prisoner by the British on the march, endeavouring to escape, was
shot within a few rods of the common. Seven men of Lexington were
killed, nine wounded; a quarter part of all who stood in arms on the
green.

Day came in all the beauty of an early spring. The trees were bud-
ding; the grass growing rankly a full month before its time; the blue bird
and the robin gladdening the genial season, and calling forth the beams
of the sun which on that morning shone with the warmth of summer;
but distress and horror gathered over the inhabitants of the peaceful town.
There on the green lay in death the gray-haired and the young; the grassy
field was red "with the innocent blood of their brethren slain," crying
unto God for vengeance from the ground.

These are the village heroes, who were more than of noble blood,
proving by their spirit that they were of a race divine. They gave their
lives in testimony to the rights of mankind, bequeathing to their country
an assurance of success in the mighty struggle which they began. The
expanding millions of their countrymen renew and multiply their praise
from generation to generation. They fulfilled their duty not from an accidental impulse of the moment; their action was the ripened fruit of
Providence and of time. The light that led them on was combined of rays
from the whole history of the race; from the traditions of the Hebrews
in the gray of the world's morning; from the heroes and sages of republican Greece and Rome; from the example of Him who died on the cross
for the life of humanity; from the religious creed which proclaimed the
divine presence in man, and on this truth, as in a life-boat, floated the
liberties of nations over the dark flood of the middle ages; from the customs of the Germans transmitted out of their forests to the councils of
Saxon England; from the burning faith and courage of Martin Luther;
from trust in the inevitable universality of God's sovereignty as taught
by Paul of Tarsus and Augustine, through Calvin and the divines of New
England; from the avenging fierceness of the Puritans, who dashed the
mitre on the ruins of the throne; from the bold dissent and creative self-
assertion of the earliest emigrants to Massachusetts; from the statesmen
who made, and the philosophers who expounded, the revolution of England; from the liberal spirit and analyzing inquisitiveness of the eighteenth century; from the cloud of witnesses of all the ages to the reality

and the rightfulness of human freedom. All the centuries bowed themselves from the recesses of the past to cheer in their sacrifice the lowly
men who proved themselves worthy of their forerunners, and whose
children rise up and call them blessed.

Heedless of his own danger, Samuel Adams, with the voice of a
prophet, exclaimed: "Oh, what a glorious morning is this!" for he saw
his country's independence hastening on, and, like Columbus in the
tempest, knew that the storm bore him more swiftly toward the undis-
covered world.

VII. CONGRESS APPOINTS GEORGE WASHINGTON
COMMANDER-IN-CHIEF

May–June 17, 1775

"UNHAPPY it is," said Washington, "to reflect that a brother's sword has
been sheathed in a brother's breast, and that the once happy and peaceful
plains of America are either to be drenched with blood or inhabited by
slaves. Sad alternative! But can a virtuous man hesitate in his choice?" He
foresaw the long contest which was to precede the successful vindication
of the liberties of America; and from the first he avowed to his friends
"his full intention to devote his life and fortune" to the cause. To mark
the necessity of immediate preparation for war, he wore in congress his
uniform as an officer.

Franklin, who knew with certainty that every method of peaceful
entreaty had been exhausted, reproved irresoluteness and delay. "Make
yourselves sheep," he would say, "and the wolves will eat you;" and
again, "God helps them who help themselves;" adding, hopefully:
"United, we are well able to repel force by force." Thus "he encouraged
the revolution," yet wishing for independence as the spontaneous action
of a united people. The people of the continent, now that independence
was become inevitable, still longed that the necessity for it might pass by.

In this state of things Dickinson seconded the motion of Jay for one
more petition to the king; but his determination to sustain Massachusetts
was never in doubt. He did not ask merely relief from parliamentary taxation; he insisted on security against the encroachments of parliament on
charters and laws so distinctly and firmly that Samuel Adams pronounced
the Farmer a thorough Bostonian.

On the twenty-fourth, the chair of the president becoming vacant
by the departure of Peyton Randolph, John Hancock of Massachusetts
was elected unanimously in his stead; and Harrison of Virginia conducted
him to the chair, saying: "We will show Britain how much we value her
proscriptions;" for the proscription of Samuel Adams and Hancock had
long been known, though it had not yet been proclaimed. On the twenty-
fifth directions were given to the provincial congress in New York to

fortify posts at the upper end of the island near King's Bridge, and on each side of Hudson river in the highlands. A post was to be taken near Lake George.

Measures were next taken for organizing and paying an American continental army. Washington, Schuyler, and others, were deputed to prepare the necessary rules and regulations. It was further resolved to enlist six companies of expert riflemen in Pennsylvania, two in Maryland, and two in Virginia; and, on the fifteenth of June, it was voted to appoint a general. Thomas Johnson of Maryland nominated George Washington; and he was elected by ballot unanimously.

Washington was then forty-three years of age. In stature, he a little exceeded six feet; his limbs were sinewy and well-proportioned; his chest broad; his figure stately, blending dignity of presence with ease. His robust constitution had been tried and invigorated by his early life in the wilderness, the habit of occupation out of doors, and rigid temperance; so that few equalled him in strength of arm, or power of endurance, or noble horsemanship. His complexion was florid; his hair dark brown; his head in its shape perfectly round. His broad nostrils seemed formed to give escape to scornful anger. The lines of his eyebrows were long and finely arched. His dark blue eyes, which were deeply set, had an expression of resignation, and an earnestness that was almost pensiveness. His forehead was sometimes marked with thought, but never with inquietude; his countenance was pleasing and full of benignity.

VIII. BUNKER HILL

June 16–17, 1775

Two days after the expedition to Concord, Gage had threatened that if the Americans should occupy Charlestown heights the town should be burnt. Its inhabitants, however, had always been willing that the threat should be disregarded. The time for the holocaust was come. Pretending that his flanking parties were annoyed from houses in the village, Howe sent a boat over with a request to Clinton and Burgoyne to burn it. The order was immediately obeyed by a discharge of shells from Copp's Hill. The inflammable buildings caught in an instant, and a party of men landed and spread the fire; but, from a sudden shifting of the wind, the movements of the British were not covered by the smoke of the conflagration.

At half past two o'clock, or a very little later, General Howe, not confining his attack to the left wing alone, advanced to a simultaneous assault on the whole front from the redoubt to Mystic river. In Burgoyne's opinion, "his disposition was soldier-like and perfect." Of the two columns which were put in motion, the one was led by Pigot against the redoubt, the other by Howe himself against the flank, which seemed protected by nothing but a fence of rails and hay easy to be scrambled over, so that [the American commander William] Prescott, when his left should be turned, would find the enemy in his rear, and be forced to surrender.

As they began to march, the battery on Copp's Hill, from which Clinton and Burgoyne were watching every movement, kept up an incessant fire, which was seconded by the Falcon and the Lively, the Somerset and the two floating batteries; the town of Charlestown, consisting of five hundred edifices of wood, burst into a blaze; and the steeple of its only church became a pyramid of fire. All the while the masts of the shipping and the heights of the British camp, the church-towers, the house-tops of a populous town, and the acclivities of the surrounding country, were crowded with spectators to watch the battle which was to take place in full sight on a conspicuous eminence.

As soon as Prescott perceived that the enemy were in motion, he commanded Robinson, his lieutenant-colonel, who conducted himself so bravely in the fight at Concord, and Henry Woods, his major, famed in the villages of Middlesex for ability and patriotism, to flank the enemy; and they executed his orders with prudence and daring. He then went through the works to encourage and animate his inexperienced soldiers. "The redcoats will never reach the redoubt," such were his words, as he himself used to narrate them, "if you will but withhold your fire till I give the order, and be careful not to shoot over their heads." After this round he took his post in the redoubt, well satisfied that the men would do their duty.

The British advanced in line in good order, steadily and slowly, pausing on the march for their artillery to prepare the way, and firing with muskets as they advanced. But they fired too soon and too high, doing but little injury.

Encumbered with their knapsacks, they ascended the steep hill with difficulty, covered as it was with grass reaching to their knees, and intersected with walls and fences. Prescott waited till the enemy had approached within eight rods as he afterward thought, within ten or twelve rods as the committee of safety of Massachusetts wrote, when he gave the word: "Fire!" At once, from the redoubt and breastwork, every gun was discharged. Nearly the whole front rank of the enemy fell, and the rest, to whom this determined resistance was unexpected, were brought to a stand. For a few minutes, fifteen or ten—who can count such minutes! —each one of the Americans, completely covered while he loaded his musket, exposed only while he stood upon the wooden platform or steps of earth in the redoubt to take aim, fought according to his own judgment and will; and a close and unremitting fire was continued and returned, till the British staggered, wavered, and then, in disordered masses, retreated precipitately to the foot of the hill, and some even to their boats.

The column of the enemy, which advanced near the Mystic under the lead of Howe, moved gallantly against the rail-fence, and, when within eighty or one hundred yards, displayed into line with the precision of troops on parade. Here, too, the Americans, commanded by Stark and Knowlton, cheered on by Putnam, who like Prescott bade them reserve their fire, restrained themselves as if by universal consent, till at the proper moment, resting their guns on the rails of the fence, they poured forth a deliberate, well-directed, fatal discharge; here, too, the British recoiled from the volley, and, after a short contest, were thrown into confusion, sounded a retreat, and fell back till they were covered by the ground.

Then followed moments of joy in that unfinished redoubt, and behind the grassy rampart, where New England husbandmen beheld veteran battalions shrink before their arms. Their hearts bounded as they congratulated each other. The night-watches, thirst, hunger, danger whether of captivity or death, were forgotten. They promised themselves victory.

As the British soldiers retreated, the officers were seen, by the spectators on the opposite shore, running down to them, using passionate gestures, and pushing them forward with their swords. After an interval of about fifteen minutes, during which Prescott moved round among his men, cheering them with praise, the British column under Pigot rallied and advanced, though with apparent reluctance, in the same order as before, firing as they approached within musket-shot. This time the Americans withheld their fire till the enemy were within six or five rods of the redoubt, when, as the order was given, it seemed more fatal than before. The enemy continued to discharge their guns, and pressed forward with spirit. "But from the whole American line there was," said Prescott, "a continuous stream of fire;" and though the British officers exposed themselves fearlessly, remonstrating, threatening, and even striking the soldiers to urge them on, they could not reach the redoubt, but in a few moments gave way in greater disorder than before. The wounded and the dead covered the ground in front of the works, some lying within a few yards of them.

On the flank the British light infantry again marched up its companies against the grass-fence, but could not penetrate it. "Indeed," wrote some of the survivors, "how could we penetrate it? Most of our grenadiers and light infantry, the moment of presenting themselves, lost three fourths, and many nine tenths of their men. Some had only eight or nine men in a company left, some only three, four, or five." On the ground where but the day before the mowers had swung the scythe in peace, "the dead," relates Stark, "lay as thick as sheep in a fold." Howe for a few seconds was left nearly alone, so many of the officers about him having been killed or wounded; and it required the utmost exertion of all, from the generals down to the subalterns, to repair the rout.

At intervals, the artillery from the ships and batteries was playing, while the flames were rising over the town of Charlestown and laying waste the places of the graves of its fathers, and streets were falling together, and ships at the yards were crashing on the stocks, and the kindred of the Americans, from the fields and hills and house-tops around, watched every gallant act of their defenders. "The whole," wrote Burgoyne, "was a complication of horror and importance beyond anything it ever came to my lot to be witness to. It was a sight for a young soldier that the longest service may not furnish again."

"If we drive them back once more," cried Prescott, "they cannot rally again." To the husbandmen about him the terrible and appalling scene was altogether new, and not one of them shrunk from duty. "We are ready for the redcoats again," they shouted, cheering their commander.

In the longer interval that preceded the third attack, a council of officers disclosed the fact that the ammunition was almost exhausted. Though Prescott had sent in the morning for a supply, he had received none, and there were not fifty bayonets in his party. A few artillery cartridges were discovered, and, as the last resource, the powder in them was distributed, with the direction that not a kernel of it should be wasted.

The royal army, exasperated at retreating before an enemy whom they had professed to despise, and by the sight of many hundreds of their men who lay dead or bleeding on the ground, prepared to renew the engagement. While the light infantry and a part of the grenadiers were left to continue the attack at the rail-fence, Howe concentrated the rest of his forces upon the redoubt. Cannon were brought to bear in such a manner as to rake the inside of the breastwork from one end of it to the other, so that the Americans were obliged to crowd within their fort. Then the British troops, having disencumbered themselves of their knapsacks, advanced in column with fixed bayonets. Clinton, who from Copp's Hill had watched the battle, at this critical moment, without orders, pushed off in a boat and put himself at the head of two battalions, the marines and the forty-seventh, which seemed to hesitate on the beach as if uncertain what to do. These formed the extreme left of the British, and advanced from the south; the fifth, the thirty-eighth, and forty-third battalions formed the centre, and attacked from the east; on their right was the fifty-second with grenadiers, who forced the now deserted intrenchments.

The Americans within the redoubt, attacked at once on three sides by six battalions, at that time numbered less than seven hundred men. Of these, some had no more than one, none more than four rounds of ammunition left. But Prescott's self-possession increased with danger. He directed his men to wait till the enemy were within twenty yards, when they poured upon them a deadly volley. The British wavered for an instant, and then sprang forward without returning the fire. The American fire slackened, and began to die away. The British reached the rampart on the southern side. Those who first scaled the parapet were shot down as they mounted. Pitcairn fell mortally wounded, just as he was entering the redoubt. A single artillery cartridge furnished powder for the last muskets which the Americans fired. The breastwork being abandoned, the ammunition expended, the redoubt half filled with regulars, at a little before four Prescott, on the point of being surrounded, gave the word to retreat. He himself was among the last to leave the fort, escaping unhurt, though with coat and waistcoat rent and pierced by bayonets, which he parried with his sword. The men, retiring through the sally-port or leaping over the walls, made their way through their enemies, each for himself, without much order, and the dust which rose from the dry earth now powdered in the sun, and the smoke of the engagement, gave them some covering. The British, who had turned the north-eastern end of the breast-work, and had come round the angle of the redoubt, were too much exhausted to use the bayonet against them with vigor, and at first the parties were so closely intermingled as to interrupt the firing; a supply of ball for the artillery, sent from Boston during the battle, was too large for the field-pieces which accompanied the detachment.

The brave men of the redoubt would have been effectually cut off but for the provincials at the rail-fence and the bank of the Mystic, who had repulsed the enemy twice, and now held them in check till the main body had left the hill. Not till then did the Connecticut companies under Knowlton, and the New Hampshire soldiers under Stark, quit the station, which they had "nobly defended." The retreat was made with more regularity than could have been expected of troops who had been for so short a time under discipline, and of whom many had never before seen an engagement. Trevett and his men drew off the only field-piece that was saved. The musket of Pomeroy was struck and marked by a ball. The redoubt, the brow of Bunker Hill, and the passage across the Charlestown causeway, were the principal places of slaughter.

Putnam, at the third onset, was absent, "employed in collecting men" for re-enforcements, and was encountered by the retreating party on the northern declivity of Bunker Hill. Acting on his own responsibility, he now for the first time during the day assumed the supreme direction. Without orders from any person, he rallied such of the fugitives as would obey him, joined them to a detachment which had not arrived in season to share in the combat, and took possession of Prospect Hill, where he encamped that very night.

Repairing to head-quarters, Prescott offered with three fresh regiments to recover his post; but for himself he sought neither promotion nor praise, and, having performed the best service, never thought that he had done more than his duty. It is the contemporary record that during the battle "no one appeared to have any command but Colonel Prescott," and that "his bravery could never be enough acknowledged and applauded." The camp long repeated the story of his self-collected valor; and a historian of the war, who best knew the judgments of the army, has rightly awarded the "highest prize of glory to Prescott and his companions."

The British were unable to continue the pursuit beyond the isthmus. They had already brought their best forces into the field; more than a third of those engaged lay dead or bleeding; and the survivors were fatigued, and overawed by the courage of their adversaries. The battle put an end to all offensive operations on the part of Gage.

The number of the killed and wounded in his army was, by his own account, at least one thousand and fifty-four. Seventy commissioned officers were wounded, and thirteen were slain. Of these, there were one lieutenant-colonel, two majors, and seven captains. For near half an hour there had been a continued sheet of fire from the provincials; and the action was hot for double that period. The oldest soldiers had never seen the like. The battle of Quebec, which won half a continent, did not cost the lives of so many officers as the battle of Bunker Hill, which gained nothing but a place of encampment.

That Howe did not fall was a marvel. The praises bestowed on his apathetic valor, on the gallantry of Pigot and Rawdon, on the conduct of Clinton, reflected honor on the untrained farmers, who, though inferior in numbers, had tasked the most strenuous exertions of their assailants before they could be dislodged from the defences which they had had but four hours to construct.

The loss of the Americans amounted to one hundred and forty-five killed and missing, and three hundred and four wounded.

Just at the moment of the retreat fell Joseph Warren, the last in the trenches. In him were combined swiftness of thought and resolve, courage, endurance, and manners which won universal love. He opposed the British government, not from interested motives nor from resentment. Guileless and intrepid, he was in truth a patriot.

The events of the day confirmed Washington in his habitual belief that the liberties of America would be preserved. To his English friends Franklin wrote: "Americans will fight; England has lost her colonies forever."

IX.   ADVANCING TOWARD INDEPENDENCE

Last Months of 1775–March 1776

THE enlistments for the army of Washington were embarrassed by the want of funds; he could neither pay off the old army nor assure the punctual payment of the militia. In January 1776, he was left with but about ten thousand dollars, and this small sum was held as a reserve. The Massachusetts council was authorized to lend him fifty thousand pounds; and it was left to Massachusetts, with the aid of Rhode Island, Connecticut, and New Hampshire, to keep up the numbers of the army while it remained on her soil.

The troops before Boston were a mixture of recruits and transient militia, requiring a constant renewal of elementary instruction. There was a dearth of bayonets, a want of at least two thousand muskets; the artillery was poor, and was chiefly a gathering from accidental sources. There was no sufficient store of powder; for members of congress, eager to give profitable occupation to ship-builders among their constituents, reserved what little was obtained for the use of vessels which could not be prepared for sea before more ample stores would arrive; and Washington, anxious as he was "to keep above water in the esteem of mankind," was compelled to conceal his want from the public, from his friends, and even from most of his officers.

To obtain heavy ordnance, Washington, in November 1775, had despatched General Knox to Ticonderoga. In obedience to his minute orders, forty-three cannon, among which one was of twenty-four pounds and eleven of eighteen pounds, with mortars, lead, and flints, were laden upon forty-two exceedingly strong sleds and drawn by eighty yoke of oxen to Cambridge. With a community of thought and purpose and secrecy that made of the army one mind and one will, Washington prepared first to take possession of Dorchester Heights which would give the command of a great part of Boston, and next of Nook Hill in immediate contiguity to the town.

To divert the attention of the British, a heavy cannonade and bombardment of the town was kept up during two nights. Soon after candle-light on the fourth of March the firing was renewed, and was returned with such zeal that a continued roar of cannon and mortars was heard till daylight. As it began, everything was ready. Every man knew his place, and the need of acting with celerity and silence. Eight hundred went in advance as a guard, one half of them taking post on the height nearest Boston, the other at the easternmost point, opposite the castle. They were followed by carts with intrenching tools, and by the working party of twelve hundred, under the command of Thomas, an officer whose great merit on this occasion is the more to be remembered from the shortness of his career. The ground, for eighteen inches deep, was frozen too hard to yield earth readily for the defences; a train of more than three hundred carts, easily drawn by oxen over the frozen marshes, brought bundles of screwed hay, to form a cover for Dorchester neck where it was exposed to a raking fire, and an amazing quantity of gabions and fascines and chandeliers for the redoubts. The drivers, as they goaded on their cattle, suppressed their voices.

The temperature of the night was most favorable for out-door work; the haze that denotes a softening of the air hung round the base of the ridge; above, the moon, which that morning had become full, was shining in cloudless lustre; hundreds of men toiled in stillness with an assiduity that knew nothing of fatigue; the teams were all in motion, making their tour, some three, some four times; beneath, in the town, reposed the British general without special watchfulness or fear; the crowd of ships in the harbor kept their watches unsuspicious of peril; the inhabitants of Boston, emaciated, pining, and as yet little cheered by hope, trembled lest their own houses should be struck; the people that were left in the villages around, chiefly women and children, driven from their beds by the rattling of their windows, could watch from the hill-tops the flight of every shell, and anxiously waited for daybreak.

At about three in the morning the first working party was relieved. The toil was continued with fresh energy, so that strong redoubts, secure against grape-shot and musketry, crowned each of the two hills; an abattis, constructed of trees felled in the neighboring orchards, protected the foot of the ridge; the top was surrounded by barrels filled with earth and stones, which, as the hillsides were steep and bare of trees and bushes, were, in case of an attack, to be rolled down against the assailing columns. At dawn on the fifth the batteries on both sides ceased to play, and a fearful quiet prevailed. Howe, as he saw the new intrenchments loom in imposing strength, reported that "they must have been the employment of at least twelve thousand men." Some of his officers said: "Perhaps there never was so much work done in so short a space of time," and that their rising as at a word recalled to them the stories in eastern romances of the invisible agency of fairy hands. "If they retain possession of the heights," said Admiral Shuldham, "I cannot keep a ship in the harbor." A council of war saw no choice but to dislodge the New England farmers. Had the British made a sally against the party at Dorchester, the Americans had floating batteries and boats ready to carry four thousand men into Boston. Howe put twenty-four hundred men under the command of Lord Percy to make the attack. When they were seen to embark, the Americans on the heights, expecting an immediate conflict, kindled with joy. But Percy took his transports no farther than the castle; in the afternoon a gale came up from the south, and about midnight drove two or three vessels on shore; rain fell in torrents on the morning of the sixth; a movement against the American lines must have ended in the ruin of the British army. A second council of war advised the instant evacuation of Boston.

There was no time even to propose a capitulation for the safety of the refugees, and the best that could be offered them was a passage in crowded transports from the cherished land of their nativity to the naked shores of Nova Scotia. The British confessed before the world their inability to protect their friends, who had risked everything in their cause. What trust could now be reposed in their promises?

On the eighth, Howe, through the selectmen of Boston, wished to come to an understanding with Washington that the town should be spared, provided he might leave it without molestation. The unauthenticated proposal could meet with no reply from the American commander-in-chief; but, from want of ammunition, he was obliged to use his artillery sparingly, while Howe was hastening his embarkation. A chosen British army, sent at the expense of more than a million pounds sterling to correct revolted subjects and assert the authority of the British parliament, after being imprisoned for many months in the town they were to have crushed, found no safety but in flight.

The British army and more than eleven hundred refugees began their embarkation at four in the morning, and in less than six hours were put on board one hundred and twenty transports; before ten they were under way, and the citizens of Boston, from every height and every wharf, could see the fleet sail out of the harbor in a line extending from the castle to Nantasket road.

Troops from Roxbury moved into Boston; others from Cambridge crossed in boats. Everywhere appeared marks of hurry in the flight of the British; among other stores, they left behind them two hundred and fifty pieces of cannon, of which one half were serviceable; twenty-five hundred chaldrons of sea-coal; twenty-five thousand bushels of wheat; three thousand bushels of barley and oats; one hundred and fifty horses; bedding and clothing for soldiers. British store-ships, ignorant of the retreat, successively entered the harbor without suspicion, and fell into the hands of the Americans; among them a ship which, in addition to carbines, bayonets, gun-carriages, and all sorts of tools necessary for artillery, had on board more than seven times as much powder as Washington's whole stock when his last movement was begun.

On the next day Washington ordered five of his best regiments to march under Heath to New York. On the twentieth the main body of the army made its entry into Boston.

X. THE RESOLUTION AND THE DECLARATION OF INDEPENDENCE

From the First to the Fourth of July 1776

ON THE morning of the first of July, the day set apart for considering the resolution of independence, John Adams, confident as if the vote had been taken, invoked the blessing of heaven to make the new-born republic more glorious than any which had gone before. Independence could be obtained only by a great expense of life; but the greater the danger, the stronger was his determination, for he held that a free constitution of civil government could not be purchased at too dear a rate.

At the appointed hour, the members [of Congress], probably on that day fifty in number, appeared in their places; among them, the delegates lately chosen in New Jersey. The great occasion had brought forth superior statesmen—men who joined moderation to energy. Every colony was found to be represented, and the delegates of all but one had received full power of action. Comprehensive instructions, reaching the question of independence without explicitly using the word, had been given by Massachusetts in January, by Georgia on the fifth of February, by South Carolina in March. North Carolina, in the words of Cornelius Harnett, on the twelfth of April, led the way in expressly directing its representatives in congress to concur in a declaration of independence. On the first of May, Massachusetts expunged the regal style from all public proceedings, and substituted the name of her "government and people;" on the fourth, Rhode Island more explicitly renounced allegiance, and made its delegates the representatives of an independent republic; Virginia on the fifteenth, the very day on which John Adams in congress carried his measure for instituting governments by the sole authority of the people, ordered her delegates at Philadelphia to propose independence, and by a circular letter communicated her resolve to all her sister colonies. The movement of Virginia was seconded almost in her words by Connecticut on the fourteenth of June, New Hampshire on the fifteenth, New Jersey on the twenty-first, the conference of committees of Pennsylvania on the twenty-fourth, Maryland on the twenty-eighth. Delaware on the twenty-second of March had still hoped for conciliation; but on the fifteenth of June she instructed her delegates to concur in forming further compacts between the united colonies, concluding treaties with foreign powers, and adopting such other measures as should be deemed necessary for promoting the liberty, safety, and interests of America. The vote of the eleventh of June showed the purpose of New York; but, under the accumulation of dangers, her statesmen waited a few days longer, that her voice for independence might have the direct authority of her people.

The business of the day began with reading various letters, among others one from Washington, who returned the whole number of his men, present and fit for duty, including the one regiment of artillery, at seven thousand seven hundred and fifty-four. Of near fourteen hundred, the firelocks were bad; more than eight hundred had none at all; three thousand eight hundred and twenty-seven, more than half the whole number of infantry, had no bayonets. Of the militia who had been called for, only about a thousand had joined the camp. With this force the general was to defend extensive lines against an army, near at hand, of thirty thousand veterans. An express from Lee made known that fifty-three ships, with Clinton, had arrived before Charleston, of which the safety was involved in doubt.

A more cheering letter, which Chase had forwarded by express from Annapolis, brought the first news of the unanimity of the Maryland convention, whose vote for independence was produced and read.

The order of the day came next, and congress resolved itself "into a committee of the whole to take into consideration the resolution respecting independency." For a few minutes, silence prevailed. In the absence of the mover of the resolution, the eyes of every one turned toward its seconder, John Adams; and the new members from New Jersey requested that the arguments used in former debates might be recapitulated. He had made no preparation for that morning; but for many months independence had been the chief object of his thoughts and his discourse, and the strongest arguments ranged themselves before his mind in their natural order. Of his sudden, impetuous, unpremeditated speech, no minutes ever existed, and no report was made. It is only remembered that he set forth the justice and the necessity, the seasonableness and the advantages of a separation from Great Britain; he dwelt on the neglect and insult with which their petitions had been treated by the king; and on the vindictive spirit manifested in the employment of German troops whose arrival was hourly expected. He concluded by urging the present time as the most suitable for resolving on independence, in as much as it had become the first wish and the last instruction of the communities they represented.

A letter from Washington, of the twenty-ninth of June, was read, from which it appeared that Howe and forty-five ships or more, laden with troops, had arrived at Sandy Hook, and that the whole fleet was expected in a day or two. "I am hopeful," wrote the general, "that I shall get some re-enforcements before they are prepared to attack; be that as it may, I shall make the best disposition I can of our troops." Not all who were round him had firmness like his own; Reed, the new adjutant-general, quailed before the inequality of the British and American force, saying: "Had I known the true posture of affairs, no consideration would have tempted me to have taken an active part in this scene." No one knew better than the commander-in-chief the exceedingly discouraging aspect of military affairs; but his serene and unfaltering courage in this hour was a support to congress. His letter was referred to the board of war which they had recently established, and of which John Adams was the president.

On the second day of July there were present in congress probably forty-nine members. Rodney had arrived from Delaware, and, joining Mackean, secured that colony. Dickinson and Morris stayed away, which enabled Franklin, Wilson, and Morton of Pennsylvania, to outvote Willing and Humphreys. The South Carolina members, still uncertain if Charleston had not fallen, for the sake of unanimity, came round; so, though New York was still unable to vote, twelve colonies, with no dissenting one, resolved: "That these united colonies are, and of right ought to be, free and independent states; that they are absolved from all allegiance to the British crown, and that all political connection between them and the state of Great Britain is, and ought to be, totally dissolved."

At the end of this great day the mind of John Adams heaved like the ocean after a storm. "The greatest question," he wrote, "was decided which ever was debated in America, and a greater, perhaps, never was nor will be decided among men. When I look back to 1761, and run through the series of political events, the chain of causes and effects, I am surprised at the suddenness as well as greatness of this revolution. Britain has been filled with folly, and America with wisdom. It is the will of heaven that the two countries should be sundered forever; it may be the will of heaven that America shall suffer calamities still more wasting and distresses yet more dreadful. If this is to be the case, the furnace of affliction produces refinement in states as well as individuals; but I submit all my hopes and fears to an overruling Providence, in which, unfashionable as the faith may be, I firmly believe."

The resolution of congress changed the old thirteen British colonies into free and independent states. It remained to set forth the reason for this act, and the principles which the new people would own as their guides. Of the committee appointed for that duty, Thomas Jefferson of Virginia had received the largest number of votes, and was in that manner singled out to draft the confession of faith of the rising empire. He owed this distinction to respect for the colony which he represented, to the consummate ability of the state papers which he had already written, and to that general favor which follows merit, modesty, and a sweet disposition; but the quality which specially fitted him for the task was the sympathetic character of his nature, by which he was able with instinctive perception to read the soul of the nation, and, having collected its best thoughts and noblest feelings, to give them out in clear and bold words, mixed with so little of himself that his country, as it went along with him, found nothing but what it recognised as its own. His profession was that of the law, in which he was methodical, painstaking, and successful; at the same time he pursued it as a science, and was well read in the law of nature and of nations. Whatever he had to do, it was his custom to prepare himself for it carefully; and in public life, when others were at fault, they often found that he had already hewed out the way; so that in council men willingly gave him the lead, which he never appeared to claim, and was always able to undertake. But he rarely spoke in public, and was less fit to engage in the war of debate than calmly to sum up its conclusions. It was a beautiful trait in his character that he was free from envy; he is the constant and best witness to the greatness of John Adams as the advocate and defender of independence. A common object now riveted the two statesmen together. At that period Jefferson, by the general consent of Virginia, stood first among her civilians. Just thirty-three years old, married, and happy in his family, affluent, with a bright career before him, he was no rash innovator by his character or his position; if his convictions drove him to demand independence, it was only because he could no longer live with honor under the British "constitution, which he still acknowledged to be better than all that had preceded it." His enunciation of general principles was fearless, but he was no visionary devotee of abstract theories; the nursling of his country, the offspring of his time, he set about the work of a practical statesman, and the principles which he set forth grew so naturally out of previous law and the facts of the past that they struck deep root and have endured.

From the fulness of his own mind, without consulting one single book, yet having in memory the example of the Swiss and the manifesto of the United Provinces of the Netherlands, Jefferson drafted the declaration, in which, after citing the primal principles of government, he presented the complaints of the United States against England in the three classes of the iniquitous use of the royal prerogative, the usurpation of legislative power over America by the king in parliament, and the measures for enforcing the acts of the British parliament. He submitted the paper separately to Franklin and to John Adams, accepted from each of them one or two verbal, unimportant corrections, and on the twenty-eighth of June reported it to congress, which, on the second of July, immediately after adopting the resolution of independence, entered upon its consideration.

This immortal state paper was "the genuine effusion of the soul of the country at that time," the revelation of its mind, when, in its youth, its enthusiasm, its sublime confronting of danger, it rose to the highest creative powers of which man is capable. The bill of rights which it promulgates is of rights that are older than human institutions, and spring from the eternal justice.

XI. THE RETREAT FROM LONG ISLAND

August 1776

THE works for the defence of New York Island, including the fortifications in Brooklyn, had been planned by Lee in concert with a New York committee and a committee from congress. Jay thought it proper to lay Long Island waste, burn New York, and retire to the Highlands; but, as it was the maxim of congress not to give up a foot of territory, Washington promised "his utmost exertions under every disadvantage;" "the appeal," he said, "may not terminate so happily as I could wish, yet any advantage the enemy may gain I trust will cost them dear." To protect New York city he was compelled to hold King's Bridge, Governor's Island, Paulus Hook, and the heights of Brooklyn. For all these posts, divided by water, and some of them fifteen miles apart, he had in the first week of August but ten thousand five hundred and fourteen men fit for duty. Of these, many were often obliged to sleep without cover, exposed to the dews. There was a want of good physicians, medicines, and hospitals; more than three thousand lay sick, and their number was increasing.

Of the effective men, less than six thousand had had any experience, and none had seen more than one year's service. Some were wholly without arms; not one regiment of infantry was properly equipped. The regiment of artillery, five hundred and eighty-eight in number, including officers, had no skilled gunners or engineers. Knox, its colonel, had been a Boston bookseller. Most of the cannon in the field-works were of iron, old and honeycombed. The constant arrival and departure of militia made good discipline impossible.

In New York the country people turned out with surprising alacrity, leaving their grain to perish for want of the sickle. The body suddenly levied in New York, the nine regiments from Connecticut, the Maryland regiment and companies, a regiment from Delaware, and two more battalions of Pennsylvania riflemen, raised the number of men fit for duty under Washington's command to about seventeen thousand; but most of them were fresh from rustic labor, ill-armed or not armed at all.

The New York convention desired that the command of the Hudson might be secured; and, on the recommendation of Putnam and Mifflin, a fort was built on the height now known as Fort Washington, two miles and a half below King's Bridge.

Of the batteries by which New York was protected, the most important was the old Fort George on the south point of the island; a barrier crossed Broadway near the Bowling Green; a redoubt was planted near the river, west of Trinity church; another, that took the name of Bunker Hill, near the site of the present Centre Market. Earthworks were thrown up here and there along the East and Hudson rivers within the settled parts of the town, and at the northern end of the island, on hills overlooking King's Bridge; but many intermediate points, favorable for landing, were defenceless. The regiment of Prescott, who commanded in the battle of Bunker Hill, and one other regiment, were all that could be spared to garrison Governor's Island.

British reinforcements arrived with Clinton and Cornwallis on the first of August, and eleven days later more than twenty-five hundred British troops from England, and more than eighty-six hundred Hessians. Sir Peter Parker brought Campbell and Dunmore, who, with Tryon and Martin, hoped from victory their restoration to their governments. On the fifteenth the Hessians, who were in excellent health after their long voyage, landed on Staten Island.

The plan of attack by General Howe was as elaborate as if he had had to encounter an equal army. A squadron of five ships under Sir Peter Parker was to menace New York and act against the right flank of the American defences; Grant, with two brigades, a regiment of Highlanders, and two companies of New York provincials, was to advance upon the coast-road toward Gowanus; the three German brigades and yagers, stationed half a mile in front of Flatbush, in a line of nearly a mile in length, were to force the direct road to Brooklyn, while at the evening gun Howe and much the larger part of the army, under Clinton, Cornwallis, and Percy, with eighteen field-pieces, leaving their tents and equipage behind, moved from Flatlands across the country through the New Lots, to turn the left of the American outposts.

At three in the morning of the twenty-seventh, the sun rose with an angry red glare, foreboding a change of weather; the first object seen from New York was the squadron of Sir Peter Parker attempting to sail up the bay as if to attack the town; but, the wind veering to the northward, it came to anchor at the change of tide, and the Roebuck was the only ship that fetched high enough to exchange shot with the battery at Red Hook. Relieved from apprehension of an attack on the city, Washington repaired to Long Island; but he rode through the lines only in time to witness disasters which were become inevitable.

The van of the British army under Clinton, guided by tory farmers of the neighborhood, having captured a patrol of American officers in the night, gained the heights on the first appearance of day. The force with Howe, after passing them without obstruction, and halting to give the soldiers time for refreshment, renewed its march. At half-past eight, or a little later, it reached Bedford, in the rear of the American left, and the signal was given for a general attack. At this moment about four thousand Americans were on the wooded passes in advance of the Brooklyn lines. They were attacked by the largest British army which appeared in the field during the war.

When the cannonading from the main army and the brigades under Grant was heard, the Hessians moved up the ridge, the yagers under Donop and some volunteers going in advance as flanking parties and clearing the way with their small cannon; the battalions followed, with a widely extended front, and in ranks but two deep, using only the bayonet. At first, Sullivan's party fired with nervous rapidity, and too high, doing little injury; then, becoming aware of the danger on their flank and rear, they turned to retreat. The Hessians took possession of their deserted redoubt, its three brass six-pounders, one howitzer, and two baggage-wagons, and chased the fugitives relentlessly through the thickets. The Americans, stopped on their way by British regiments, were thrown back upon the Hessians. For a long time the forest rung with the cries of the pursuers and the pursued, the noise of musketry and artillery, the notes of command given by trumpets and hautboys; the ground was strewn with the wounded and the dead. The Jersey militia fought well, till Johnston, their colonel, was shot in the breast, after showing the most determined courage. Sullivan, seeing himself surrounded, desired his men to shift for themselves. Some of them, fighting with desperate valor, cleaved a passage through the British to the American lines; others, breaking into small parties, hid themselves in the woods, from which they escaped to the lines, or were picked up as prisoners. Sullivan was found by three Hessian grenadiers, hiding in a field of maize.

The contest was over at the east and at the centre. Near the bay Stirling still maintained his position. Lord Howe, having learned that Grant's division, which halted at the edge of the woods, was in want of ammunition, went himself with a supply from his ship, sending his boat's crew with it on their backs up the hill, while further supplies followed from the store-ships. Early in the day Parry, lieutenant-colonel under Atlee, was shot in the head as he was encouraging his men. Parsons left his men, concealed himself in a swamp, and came into camp the next morning by way of the East river. His party were nearly all taken prisoners; among them Jewett of Lyme, captain of volunteers, who after his surrender was run through the body by the officer to whom he gave up his sword.

None remained in the field but Stirling, with the regiment of Maryland and that of Delaware. For nearly four hours they stood in their ranks with colors flying, when, perceiving the main body of the British army rapidly coming behind him, he gave them the word to retreat. They withdrew in perfect order; twenty marines were brought off as prisoners.

A bleak northeasterly wind sprung up at evening. The British army, whose tents had not yet been brought up, slept in front of the lines at Brooklyn, wrapped in blankets and warmed by fires. Of the patriot army many passed the night without shelter. Their dead lay unburied in the forest; the severely wounded languished where they fell. The captives were huddled together in crowded rooms or prison-ships, cut off from good air and wholesome food, and suffered to waste away and die.

The next morning was chill and lowering. Unable to rely on either of his major-generals, Washington, at the break of day, renewed the inspection of the American works, which from their great extent left many points exposed. The British encampments appeared large enough for twenty thousand men; wherever he passed, he encouraged the soldiers to engage in continual skirmishes. During the morning Mifflin brought over from New York a reinforcement of nearly one thousand men, composed of Glover's regiment of Massachusetts fishermen, and the Pennsylvania regiments of Shee and Magaw, which were "the best disciplined of any in the army." Their arrival was greeted with cheers. In the afternoon rain fell heavily; the lines were at some places so low that men employed in the trenches stood in water; provisions could not be regularly served, and whole regiments had nothing to eat but raw pork and bread; but their commander-in-chief was among them, exposing himself more than any one to the storm, and the sight of their general, enduring hardships equally with themselves, reconciled them to their sufferings. For eight-and-forty hours he gave no moment to sleep, and for nearly all that time, by night and by day, was on horseback in the lines.

All the following night Washington, who was fixed in the purpose "to avoid a general action," kept watch over the British army and his own. In Philadelphia, rumor quadrupled his force; congress expected him to stay the enemy at the threshold, as had been done at Charlestown; but the morning of Thursday showed him that the British had broken ground within six hundred yards of the height now known as Fort Greene, and that they intended to force his lines by regular approaches, which the nature of the ground and his want of heavy cannon extremely favored; all Long Island was in their hands, except only the neck on which he was intrenched, and a part of his camp would soon be exposed to their guns; his men were falling sick from hard service, exposure, and bad food; on a change of wind, he might be encircled by the entrance of the British fleet into the East river. It was no longer safe to delay a retreat, of which the success would depend on preparing for it with impenetrable secrecy.

Through Mifflin, in whom he confided more than in any general on the island and who agreed with him in opinion, he despatched, at an early hour, a written command to Heath, at King's Bridge, "to order every flat-bottomed boat and other craft at his post, fit for transporting troops, down to New York as soon as possible, without the least delay." In like manner, before noon, he sent Trumbull, the commissary-general, to New York, with orders for Hugh Hughes, the assistant quartermaster-general, "to impress every kind of water-craft, on either side of New York, that could be kept afloat, and had either oars or sails, or could be furnished with them, and to have them all in the East river by dark."

The whole American army who were on Long Island, with their provisions, military stores, field-artillery, and ordnance, except a few worthless iron cannon, landed safely in New York.

"Considering the difficulties," wrote Greene, "the retreat from Long Island was the best effected retreat I ever read or heard of."

XII. THE RETREAT THROUGH THE JERSEYS

November 17–December 13, 1776

EARL CORNWALLIS took the command in New Jersey. His first object was Fort Lee, which lay on the narrow ridge between the Hudson and Hackensack rivers. Drop after drop of sorrow was fast falling into the cup of Washington. On the seventeenth of November he gave orders to Lee with his division to join him, but the orders were wilfully slighted. In the following weeks they were repeated constantly, mixed with reasoning and entreaty, and were always disobeyed with stolid and impertinent evasions.

In the night of the nineteenth two battalions of Hessian grenadiers, two companies of yagers, and the eight battalions of the English reserve, at least five thousand men, marched up the east side of the Hudson, and the next morning, about daybreak, crossed with their artillery to Closter landing, five miles above Fort Lee. Greene had placed on the post neither guard nor watch, being certain in his own mind that the British would not make their attack by that way; so that the nimble seamen were unmolested as they dragged the cannon for near half a mile up the narrow, steep, rocky road, to the top of the palisades. Receiving a report of the near approach of the enemy, Greene sent an express to the commander-in-chief, and, having ordered his troops under arms, took to flight with more than two thousand men, leaving blankets and baggage, except what his few wagons could bear away, a large amount of provisions, camp-kettles on the fire, above four hundred tents standing, and all his cannon except two twelve-pounders, but no military stores. With his utmost speed he barely escaped being cut off; but Washington, first ordering Grayson, his aide-de-camp, to renew the summons for Lee to cross the river, gained the bridge over the Hackensack by a rapid march, and covered the retreat of the garrison, so that less than ninety stragglers were taken prisoners. The main body of those who escaped were without tents, or blankets, or camp utensils, but such as they could pick up as they went along.

To prevent being hemmed in on the narrow peninsula between the Hackensack and Passaic rivers, which meet in Newark bay, orders were given on the twenty-first for moving beyond the Passaic. The governor of New Jersey was reminded that the enlistment of the flying camp belonging to that state, Pennsylvania, and Maryland was near expiring, so that the enemy could be stopped only by the immediate uprising of the militia. At Newark, where Washington arrived on the night of the twenty-second, he maintained himself for five days, devising means to cover the country, and awaiting the continental force under Lee and volunteers of New Jersey.

On the twenty-third he sent Reed, who was a native of New Jersey, to the legislature of that state then at Burlington, and Mifflin to congress. Reed, who had been charged to convey to the New Jersey government "a perfect idea of the critical situation of affairs, the movements of the enemy, and the absolute necessity of further and immediate exertions," shrinking from further duty, returned his commission to the president of congress; but a cold rebuke from Washington drove him, at the end of four days, to retract his resignation, though he could not overcome his reluctance at "following the wretched remains of a broken army."

Congress called on the associators in Philadelphia and the nearest four counties to join the army, if but for six months; begged blankets and woollen stockings for the soldiers; and wrote North and South for troops and stores. The state of Pennsylvania was paralyzed by disputes about its new constitution; but Mifflin successfully addressed the old committee of safety and the new assembly; he reviewed and encouraged the city militia; with Rittenhouse in the chair, and the general assembly and council of safety in attendance, he spoke to the people of Philadelphia in town-meeting with fervor, and was answered by acclamations. All this while the British officers were writing home from New York: "Lord Cornwallis is carrying all before him in the Jerseys; peace must soon be the consequence of our success." On the twenty-eighth the advanced guard of Cornwallis reached Newark, just as it was left by the rear of the Americans.

At Brunswick, where the American army arrived on the evening of the twenty-eighth, it found short repose. Lee, though importuned daily, and sometimes twice a day, lingered on the east of the Hudson; Pennsylvania had no government; the efforts of congress were ineffective; and the appeal of the governor of New Jersey to its several colonels of militia could not bring into the field one full company. All this while Washington was forced to hide his weakness and bear loads of censure from false estimates of his strength. To expressions of sympathy from William Livingston he answered: "I will not despair." As he wrote these words, on the last day of November, he was parting with the New Jersey and Maryland brigades, which formed nearly half his force and claimed their discharge now that their engagement expired; while the brothers, Lord and Sir William Howe, were publishing a new proclamation of pardon and amnesty to all who within sixty days would promise not to take up arms against the king.

On the first of December, just as Washington was leaving Brunswick, he renewed his urgency with Lee: "The enemy mean to push for Philadelphia. I must entreat you to hasten your march, or your arrival may be too late." On the evening of that day Cornwallis entered Brunswick. Washington, as he retreated, broke down a part of the bridge over the Raritan, and a sharp cannonade took place across the river, in which it is remembered that an American battery was commanded by Alexander Hamilton. With but three thousand men, he marched by night to Princeton. Leaving Stirling and twelve hundred men at that place to watch the motions of the enemy, he went with the rest to Trenton, where he found time to counsel congress how to provide resources for the campaign of the next year. Having transferred his baggage and stores beyond the Delaware, he faced about with such troops as were fit for service. But, on the sixth, Cornwallis was joined by Howe and nearly a full brigade of fresh troops. Washington, on his way to Princeton, met the detachment of Stirling retreating before a vastly superior force; he therefore returned with his army to Trenton, and crossed the Delaware.

No hope remained to the United States but in Washington. His retreat of ninety miles through the Jerseys, protracted for eighteen or nineteen days, in winter, often in sight and within cannon-shot of his enemies, his rear pulling down bridges and their van building them up, had for its purpose to effect delay till midwinter and impassable roads should offer their protection. The actors, looking back upon the crowded disasters which fell on them, hardly knew by what springs of animation they had been sustained.

XIII. TRENTON

December 11–26, 1776

The British posts on the eastern side of the Delaware drew near to Philadelphia; rumor reported ships-of-war in the bay; the wives and children of the inhabitants were escaping with their papers and property; and the contagion of panic broke out in congress. On the eleventh of December they called on the states to appoint, each for itself, a day of fasting and humiliation; on the twelfth, after advice from Putnam and Mifflin, they voted to adjourn to Baltimore. It is on record that Samuel Adams, whom Jefferson has described as "exceeded by no man in congress for depth of purpose, zeal, and sagacity," mastered by enthusiasm and excitement which grew with adversity, vehemently opposed a removal.

At New York, where all was mirth and jollity, Howe met the messenger who, in return for the victory on Long Island, brought him encomiums from the minister and honors from the king. The young English officers were preparing to amuse themselves by the performance of plays at the theatre for the benefit of the widows and children of sufferers by the war. The markets were well supplied, balls were given to satiety, and the dulness of evening parties was dispelled by the faro-table, where sub-alterns competed with their superiors and ruined themselves by play. Howe fired his sluggish nature by wine and good cheer; his mistress spent his money prodigally, but the continuance of the war promised him a great fortune. The refugees grumbled because Lord Howe would not break the law by suffering them to fit out privateers; and they envied the floods of wealth which poured in upon him from his eighth part of prize-money on captures made by his squadron. As the fighting was over, Corn-wallis sent his baggage on board the packet for England. The brothers gave the secretary of state under their joint hands an assurance of the conquest of all New Jersey; and every one in New York was looking out for festivals on the investiture of Sir William Howe as knight of the Bath. His flatterers wrote home that, unless there should be more tardiness in noticing his merit, the king would very soon use up all the honors of the peerage in rewarding his victories.

The day arrived for the concerted attack on the British posts along the Delaware; and complete success could come only from the exact co-operation of every part. Gates wilfully turned his back on danger, duty, and honor. He disapproved of Washington's station above Trenton: the British would secretly construct boats, pass the Delaware in his rear, and take Philadelphia; Washington ought to retire to the south of the Susque-hannah. Eager to intrigue with congress at Baltimore for the chief com-mand in the northern district, Gates, with Wilkinson, rode away from Bristol. Griffin, flying before Donop, had abandoned New Jersey; Putnam would not think of conducting an expedition across the river.

At nightfall General John Cadwalader, who was left in sole command at Bristol, marched to Dunk's ferry; it was the time of the full moon, but the clouds were thick and dark. For about an hour that remained of the ebb-tide the river was passable in boats, and Reed, who just then arrived from a visit to Philadelphia, was able to get over with his horse; but the tide, beginning to rise, threw back the ice in such heaps on the Jersey shore that, though men on foot still could cross, neither horses nor artil-lery could reach the land. Sending word that it was impossible to carry out their share in Washington's plan, and leaving the party who had crossed the river to return as they could, Reed sought shelter within the enemy's lines at Burlington. Meanwhile, during one of the worst nights of December, the men waited with arms in their hands for the floating ice to open a passage; and, only after the vain sufferings of many hours, re-turned to their camp. Cadwalader and the best men about him were confi-dent that Washington, like themselves, must have given up the expedi-tion. Ewing did not even make an effort to cross at Trenton; and Moylan, who set off on horseback to overtake Washington and share the honors of the day, became persuaded that no attempt could be made in such a storm, and stopped on the road for shelter.

At that hour an American patrol of twenty or thirty men, led by Captain Anderson to reconnoitre Trenton, made a sudden attack upon the post of a Hessian subaltern, and wounded five or six men. The alarm was sounded, the Hessian brigade put under arms, and a part of Rall's regiment sent in pursuit. On their return, they reported that they could discover nothing; the attack, like those which had been made repeatedly before, was held to be of no importance. The post was strengthened; additional patrols were sent out; but every apprehension was put to rest; and Rall, till late into the night, sat by his warm fire, in his usual revels, while Washington was crossing the Delaware.

"The night," writes Thomas Rodney, "was as severe a night as ever I saw;" the frost was sharp, the current difficult to stem, the ice increasing, the wind high, and at eleven it began to snow. It was three in the morning of the twenty-sixth before the troops and cannon were all over; and another hour passed before they could be formed on the Jersey side. A violent north-east storm of wind and sleet and hail set in as they began their nine miles' march to Trenton, against an enemy in the best condition to fight. The weather was terrible for men clad as the Americans were, and the ground slipped under their feet. For a mile and a half they had to climb a steep hill, from which they descended to the road that ran for about three miles between hills and through forests of hickory, ash, and black oak. At Birmingham the force was divided; Sullivan continued near the river, and Washington passed up into the Pennington road. While Sullivan, who had the shortest route, halted to give time for the others to arrive, he reported to Washington by one of his aids that the arms of his party were wet. "Then tell your general," answered Washington, "to use the bayonet, and penetrate into the town." The return of the aide-de-camp was watched by the soldiers; and hardly had he spoken when those who had bayonets fixed them without waiting for a command.

It was now broad day. The slumber of the Hessians had been undisturbed; their patrols reported that all was quiet; and the night-watch of yagers had turned in, leaving the sentries at their seven advanced posts, to keep up the communication between their right and left wings. The storm beat violently in the faces of the Americans; the men were stiff with cold and a continuous march of fifteen miles; but now that they were near the enemy, they thought of nothing but victory. Washington's party began the battle with an attack on the outermost picket on the Pennington road; the men with Stark, who led the van of Sullivan's party, gave three cheers, and with the bayonet rushed upon the enemy's picket near the river. A company came out of the barracks to protect the patrol; but, astonished at the fury of the charge, they all, including the yagers, fled in confusion, escaping across the Assanpink, followed by the dragoons and the party which was posted near the river bank. Washington entered the town by King and Queen streets, now named after Warren and Greene; Sullivan moved by the river-road into Second street, cutting off the way to the Assanpink bridge; and both divisions pushed forward with such equal ardor as never to suffer the Hessians to form completely. The two cannon which stood in front of Rall's quarters were from the first separated from the regiment to which they belonged. The Americans were coming into line of battle, when Rall made his appearance, received a report, rode up in front of his regiment, and cried out: "Forward, march; advance, advance," reeling in the saddle like one not yet recovered from a night's debauch. Before his own regiment could form in the street a party pushed on rapidly and dismounted its two cannon, with no injury but slight wounds to Captains William Washington and James Monroe. Under Washington's own direction, Forest's American battery of six guns was opened upon two regiments at a distance of less than three hundred yards. His position was near the front, a little to the right, a conspicuous mark for musketry; but he remained unhurt, though his horse was wounded under him. The moment for breaking through the Americans was lost by Rall, who drew back the Lossberg regiment and his own, but without artillery, into an orchard east of the town, as if intending to reach the road to Princeton by turning Washington's left. To check this movement, Hand's regiment was thrown in his front. By a quick resolve the passage might still have been forced; but the Hessians had been plundering ever since they landed in the country; and, loath to leave behind the wealth which they had amassed, they urged Rall to recover the town. In the attempt to do so, his force was driven by the impetuous charge of the Americans farther back than before; he was himself struck by a musketball; and the two regiments were mixed confusedly and almost surrounded. Riding up to Washington, Baylor could now report: "Sir, the Hessians have surrendered."

Until that hour the life of the United States flickered like a dying flame. "But the Lord of hosts heard the cries of the distressed, and sent an angel for their deliverance," wrote the praeses of the Pennsylvania Lutherans. "All our hopes," said Lord George Germain, "were blasted by the unhappy affair at Trenton." That victory turned the shadow of death into the morning.

XIV. ASSANPINK AND PRINCETON

December 26, 1776–January 1777

AFTER snatching refreshments from the captured stores, the victorious troops, worn out by cold, rain, snow, and storm, the charge of nearly a thousand prisoners, and the want of sleep, set off again in sleet driven by a north-east wind, and, passing another terrible night at the ferry, recrossed the Delaware. But Stirling and one half of the soldiers were disabled, and two men were frozen to death.

An hour before noon on the twenty-seventh Cadwalader at Bristol heard of Washington at Trenton, and took measures to cross into New Jersey. Hitchcock's remnant of a New England brigade could not move for want of shoes, stockings, and breeches; but these were promptly supplied from Philadelphia. Donop, on hearing of the defeat of Rall, had precipitately retreated by way of Crosswicks and Allentown to Princeton, abandoning his stores and his sick and wounded at Bordentown, and leaving Burlington to be occupied by the detachment under Cadwalader.

Washington on the twenty-seventh communicated to Cadwalader his scheme for driving the enemy to the extremity of New Jersey. Intending to remain on the east side of the Delaware, he wrote urgent letters to Macdougall and Maxwell to collect troops at Morristown; for, said he, "if the militia of Jersey will lend a hand, I hope and expect to rescue their country." To Heath, who was receiving large reinforcements from New England, he sent orders to render aid by way of Hackensack. Through Lord Stirling he entreated the governor of New Jersey to convene the legislature of that state, and make the appointments of their officers according to merit. He took thought for the subsistence of the troops, which, when they should all be assembled, would form a respectable force. On the twenty-ninth, while his army, reduced nearly one half in effective numbers by fatigue in the late attack on Trenton, was again crossing the Delaware, he announced to congress his purpose "to pursue the enemy and try to beat up more of their quarters, and, in a word, in every instance, adopt such measures as the exigency of our affairs requires and our situation will justify."

On New Year's morning Robert Morris went from house to house in Philadelphia, rousing people from their beds to borrow money of them; and early in the day he sent Washington fifty thousand dollars, with the message: "Whatever I can do shall be done for the good of the service; if further occasional supplies of money are necessary, you may depend upon my exertions either in a public or private capacity." Washington brought with him scarcely more than six hundred trusty men, and in the choice of measures, all full of peril, he resolved to concentrate his forces at Trenton. Obedient to his call, the volunteers joined him in part on the first of January; in part, after a night-march, on the second; yet making collectively a body of less than five thousand men, of whom three fifths or more were just from their families and warm houses, ignorant of war.

On the second of January 1777, Cornwallis, leaving three regiments and a company of cavalry at Princeton, "advanced upon" the Americans with the flower of the British army, just as Washington had expected. The air was warm and moist, the road soft, so that their march was slow. From Maidenhead, where they were delayed by skirmishers, and where one brigade under Leslie remained, they pressed forward with more than five thousand British and Hessians. At Five Mile Run they fell upon Hand and his riflemen, who continued to dispute every step of his progress. At Shabbakonk creek, troops secreted within the wood on the flanks of the road embarrassed them for two hours. On the hill less than a mile above Trenton they were confronted by about six hundred musketeers and two skilfully managed field-pieces, supported by a detachment under

Greene. This party, when attacked by artillery, withdrew in good order.

At four in the afternoon Washington took command of the rear of the army, and, while Cornwallis sought to outflank him, detained the British until those of his own army who had passed the Assanpink gained time to plant their cannon beyond the rivulet. The enemy, as they advanced, were worried by musketry from houses and barns. Their attempt to force the bridge was repulsed. The Americans had all safely passed over; the Assanpink could not be forded without a battle, for beyond it stood the main body of the American army, silent in their ranks and already protected by batteries. Late as it was in the day, Simcoe advised at once to pass over the Assanpink to the right of "the rebels" and bring on a general action; and Sir William Erskine feared that, if it were put off, Washington might get away before morning. But the sun was nearly down; the night threatened to be foggy and dark; the British troops were worn out with skirmishes and a long march over heavy roads; the attitude of the American army was imposing. Cornwallis sent messengers in all haste for the brigade at Maidenhead, and for two of the three regiments at Princeton, and put off the fight till the next morning. The British army, sleeping by their fires, bivouacked on the hill above Trenton, while their pickets were pushed forward along the Assanpink, to watch the army of Washington. Confident in their vigilance, the general officers took their repose.

Not so Washington. From his slow retreat through the Jerseys, and his long halt in the first week of December at Trenton, he knew the byways leading out of the place, and the roads to Brunswick, where the baggage of the British troops was deposited. He first ascertained by an exploring party that the path to Princeton on the south side of the Assanpink was unguarded. He was aware that there were but few troops at Princeton, and that Brunswick had retained but a small guard for its rich magazines. He therefore followed out the plan which had existed in germ from the time of his deciding to re-enter New Jersey, and prepared to turn the left of Cornwallis, overwhelm the party at Princeton, and push on if possible to Brunswick, or, if there were danger of pursuit, to seek the high ground on the way to Morristown. When it became dark he ordered the baggage of his army to be removed noiselessly to Burlington.

Soon after midnight, sending word to Putnam to occupy Crosswicks, Washington "marched his army round the head of the creek into the Princeton road." The wind veered to the north-west; the weather suddenly became cold; and the by-road, lately difficult for artillery, was soon frozen hard. Guards were left to replenish the American camp-fires which flamed along the Assanpink for more than half a mile, and the drowsy British night-watch surmised nothing.

Arriving about sunrise in the south-east outskirts of Princeton, Washington and the main body of the army wheeled to the right by a back road to the colleges, while Mercer was detached toward the west, with about three hundred and fifty men, to break down the bridge over Stony brook, on the main road to Trenton. Two British regiments were already on their march to join Cornwallis; the seventeenth with three companies of horse, under Mawhood, was more than a mile in advance of the fifty-fifth, and had already passed Stony brook. On discovering in his rear a small body of Americans, apparently not larger than his own, he recrossed the rivulet, and, forming a junction with a part of the fifty-fifth and other detachments on their march, hazarded an engagement with Mercer. The parties were nearly equal in numbers; each had two pieces of artillery; but the English were fresh from undisturbed repose, while the Americans were suffering from a night-march of eighteen miles. Both parties moved toward high ground that lay north of them, on the right of the Americans. A heavy discharge from the English artillery was returned by Neil from two New Jersey field-pieces. After a short but brisk cannonade, the Americans, climbing over a fence to confront the British, were the first to use their guns; Mawhood's infantry returned the volley, and soon charged with their bayonets; the Americans, for the most part riflemen without bayonets, gave way, abandoning their cannon. Their gallant officers, loath to fly, were left in their rear, endeavoring to call back the fugitives. In this way fell Haslet, the brave colonel of the Delaware regiment; Neil, who stayed by his battery; Fleming, the gallant leader of all that remained of the first Virginia regiment; and other officers of promise; and the able General Mercer, whose horse had been disabled under him, was wounded, knocked down, and then stabbed many times with the bayonet. Just then Washington, who had turned at the sound of the cannon, came upon the ground by a movement which intercepted the main body of the British fifty-fifth regiment. The Pennsylvania militia, supported by two pieces of artillery, were the first to form their line. "With admirable coolness and address," Mawhood attempted to carry their battery; the way-worn novices began to waver; on the instant, Washington, from "his desire to animate his troops by example," rode within less than thirty yards of the British, and reined in his horse with its head toward them. Each party at the same moment gave a volley, but Washington remained untouched. Hitchcock, for whom a burning hectic made this day nearly his last, brought up his brigade; and the British, seeing Hand's riflemen beginning to turn their left, fled over fields and fences up Stony brook. The action, from the first contact with Mercer, did not last more than twenty minutes. Washington on the battleground took Hitchcock by the hand and thanked him for his service. Mawhood left two brass field-pieces, which, from want of horses, the Americans could not carry off. He was chased three or four miles, and many of his men were taken prisoners.

The fifty-fifth British regiment, after resisting gallantly the New England troops of Stark, Poor, Patterson, Reed, and others, retreated with the fortieth to the college; and, when pieces of artillery were brought up, escaped across the fields into a back road toward Brunswick. The British lost on that day about two hundred killed and wounded, and two hundred and thirty prisoners; the American loss was small, except of officers.

At Trenton, on the return of day, the generals were astonished at not seeing the American army; the noise of cannon at Princeton first revealed whither it was gone. In consternation for the safety of the magazines at Brunswick, Cornwallis roused his army and began a swift pursuit. His advanced party from Maidenhead reached Princeton just as the town was left by the American rear. It had been a part of Washington's plan as he left Trenton to seize Brunswick, which was eighteen miles distant; but many of his brave soldiers, such is the concurrent testimony of English and German officers as well as of Washington, were "quite barefoot, and were badly clad in other respects;" all were exhausted by the service of two days and a night, from action to action, almost without refreshment; and the army of Cornwallis was close upon their rear. So, with the advice of his officers, after breaking up the bridge at Kingston over the Millstone river, Washington made for the highlands, and halted for the night at Somerset court-house. There, in the woods, worn-out men sank down on the frozen ground and fell asleep.

The example and the orders of Washington roused the people around him to arms. On the fifth, the day of his arrival at Morristown, a party of Waldeckers, attacked at Springfield by an equal number of the New Jersey militia under Oliver Spencer, were put to flight, losing forty-eight men, of whom thirty-nine were prisoners. On the same day, at the approach of George Clinton with troops from Peekskill, the British force at Hackensack saved their baggage by a timely flight. Newark was abandoned; Elizabethtown was surprised by Maxwell, who took much baggage and a hundred prisoners.

The eighteenth, which was the king's birthday, was chosen for investing Sir William Howe with the order of the Bath. But it was become a mockery to call him a victorious general; and both he and Germain had a foresight of failure, for which each of them was preparing to throw the blame on the other.

In New Jersey all went well. On the twentieth, General Philemon Dickinson, with about four hundred raw troops, forded the Millstone river, near Somerset court-house, and defeated a foraging party, taking a few prisoners, sheep and cattle, forty wagons, and upward of a hundred horses of the English draught breed. Washington made his head-quarters at Morristown; and there, and in the surrounding villages, his troops found shelter. The largest encampment was in Spring valley, on the southern slope of Madison Hill; the outposts extended to within three miles of Amboy; and, though there was but the phantom of an army, the British in New Jersey were confined to Brunswick, Amboy, and Paulus Hook.

Under the last proclamation of the brothers, two thousand seven hundred and three Jerseymen, besides eight hundred and fifty-one in Rhode Island, and twelve hundred and eighty-two in the rural districts and city of New York, subscribed a declaration of fidelity to the British king; on the fourteenth of January, just as the period for subscription was about to expire, Germain, who grudged every act of mercy, sent orders to the

Howes not to let "the undeserving escape that punishment which is due to their crimes, and which it will be expedient to inflict for the sake of example to futurity." Eleven days after the date of this order, Washington, the harbinger and champion of union, was in a condition to demand, by a proclamation in the name of the United States, that those who had accepted British protections "should withdraw within the enemy's lines, or take the oath of allegiance to the United States of America." The indiscriminate rapacity of the British and Hessians, their lust, their unrestrained passion for destruction, united the people of New Jersey in courage and the love of liberty.

The result of the campaign was inauspicious for Britain. New England, except the island of Rhode Island, all central, northern, and western New York except Fort Niagara, all the country from the Delaware to Florida, were free.

XV. THE WINTER AT VALLEY FORGE

November 1777–April 1778

WHEN at last Washington was joined by troops from the northern army, a clamor arose for the capture of Philadelphia. Protected by the Schuylkill and the Delaware, the city could be approached only from the north, and on that side a chain of fourteen redoubts extended from river to river. Moreover, the army by which it was occupied, having been reinforced from New York by more than three thousand men, exceeded nineteen thousand. Four American officers voted in council for an assault upon the lines of this greatly superior force; but the general, sustained by eleven, disregarded the murmurs of congress and rejected "the mad enterprise."

With quickness of eye he selected in the woods of Whitemarsh strong ground for an encampment, and there, within fourteen miles of Philadelphia, awaited the enemy, of whose movements he received exact and timely intelligence. On the severely cold night of the fourth of December the British, fourteen thousand strong, marched out to attack the American lines. Before daybreak on the fifth their advance party halted on a ridge beyond Chestnut Hill, eleven miles from Philadelphia, and at seven their main body formed in one line, with a few regiments as reserves. The Americans occupied thickly wooded hills, with a morass and a brook in their front. Opposite the British left wing a breastwork defended the only point where the brook could be easily forded. At night the British force rested on their arms. Washington passed the hours in strengthening his position; and though, according to Kalb who was present, he had but seven thousand really effective men, he wished for an engagement. Near the end of another day Howe marched back to Germantown, and on the next, as if intending a surprise, suddenly returned upon the American left, which he made preparations to assail. Washington delivered in person to each brigade his orders on the manner of receiving their enemy, exhorting to a reliance on the bayonet. All day long, and until eight in the evening, Howe kept up his reconnoitring, but found the American position everywhere strong by nature and by art. Nothing occurred but a sharp action on Edge Hill between light troops under Gist and Morgan's riflemen and a British party led by General Grey. The latter lost eighty-nine in killed and wounded; the Americans, twenty-seven, among them the brave Major Morris of New Jersey. On the eighth, just after noon, the British suddenly marched by the shortest road to Philadelphia. Their loss in the expedition exceeded one hundred. The rest of the season Howe made no excursions except for food or forage; and Washington had no choice but to seek winter-quarters for his suffering soldiers; while Gates, with Conway and Mifflin, formed a cabal to drive Washington into retirement and put Gates in his place.

The problem which Washington must next solve was to keep together through the cold winter an army without tents, and to confine the British to the environs of Philadelphia. There was no town which would serve the purpose. Valley Forge, on the Schuylkill, but twenty-one miles from Philadelphia, admitted of defence against the artillery of those days, and had more than one route convenient for escape into the interior. The ground lay between two ridges of hills, and was covered by a thick forest. As his men moved toward the spot, they were in need of clothes and blankets and shoes, as well as tents, and were almost as often without provisions as with them. On the nineteenth they arrived at Valley Forge, with no covering. From his life in the woods, Washington could see in the trees a town of log cabins, built in regular streets, and affording shelter enough to save the army from dispersion. The order for their erection was received by officers and men as impossible of execution; and they were astonished at the ease with which, as the work of their Christmas holidays, they changed the forest into huts thatched with boughs in the order of a regular encampment.

Washington was followed to Valley Forge by letters from congress transmitting the remonstrance of the council and assembly of Pennsylvania against his going into winter-quarters. To this reproof Washington, on the twenty-third, after laying deserved blame upon Mifflin for neglect of duty as quartermaster-general, replied: "For the want of a two days' supply of provisions, an opportunity scarcely ever offered of taking an advantage of the enemy that has not been either totally obstructed or greatly impeded. Men are confined to hospitals, or in farmers' houses for want of shoes. We have this day no less than two thousand eight hundred and ninety-eight men in camp unfit for duty, because they are barefoot and otherwise naked. Our whole strength in continental troops amounts to no more than eight thousand two hundred in camp fit for duty. Since the fourth instant our numbers fit for duty from hardships and exposures have decreased nearly two thousand men. Numbers still are obliged to sit all night by fires. Gentlemen reprobate the going into winter-quarters as much as if they thought the soldiers were made of stocks or stones. I can assure those gentlemen that it is a much easier and less distressing thing to draw remonstrances in a comfortable room by a good fireside than to occupy a cold, bleak hill, and sleep under frost and snow without clothes or blankets. However, although they seem to have little feeling for the naked and distressed soldiers, I feel superabundantly for them, and from my soul I pity those miseries which it is neither in my power to relieve or prevent."

While the shivering soldiers were shaping the logs for their cabins, the clamor of the Pennsylvanians continued; and, the day after Christmas, Sullivan, who held with both sides, gave his written advice to Washington to yield and attack Howe in Philadelphia, "risking every consequence in an action."

The next year opened gloomily at Valley Forge. To the touching account of the condition of the army, congress, which had not provided one magazine for winter, made no response except a promise to the soldiers of one month's extra pay, and a renewal of authority to take the articles necessary for their comfortable subsistence. On the fifth of January 1778, Washington renewed his remonstrances: "It will never answer to procure supplies of clothing or provision by coercive measures. Such procedures may give a momentary relief, but, if repeated, besides spreading disaffection, jealousy, and fear among the people, never fail, even in the most veteran troops under the most rigid and exact discipline, to raise in the soldiery a disposition to plunder, difficult to suppress, and not only ruinous to the inhabitants, but, in many instances, to armies themselves. I regret the occasion that compelled us to the measure the other day, and shall consider it among the greatest of our misfortunes if we should be under the necessity of practicing it again." Still, congress did no more than, on the tenth and twelfth of January, appoint Gates and Mifflin, with four or five others, to repair to head-quarters and concert reforms.

Even so late as the eleventh of February, Dana, one of the committee, reported that men died for the want of straw or other bedding to raise them from the cold, damp earth. Inoculation was for a like reason delayed. Almost every species of camp-transportation was performed by men who, without a murmur, yoked themselves to little carriages of their own making, or loaded their fuel and provisions on their backs. Sometimes fuel was wanting, when for want of shoes and stockings they could not walk through the snow to cut it in the neighboring woods. Some brigades had been four days without meat. For days together the army was without bread. There was danger that the troops would perish from famine or disperse in search of food.

All this time the British soldiers in Philadelphia were well provided for, and the officers quartered upon the inhabitants. The days were spent in pastime, the nights in entertainments. By a proportionate tax on the pay and allowances of each officer, a house was opened for daily resort and for weekly balls, with a gaming-table, and a room devoted to the players of chess. Thrice a week dramas were enacted by amateur performers. The curtain painted by André was greatly admired. The officers, among whom all ranks of the British aristocracy were represented, lived in open licentiousness. At a grand review, an English girl, mistress of a colonel and dressed in the colors of his regiment, drove down the line in her open carriage with great ostentation. The pursuit of pleasure was so eager that an attack in winter was not added to the trials of the army at Valley Forge, even though at one time it was reduced to five thousand men.

XVI. THE LAST CAMPAIGN OF THE AMERICAN WAR

1781

Sir Henry Clinton persevered in the purpose of holding a station in the Chesapeake bay; and, on the second of January 1781, [Benedict] Arnold, with sixteen hundred men, appeared by his order in the James river. The commonwealth of Virginia having sent its best troops and arms to the more southern states, Governor Jefferson promptly called the whole militia from the adjacent counties; but, in the region of planters with slaves, there were not freemen enough at hand to meet the invaders. Arnold offered to spare Richmond if he might unmolested carry off its stores of tobacco; the proposal being rejected with scorn, on the fifth and sixth its houses and stores, public and private, were set on fire. Washington used his knowledge of the lowlands of Virginia to form for the capture of Arnold a plan of which the success seemed to him certain. From his own army he detached about twelve hundred men of the New England and New Jersey lines under the command of Lafayette, and asked the combined aid of the whole French fleet at Newport and a detachment from the land forces under Rochambeau. But d'Estouches, the French admiral, had already sent out a sixty-four-gun ship and two frigates, and did not think it prudent to put to sea with the residue of the fleet. The ships-of-war, which arrived safely in the Chesapeake, having no land troops, could not reach Arnold; but, on their way back to Rhode Island, they captured a British fifty-gun frigate. Washington, on the sixth of March, met Rochambeau and d'Estouches in council on board the flag-ship of the French admiral at Newport, and the plan of Washington, for a combined expedition of the French fleet and land forces into Virginia, was adopted.

On the twenty-sixth of March, General Phillips, who brought from New York a reinforcement of two thousand picked men, took the command in Virginia. All the stores of produce which its planters in five quiet years had accumulated had been carried off or destroyed. Their negroes, so desired in the West Indies, formed the staple article of plunder.

By a courier from Washington Lafayette received information that Virginia was to become the centre of active operations, and was instructed to defend the state as well as his means would permit. His troops, who were chiefly from New England, dreaded the climate of lower Virginia, and, besides, were destitute of everything; yet when Lafayette, from the south side of the Susquehannah, in an order of the day, offered leave to any of them to return to the North, not one would abandon him. At Baltimore he borrowed two thousand pounds sterling, supplied his men with shoes and hats, and bought linen, which the women of Baltimore made into summer garments. Then, by a forced march of two hundred miles, he arrived at Richmond on the twenty-ninth of April, the evening before Phillips reached the opposite bank of the river. Having in the night been joined by Steuben with militia, Lafayette was able to hold in check the larger British force. The line of Pennsylvania was detained in that state week after week for needful supplies; while Clinton, stimulated by Germain's praises of the activity of Cornwallis, sent another considerable detachment to Virginia.

On the thirteenth of May, General Phillips died of malignant fever. Arnold, on whom the command devolved, though only for seven days, addressed a letter to Lafayette, who returned it, refusing to correspond with a traitor. Arnold rejoined by threatening to send to the Antilles all American prisoners, unless a cartel should be immediately concluded. On the twentieth Cornwallis arrived at Petersburg, and ordered Arnold back to New York.

Cornwallis now found himself where he had so persistently desired to be—in Virginia, at the head of seven thousand effective men, with not a third of that number to oppose him by land, and with undisputed command of the water. "Wanting a rudder in the storm," said Richard Henry Lee, "the good ship must inevitably be cast away;" and he proposed to send for General Washington immediately and invest him with "dictatorial powers." But Jefferson reasoned: "The thought alone of creating a dictator is treason against mankind, giving to their oppressors a proof of the imbecility of republican government in times of pressing danger. The government, instead of being braced for greater exertions, would be thrown back." As governor of Virginia, speaking for its people and representing their distresses, he wrote to Washington: "Could you lend us your personal aid? The presence of their beloved countryman would restore full confidence, and render them equal to whatever is not impossible. Should you repair to your native state, the difficulty would then be how to keep men out of the field."

The French government declined to furnish means for the siege of New York. After the arrival of its final instructions, Rochambeau, attended by Chastellux, in a meeting with Washington at Weathersfield on the twenty-first of May, settled the preliminaries of the campaign. The French land force was to march to the Hudson river, and, in conjunction with the American army, be ready to move to the southward. De Grasse was charged anew on his way to the North to enter the Chesapeake. In the direction of the war for the coming season there would be union; for congress had lodged the highest power in the northern and southern departments in the hands of Washington, and France had magnanimously placed her troops under his command.

Before his return, the American general called upon the governors of the New England states, "in earnest and pointed terms," to complete their continental battalions, to hold bodies of militia ready to march in a week after being called for, and to adopt effective modes of supply. Governor Trumbull of Connecticut cheered him with the opinion that he would obtain all that he needed.

In June the French contingent, increased by fifteen hundred men newly arrived in ships-of-war, left Newport for the Hudson river. The inhabitants crowded around them on their march, glad to recognise in them allies and defenders. The rights of private property were scrupulously respected, and the petty exigencies of local laws good-naturedly submitted to.

Cornwallis began his career on the James river in Virginia by seizing horses, which were of the best breed, and mounting five or six hundred men. He then started in pursuit of Lafayette, who, with about one thousand continental troops, was posted between Wilton and Richmond, waiting for reinforcements from Pennsylvania. The youthful major-general warily kept to the north of his pursuer; and on the seventh of June made a junction with Wayne not far from Raccoon ford. Small as was his force, he compared the British in Virginia to the French in the German kingdom of Hanover at the time of the seven years' war, and confidently predicted analogous results. Cornwallis advanced as far as the court-house of the Virginia county of Hanover, then crossed South Anna, and, not encountering Lafayette, encamped on the James river, from the Point of Fork to a little below the mouth of Byrd creek. For the next ten days his headquarters were at Elk Hill, on a plantation belonging to Jefferson.

From his camp on Malvern Hill, Lafayette urged Washington to march to Virginia in force; and he predicted in July that, if a French fleet should enter Hampton Roads, the English army must surrender. On the eighth of the same month Cornwallis, in reply to Clinton, reasoned earnestly against a defensive post in the Chesapeake: "It cannot have the smallest influence on the war in Carolina: it only gives us some acres of an unhealthy swamp, and is forever liable to become a prey to a foreign enemy with a temporary superiority at sea." Thoroughly disgusted with the aspect of affairs in Virginia, he asked leave to transfer the command to General Leslie, and go back to Charleston. Meantime, transport ships arrived in the Chesapeake; and, in a letter which he received on the twelfth, he was desired by his chief so to hasten the embarkation of three thousand men that they might sail for New York within forty-eight hours; for, deceived by letters which were written to be intercepted, he believed that the enemy would certainly attack that post.

The engineers of Cornwallis, after careful and extensive surveys, reported unanimously that a work on Point Comfort would not secure ships at anchor in Hampton Roads. To General Phillips, on his embarkation in April, Clinton's words had been: "With regard to a station for the protection of the king's ships, I know of no place so proper as Yorktown." Nothing therefore remained but, in obedience to the spirit of Clinton's orders, to seize and fortify York and Gloucester. Cornwallis accordingly, in the first week of August, embarked his troops successively, and evacuating Portsmouth, transferred his force to Yorktown and Gloucester. Yorktown was then but a small village on a high bank, where the long peninsula dividing the York from the James river is less than eight miles wide. The water is broad, bold, and deep; so that ships of the line may ride there in safety. On the opposite side lies Gloucester, a point of land projecting into the river and narrowing till it becomes but one mile wide. These were occupied by Cornwallis, and fortified with the utmost diligence; though, in his deliberate judgment, the measure promised no honor to himself and no advantage to Great Britain.

On the other hand, Lafayette, concentrating his forces in a strong position at a distance of about eight miles, indulged in the happiest prophecies.

On the very day on which Cornwallis took possession of York and Gloucester, Washington, assured of the assistance of de Grasse, turned his whole thoughts toward moving with the French troops under Rochambeau and the best part of the American army to the Chesapeake. While hostile divisions and angry jealousies increased between the two chief British officers in the United States, on the American side all things conspired happily together. De Barras, who commanded the French squadron at Newport, wrote as to his intentions: "De Grasse is my junior; yet, as soon as he is within reach, I will go to sea to put myself under his orders." The same spirit insured unanimity in the mixed council of war. The rendezvous was given to de Grasse in Chesapeake bay; and, at the instance of Washington, he was to bring with him as many land troops as could be spared from the West Indies.

In the allied camp all was joy. The enthusiasm for political freedom took possession not of the French officers only, but of the soldiers. Every one of them was proud of being a defender of the young republic. On the fifth of September they encamped at Chester. Never had the French seen a man penetrated with a livelier or more manifest joy than Washington when he there learned that, on the last day but one in August, the Count de Grasse, with twenty-eight ships of the line and nearly four thousand land troops, had entered the Chesapeake, where, without loss of time, he had moored most of the fleet in Lynnhaven bay, blocked up York river, and, without being in the least annoyed by Cornwallis, had disembarked at James Island three thousand men under the command of the Marquis de Saint-Simon. Here, too, prevailed unanimity. Saint-Simon, though older in military service as well as in years, placed himself and his troops as auxiliaries under the orders of Lafayette, because he was a major-general in the service of the United States. The combined army in their encampment could be approached only by two passages, which were in themselves difficult and were carefully guarded, so that Cornwallis could not act on the offensive, and found himself effectually blockaded by land and by sea.

One more disappointment awaited Cornwallis. Lord Sandwich, after the retirement of Howe, gave the naval command at New York to officers without ability; and the aged Arbuthnot was succeeded by Graves, a coarse and vulgar man, of mean ability and without skill in his profession.

There was no want of information at New York, yet the British fleet did not leave Sandy Hook until the day after de Grasse had arrived in the Chesapeake. Early on the fifth of September, Graves discovered the French fleet at anchor in the mouth of that bay. De Grasse, though eighteen hundred of his seamen and ninety officers were on duty in James river, ordered his ships to slip their cables, turn out from the anchorage ground, and form the line of battle. The action began at four o'clock in the afternoon, and continued till about sunset. The British sustained so great a loss that, after remaining five days in sight of the French, they returned to New York. On the first day of their return voyage they evacuated and burned The Terrible, a ship of the line, so much had it been damaged in the engagement. De Grasse, now undisturbed master of the Chesapeake, on his way back to his anchoring ground captured two British ships, each of thirty-two guns, and he found de Barras safely at anchor in the bay.

Leaving the allied troops to descend by water from Elk river and Baltimore, Washington, with Rochambeau and Chastellux, riding sixty miles a day, on the evening of the ninth reached his "own seat at Mount Vernon." It was the first time in more than six years that he had seen his home. From its natural terrace above the Potomac his illustrious guests commanded a noble river, a wide and most pleasing expanse of country, and forest-clad heights, which were soon to become the capital of the united republic.

Two days were given to domestic life. On the fourteenth the party arrived at Williamsburg, where Lafayette, recalling the moment when in France the poor rebels were held in light esteem, and when he nevertheless came to share with them all their perils, had the pleasure of welcoming Washington as generalissimo of the combined armies of the two nations.

One peril yet menaced Washington. Count de Grasse, hearing of a reinforcement of the fleet at New York, was bent on keeping the sea, leaving only two vessels at the mouth of the York river. Against this Washington, on the twenty-fifth, addressed the plainest and most earnest remonstrance: "I should esteem myself deficient in my duty to the common cause of France and America, if I did not persevere in entreating you to resume the plans that have been so happily arranged." The letter was taken by Lafayette, who joined to it his own explanations and reasonings; and de Grasse, though reluctant, was prevailed upon to remain within the capes.

The troops from the North having been safely landed at Williamsburg, on the twenty-eighth the united armies marched for the investiture of Yorktown, drove everything on the British side before them, and lay on their arms during the night.

The fortifications of Yorktown, which were nothing but earthworks freshly thrown up, consisted on the right of redoubts and batteries, with a line of stockade in the rear, which supported a high parapet. Over a marshy ravine in front of the right a large redoubt was placed. The morass extended along the centre, which was defended by a stockade and batteries. Two small redoubts were advanced before the left. The ground in front of the left was in some parts level with the works, in others cut by ravines; altogether very convenient for the besiegers. The space within the works was exceedingly narrow, and, except under the cliff, was exposed to enfilade.

The twenty-ninth was given to reconnoitring and forming a plan of attack and approach. The French entreated Washington for orders to storm the exterior posts of the British; in the course of the night before the thirtieth, Cornwallis ordered them all to be abandoned, and thus prematurely conceded to the allied armies ground which commanded his line of works in a very near advance, and gave great advantages for opening the trenches.

In the night before the sixth of October, everything being in readiness, trenches were opened at six hundred yards' distance from the works of Cornwallis—on the right by the Americans, on the left by the French; and the labor was executed in friendly rivalry, with so much secrecy and dispatch that it was first revealed to the enemy by the light of morning. Within three days the first parallel was completed, the redoubts were finished, and batteries were employed in demolishing the embrasures of the enemy's works and their advanced redoubts. On the night before the eleventh the French battery on the left, using red-hot shot, set on fire the frigate Charon, of forty-four guns, and three large transport ships which were entirely consumed.

On the eleventh, at night, the second parallel was begun within three hundred yards of the lines of the besieged. This was undertaken so much sooner than the British expected, that it could be conducted with the same secrecy as before; and they had no suspicion of the working parties till daylight discovered them to their pickets.

All day on the fourteenth the American batteries were directed against the abattis and salient angles of two advanced redoubts of the British, both of which needed to be included in the second parallel; and breaches were made in them sufficient to justify an assault. That on the right near York river was garrisoned by forty-five men, that on the left by thrice as many. The storming of the former fell to the Americans under the command of Lieutenant-Colonel Alexander Hamilton; that of the latter to the French, of whom four hundred grenadiers and yagers of the regiments of Gatinois and of Deux Ponts, with a large reserve, were intrusted to Count William de Deux Ponts and to Baron de l'Estrade.

At the concerted signal of six shells consecutively discharged, the corps under Hamilton advanced in two columns without firing a gun—the right composed of his own battalion, led by Major Fish, and of another commanded by Lieutenant-Colonel Gimat; the left, of a detachment under Lieutenant-Colonel Laurens, destined to take the enemy of reverse and intercept their retreat. All the movements were executed with exactness, and the redoubt was at the same moment enveloped and carried in every part. Lieutenant Mansfield conducted the vanguard with coolness and punctuality, and was wounded with a bayonet as he entered the work. Captain Olney led the first platoon of Gimat's battalion over the abattis and palisades, and gained the parapet, receiving two bayonet wounds in the thigh and in the body, but not till he had directed his men to form. Laurens was among the foremost to climb into the redoubt, making prisoner of Major Campbell, its commanding officer. Animated by his example, the battalion of Gimat overcame every obstacle by their order and resolution. The battalion under Major Fish advanced with such celerity as to participate in the assault. Incapable of imitating precedents of barbarity, the Americans spared every man that ceased to resist; so that the killed and wounded of the enemy did not exceed eight. The conduct of the affair brought conspicuous honor to Hamilton.

Precisely as the signal was given, the French on the left, in like manner, began their march in the deepest silence. At one hundred and twenty paces from the redoubt they were challenged by a German sentry from the parapet; they pressed on at a quick time, exposed to the fire of the enemy. The abattis and palisades, at twenty-five paces from the redoubt, being strong and well preserved, stopped them for some minutes and cost them many lives. So soon as the way was cleared by the brave carpenters, the storming party threw themselves into the ditch, broke through the fraises, and mounted the parapet. Foremost was Charles de Lameth, who had volunteered for this attack, and who was wounded in both knees by two different musket-balls. The order being now given, the French leaped into the redoubt and charged the enemy with the bayonet. At this moment the Count de Deux Ponts raised the cry of "Vive le roi," which was repeated by all of his companions who were able to lift their voices. De Sireuil, a very young captain of yagers who had been wounded twice before, was now wounded for the third time and mortally. Within six minutes the redoubt was mastered and manned; but in that short time nearly one hundred of the assailants were killed or wounded.

On that night "victory twined double garlands around the banners" of France and America. Washington acknowledged the emulous courage, intrepidity, coolness, and firmness of the attacking troops. Louis XVI. distinguished the regiment of Gatinois by naming it "the Royal Auvergne."

By the unwearied labor of the French and Americans, both redoubts were included in the second parallel in the night of their capture. Just before the break of day of the sixteenth the British made a sortie upon a part of the second parallel and spiked four French pieces of artillery and two of the Americans; but, on the quick advance of the guards in the trenches, they retreated precipitately. The spikes were easily extracted; and in six hours the cannon again took part in the fire which enfiladed the British works.

On the seventeenth, Cornwallis, who could neither hold his post nor escape, proposed to surrender. On the eighteenth, Colonel Laurens and the Viscount de Noailles as commissoners on the American side met two high officers of the army of Cornwallis, to draft the capitulation. All the troops were to be prisoners of war; all public property was to be delivered up. Runaway slaves and the plunder taken by officers and soldiers in their marches through the country might be reclaimed; with this limitation, private property was to be respected. All royalists were left to be dealt with according to the laws of their own countrymen; but Cornwallis, in the packet which took his dispatches to Sir Henry Clinton, was suffered silently to send away such persons as were most obnoxious.

Of prisoners, there were seven thousand two hundred and forty-seven regular soldiers, the flower of the British army in America, beside eight hundred and forty sailors. The British loss during the siege amounted to more than three hundred and fifty. Two hundred and forty-four pieces of cannon were taken, of which seventy-five were of brass. The land forces and stores were assigned to the Americans, the ships and mariners to the French. At four o'clock in the afternoon of the nineteenth, Cornwallis remaining in his tent, Major-General O'Hara marched the British army past the lines of the combined armies and, not without signs of repugnance, made his surrender to Washington. His troops then stepped forward decently and piled their arms on the ground.

The English soldiers affected to look at the allied army with scorn; their officers conducted themselves with decorum, yet felt most keenly how decisive was their defeat.

Nor must impartial history fail to relate that the French provided for the siege of Yorktown thirty-six ships of the line; and that while the Americans supplied nine thousand troops, the contingent of the French consisted of seven thousand.

There was no day before it or after it like that on which the elder Bourbon king, through his army and navy, assisted to seal the victory of the rights of man and to pass from nation to nation the lighted torch of freedom.

When the letters of Washington announcing the capitulation reached congress, that body, with the people streaming in their train, went in procession to the Dutch Lutheran church to return thanks to Almighty God. Every breast swelled with joy. In the evening Philadelphia was illuminated with greater splendor than ever before. Congress voted honors to Washington, to Rochambeau, and to de Grasse, with special thanks to the officers and troops. The promise was given of a marble column to be erected at Yorktown, with emblems of the alliance between the United States and his most Christian majesty.

The Duke de Lauzun, chosen to take the news across the Atlantic, arrived in twenty-two days at Brest, and reached Versailles on the nineteenth of November. The king, who had just been made happy by the birth of a dauphin, received the glad news in the queen's apartment. The very last sands of the life of the Count de Maurepas were running out; but he could still recognise de Lauzun, and the tidings threw a halo round his death-bed. No statesman of his century had a more prosperous old age or such felicity in the circumstances of his death. The joy at court penetrated the people, and the name of Lafayette was pronounced with veneration. "History," said Vergennes, "offers few examples of a success so complete." "All the world agree," wrote Franklin to Washington, "that no expedition was ever better planned or better executed. It brightens the glory that must accompany your name to the latest posterity."

THE RISE OF AMERICAN CIVILIZATION

---

by

CHARLES A. BEARD
MARY R. BEARD

CONTENTS

The Rise of American Civilization

CHARLES A. BEARD

1874-

MARY R. BEARD

1876-

CHARLES A. BEARD was born in Knightstown, Indiana, in 1874. Two years later, in Indianapolis, Indiana, was born Mary Ritter, who ultimately joined him as wife and collaborator. Both the Beards attended De Pauw University, Mary Ritter being graduated in 1897 and Charles Beard the following year. Both pursued graduate studies at Columbia University, Charles having first spent a year each at Oxford and Cornell. In 1900 Mary Ritter and Charles A. Beard were married. They traveled abroad together to lecture at Oxford University's labor college, known as Ruskin, and to become acquainted with British labor and its problems.

For many years Charles A. Beard was identified with Columbia University. In 1904 he received his Ph.D. degree from that institution and subsequently served as adjunct professor, associate professor, and professor of politics. Leaving Columbia in 1917, Professor Beard became director of the Training School for Public Service in New York, a post which he filled until called to Japan in 1922 to serve as adviser to the Institute for Municipal Research in Tokyo. After the earthquake in 1923 Professor Beard became adviser to the Japanese Minister of Home Affairs, Viscount Goto, in planning the rebuilding of the city. Some years later, in 1927–1928, he was called to Yugoslavia to fill a similar advisory role.

Professor Beard's early interest in European history found expression in a collaboration with James Harvey Robinson in the writing of *The Development of Modern Europe,* the two volumes of which were issued in 1907 and 1908. However, he soon directed his interest to the field of American history and politics, producing in 1910 *American Goverment and Politics,* and in 1912 *American City Government.* While rearing her family, Mrs. Beard maintained an active interest in the American labor movement and in the part played by women in American public life. In 1913 there appeared the volume entitled *American Citizenship,* a work of collaboration between husband and wife. Two years later Mary Beard produced *Woman's Work in the Municipalities,* followed, in 1920, by *A Short History of the American Labor Movement.* Meanwhile, Professor Beard's *Economic Interpretation of the Constitution* (1913), *The Economic Origins of Jeffersonian Democracy* (1915), and *The Economic Basis of Politics* (1922) recorded a growing preoccupation with the influence of economic factors upon the formation of American political institutions and behavior.

The *History of the United States* by Charles and Mary Beard, published in 1921, introduced a period of fruitful collaboration between husband and wife in the writing, or rewriting, of American history. With the publication of the two-volume *Rise of American Civilization* in 1927 the high attainment possible to that collaboration was realized. Years of thought, scholarly search, writing experience, and intellectual compatibility produced a work that was consistent in thesis and plan. Cause and effect linked the historical narrative. A variety of fresh illustrative material enlivened an account presented in a style marked by vigor and clarity. The study of the influence of material factors in shaping the pattern of American life and the ultimate effect of those forces upon American political thought and action assumed, in this work, a new dignity and authority. The work was immediately popular and its popularity has endured. These factors have determined its selection as the only contemporary work to be contained in this volume. Subsequent to the publication of the two volumes abridged herein, the Beards have added two more to their account of American civilization, *America in Midpassage* (1939), and *The American Spirit* (1942). In 1944 they published *A Basic History of the United States.*

As the reader follows the clear and unfaltering narrative represented in the following abridgment, he will recognize the qualities which justified the inclusion of *The Rise of American Civilization* in this collection of masterworks. The lucidity of the account is the product of matured literary craftsmanship, of a firm grasp of the historical materials, and of well-defined ideas. The thesis illuminates the facts, the facts illustrate and support the thesis. The arguments are persuasive. The material factors of the American environment did give powerful motivation and direction to the development of civilization in America, they do explain the consequences described by the Beards, and both the causes and the effects noted are real facts of American history. They are not the only facts nor the only factors which contributed to the results observed. The forces of political and social tradition, of religious and philosophic thought, of emotional and cultural atmospheres also played their parts in shaping the civilization of America. But in limiting the focus of their interest to the material aspects of American life the Beards have disclosed the pervasive influence of economics in a historical narrative that will long be read with enjoyment and enlarged understanding.

THE RISE OF AMERICAN CIVILIZATION

I. POPULISM AND REACTION

Nearly nine years after the battle of Lexington, to be exact, on December 4, 1783, General Washington bade farewell to his officers in the great room of Fraunces' Tavern in New York City. When the simple but moving ceremony was over, the Commander marched down the streets through files of soldiers and throngs of civilians to the barge at Whitehall Ferry that was to bear him across the Hudson on his way home to Mount Vernon. Cannon boomed, bells in the church steeples clashed, crowds cheered as the tall Virginia gentleman stood in the boat, bared his gray head, and bowed his final acknowledgments.

When his familiar form faded away on the Jersey shore, the multitudes in the city turned to celebrating the triumph of the Revolution. The last of the British soldiers had disappeared down the bay a few days before and the last symbols of British dominion, except in the distant frontier forts, had passed as in a dream. America was now an independent republic. Those who had assumed leadership in this stirring drama found themselves in a course far beyond all the headlands they had seen in the fateful hours when the quarrel with the mother country was impending. Undoubtedly a few bold thinkers had early envisaged independence as the outcome of revolt but their little designs had not encompassed its full import. Thus do the achievements of people outrun their conscious purposes.

In the march of events, profound social and political changes had come to pass. Seven years of war, waged by an improvised Continental Congress without traditions, authority or strength, had thrown all economic functions into confusion and disorganized society in every direction. In colonial times the prosperity of the people depended largely upon the exchange of raw materials for manufactured products in British markets, a traffic that supplied American farmers and artisans with most of the implements and tools used in agriculture and industry, enriched American merchants, brought a steady stream of British capital to these shores, and furnished nearly all the refinements for the homes of the upper classes. This commerce the outbreak of the Revolution ruined—except for the smuggling and trading with the enemy that went on in spite of the war—and the British blockade prevented the opening of new channels sufficient to take its place.

Moreover, the armed struggle itself disrupted over wide areas the ordinary processes of agriculture and industry upon which the people relied for their living, put an intolerable drain upon the slender resources of the backwoods civilization, destroyed by fire and pillage properties of immense value, afforded the occasion for a serious confiscation and transfer of estates, tore cities and communities asunder, introduced varied and fluctuating currencies which made the orderly transaction of business impossible, and delayed the payments of debts while depreciating the medium for discharging them. At the same time it proscribed and drove from the country a large part of the governing class—British executives, judges, merchants, capitalists, and owners of property in general who remained loyal to the Crown.

In many, if not all, respects, the immediate outcome of the Revolution, radical as it was, displayed the deeper purposes of the intransigent leaders who engineered it, especially the dynamic personalities of the second social rank nearest the fighting populace; for they wanted to rid themselves entirely of British political, economic, and judicial interference. When the conflict opened, the thirteen colonies were mere provinces of the British empire under whose dominion they had been forbidden to emit bills of credit, to make paper money legal tender in the payment of debts, and to restrain foreign and intercolonial commerce. Under British authority their industry and trade had been regulated in the interest of British merchants and manufacturers, subduing American agriculture to the rules prescribed by the capitalist process in London. Under the same authority, control over the western lands had been wrested from the grip of American pioneers and politicians and vested in Crown officials. To make secure the economic sovereignty, a highly centralized scheme of judicial and administrative supremacy held the legislatures of the colonies strictly within the bounds of business propriety. In short, while the colonists had been gaining strength in local government, their powers had been limited and the higher functions of diplomacy, defence, and ultimate social control had rested in British hands.

This was the system which the Revolutionists overthrew, pulling down the elaborate superstructure and making the local legislatures, in which farmers had the majorities, supreme over all things. No Crown, no royal governor, no board of trade in London, no superior judge could now defeat the desires of agrarians. They had demanded autonomy; they achieved independence.

Having rid themselves of a great, centralized political and economic machine, the radical leaders realized their ideal in a loose association of sovereign states; in the Articles of Confederation, their grand ideals were fairly mirrored. The sole organ of government set up by that instrument was a Congress composed of delegates from each state, elected by the legislatures, and paid from the state treasury, if paid at all. Enjoying no independent and inherent powers drawn directly from the people, this government was the creature of the states and the victim of the factional disputes that filled the local theaters of politics. It was in effect little more than a council of diplomatic agents engaged in promoting thirteen separate interests, without authority to interfere with the economic concerns of any. In determining all vital questions, the states were equal: each had one vote; Delaware was as powerful as Virginia, Rhode Island, the peer of Massachusetts.

The functions essential to any government of substance—the powers which the colonists had resisted when exercised by the British Crown and Parliament—were, naturally enough, withheld from the Congress which the revolutionists created under the Articles of Confederation. As a matter of course, the solemn duty of defending the country was laid upon it: it could declare war, raise an army, and provide a navy; but it could not draft a single soldier or sailor; it could only ask the states to supply quotas of men according to a system of apportionment. Even if the Congress could have raised the men by this process, it could never have been sure of the materials necessary to support them.

It had power, no doubt, to appropriate money but no authority to levy upon the strong box or economic resources of any citizen. For every penny that went into the common treasury, it had to ask the local legislatures. When it determined the amount of money needed for any fiscal period or for any specific purpose, it apportioned the total among the thirteen states on the basis of the value of the lands and improvements in each, leaving the legislatures free to decide how the quotas assigned were to be met—or not met at all, according to the mood of the party in control at the time. In fact, therefore, the Congress had to assume the rôle of a beggar, hat in hand, at the capitals of the several commonwealths. In practice it experienced what beggars usually do: more rebuffs than pleasant receptions.

If such was the weakness of the Confederation with respect to those prime considerations, military power and money, it is not strange to find the same incompetence in other spheres. Conforming to colonial agrarian traditions, the Congress was given no control over currency and banking, such as the government of Great Britain had exercised in America before independence; on the contrary, these vital economic functions were left to the discretion of the individual states. Nor could the Congress regulate trade among the states or with other countries; England had done too much of that.

Although it could make treaties with foreign countries affecting commercial matters, the Congress had no power to enforce its agreements against the will of recalcitrant states—in fact, no control over the latter in any important respect.

To the eight years of government under these Articles of Confederation, the term "critical period" has been applied and it has become the fashion to draw a doleful picture of the age, to portray the country sweeping toward an abyss from which it was rescued in the nick of time by the heroic framers of the Constitution. Yet an analysis of the data upon which that view is built raises the specter of skepticism. The chief sources of information bearing on this thesis are the assertions and lamentations of but one faction in the great dispute and they must, therefore, be approached with the same spirit of prudence as Whig editorials on Andrew Jackson or Republican essays on Woodrow Wilson.

Undoubtedly the period that followed the close of the Revolutionary War was one of dissolution and reconstruction; that is the story of every great social dislocation. Still there is much evidence to show that the country was in many respects steadily recovering order and prosperity even under the despised Articles of Confederation. If seven of the thirteen states made hazardous experiments with paper money, six clung to more practical methods and two or three of those that had embarked on un-limited inflation showed signs of turning back on their course. While a few states displayed a heartless negligence in paying their revolutionary debts, others gave serious attention to the matter.

No doubt shipping in New England and manufacturing in general suffered from the conflicting tariff policies, domestic and foreign, which followed the war, but, at the opening of 1787, Benjamin Franklin declared that the prosperity of the nation was so great as to call for thanksgiving. According to his judgment, the market reports then showed that the farmers were never better paid for their produce, that farm lands were continually rising in value, and that in no part of Europe were the labor-ing poor in such a fortunate state. Admitting that there were economic grievances in some quarters, Franklin expressed a conviction that the country at large was in a sound condition.

Nevertheless, when the best possible case is made for the critical period, there remain standing in the record of those years certain im-pressive facts that cannot be denied or explained away. Beyond all ques-tion the financiers had grounds for complaint. Though the principal of the continental debt was slightly reduced under the confederation, the arrears of interest increased nearly fourfold and the unpaid interest on the foreign obligations piled steadily higher. In an equally chaotic con-dition were the current finances. The Congress in due course made requisitions on the states to pay its bills, but it was fortunate if it received in any year one-fourth of the amount demanded, and during the last fourteen months of its life less than half a million in paper money was paid into the treasury—not enough to meet the interest on the foreign debt alone.

Hence all who held claims against the confederacy had sufficient cause for discontent. Holders of government bonds, both original sub-scribers who had made sacrifices and speculators who had bought up depreciated paper by the ream, had good reasons for desiring a change in the existing form of government. To them were added the soldiers of the late revolutionary army, especially the officers whose bonus of full pay for five years still remained in the form of paper promises.

Industry and commerce as well as government finances were in a state of depression. When peace came and the pent-up flood of British goods burst in upon the local market, greatly to the joy of the farmers and planters, American manufacturers, who had built up enterprises of no little importance during the suspension of British trade, found their monopoly of domestic business rudely broken. Nothing but a protective tariff, they thought, could save them from ruin.

In an equally unhappy position were the domestic merchants. They had at hand no national currency uniform in value through the length and breadth of the land—nothing but a curious collection of coins uncertain in weight, shaven by clippers, debased by counterfeiters, and paper notes fluctuating as new issues streamed from the press. Worse than the monetary system were the impediments in the way of interstate commerce. Under local influences legislatures put tariffs on goods coming in from neighboring states just as on foreign imports, waged commercial wars of retaliation on one another, raised and lowered rates as factional disputes oscillated, reaching such a point in New York that duties were levied on firewood from Connecticut and cabbages from New Jersey.

If a merchant surmounted the obstacles placed in his way by anarchy in the currency and confusion in tariff schedules and succeeded in building up an interstate business, he never could be sure of collections, for he was always at the mercy of local courts and juries—agencies that were seldom tender in dealing with the claims and rights of distant creditors as against the clamors of their immediate neighbors. While the Articles of Confederation lasted there was no hope of breaching such invincible barriers to the smooth and easy transaction of interstate business.

In short, the financial, creditor, commercial, and speculating classes in the new confederate republic were harassed during the critical period just as such classes had been harassed by rebellious patriots on the eve of the Revolution. From every point of view, as they saw the matter, they had valid reasons for wanting to establish under their own auspices on American soil a system of centralized political, judicial, and economic control similar in character to that formerly exercised by Great Britain. They wanted debts paid, a sound currency established, commerce regulated, paper money struck down, and western lands properly distributed; they desired these things quite as much as the governing classes of England had desired them in colonial times. No more than the stoutest Tory of London or Boston did they relish agrarian politics; commerce simply could not thrive in that economic atmosphere.

In the commonwealth of Massachusetts a conservative party of merchants, shippers, and money lenders had managed by a hard won battle to secure in 1780 a local constitution which gave their property special defenses in the suffrage, in the composition of the Senate, and in the qualifications of office holders administering the law. Heavy taxes were then levied to pay the revolutionary debt of the state, a large part of which had passed into the hands of speculators. And just when this burden fell on the people, private creditors in their haste to collect outstanding accounts deluged the local courts with lawsuits and foreclosures of farm mortgages.

The answer to this economic pressure was a populist movement led by a former soldier of the Revolution, Daniel Shays. Inflamed by new revolutionary appeals, resurgent agrarians now proposed to scale down the state debt, strike from the constitution the special privileges enjoyed by property, issue paper money, and generally ease the position of debtors and the laboring poor in town and country. Indeed, there were dark hints that the soldiers who had fought for independence would insist that property owners must sacrifice their goods for the cause. In various guises the agitation continued until in 1786 it culminated in an armed uprising known as Shays' Rebellion.

Although the insurrection was crushed, it sent alarms throughout the higher social orders of America. If Jefferson was unmoved because he thought that a little bloodshed was occasionally necessary to keep alive the spirit of agrarian liberty, Washington was thoroughly frightened. On hearing the news, he redoubled his efforts to obtain a stronger constitution—one that would afford national aid in suppressing such local disturbances. There was even talk of a counter-revolution, a military dictatorship supported by funds from merchants.

In foreign relations there were perils as menacing as the difficulties of domestic administration. When John Adams, as minister of the United States, appeared at the Court of the King he met a frosty reception, made several degrees chillier by constant reminders that the government he represented was really impotent. If he hinted that British soldiers should be withdrawn from the western part of the United States or that the ports of the British West Indies should be opened once more to American ships on favourable terms, he was reminded that his fellow countrymen had not paid the debts due British merchants and he was shown acts of Parliament which, not without reason, treated Americans as aliens.

Though nominally isolated in the New World, the confederacy was bounded on the landward side by immense territories belonging to England and Spain, both countries that had been contending for mastery in America for two hundred years. At any moment a new storm might break, involving the weak republic at the very threshold of its career. Even the most case-hardened agrarians could not avoid seeing the possibility of renewed strife among the European powers—which came in 1793—the dangers of foreign intervention in domestic politics, and the perils of disruptive rivalry among the states. If they were indifferent to the demands of public creditors, financiers, and merchants clamoring for relief, they could not ignore the menaces from foreign quarters. Such were the circumstances in which rose and flourished a movement for a drastic revision of the Articles of Confederation.

Among the many historic assemblies which have wrought revolutions in the affairs of mankind, it seems safe to say that there has never been one that commanded more political talent, practical experience, and sound substance than the Philadelphia convention of 1787. In all, sixty-two delegates were formally appointed by the states; fifty-five attended the sessions with more or less regularity; and thirty-nine signed the final draft of the new Constitution. On the list were men trained in war and diplomacy, skilled in legislation and administration, versed in finance and commerce, and learned in the political philosophy of their own and earlier times. Seven had been governors of states and at least twenty-eight had served in the Congress of the union either during the Revolution or under the Articles of Confederation. Eight had been signers of the Declaration of Independence. At the head stood Washington, who, with one voice, was chosen president of the convention. Among those who sat under him were such men as the two Morrises, the two Pinckneys, Madison, Hamilton, Franklin, Rutledge, Gerry, Ellsworth, Wilson, Randolph, Wythe, Dickinson, and Sherman, nearly all of whom represented the conservative wing of the old revolutionary party.

At all events none of the fiery radicals of 1774 was present. Jefferson, then serving as the American minister in Paris, was out of the country; Patrick Henry was elected but refused to attend because, he said, he "smellt a rat"; Samuel Adams was not chosen; Thomas Paine left for Europe that very year to exhibit an iron bridge which he had designed and to wage war on tyranny across the sea. So the Philadelphia assembly, instead of being composed of left-wing theorists, was made up of practical men of affairs—holders of state and continental bonds, money lenders, merchants, lawyers, and speculators in the public land—who could speak with knowledge and feeling about the disabilities they had suffered under the Articles of Confederation. More than half the delegates in attendance were either investors or speculators in the public securities which were to be buoyed up by the new Constitution. All knew by experience the relation of property to government.

When the convention assembled late in May, 1787, there arose at once the question whether the proceedings should be thrown open to the general public or be held behind closed doors. The body was small, oratory was evidently out of place, and none of the members was especially eager to appeal to the gallery. As realistic statesmen, they knew that negotiation and accommodation would be more effective in the attainment of their ends than Ciceronian eloquence and tattered passion. It was well understood that the dissensions bound to arise in the convention would be magnified if irresponsible partisans on the outside learned about them and continually prodded the delegates with popular agitations. It was also known how sharply the country at large was divided over the problems to be solved and how easily timid members might be frightened into voting against their own judgment by the demands of excited constituents.

So, without much argument, the members resolved that the proceedings of the convention should be secret and no one permitted to give out in any form any information respecting its deliberations. In harmony with this decision they likewise agreed that no official record of the debates should be kept, that nothing should be set down in black and white save a bare minute of the propositions before the house and the votes cast for and against them. In their anxiety for security the delegates took every precaution against publicity; they even had a discreet colleague accompany the aged Franklin to his convivial dinners with a view to checking that amiable gentleman whenever, in unguarded moments, he threatened to divulge secrets of state.

Having come to accomplish results rather than to chop logic, the majority of the members accepted the liberal view of the matter and refused to be bound by the letter of the existing law. They did not amend the Articles of Confederation; they cast that instrument aside and drafted a fresh plan of government. Nor did they merely send the new document to the Congress and then to the state legislatures for approval; on the contrary they appealed over the heads of these authorities to the voters of the states for a ratification of their revolutionary work. Finally, declining to obey the clause of the Articles which required unanimous approval for every amendment, they frankly proposed that the new system of government should go into effect when sanctioned by nine of the thirteen states, leaving the others out in the cold under the wreck of the existing legal order, in case they refused to ratify.

After listening carefully to the debates for several weeks, Madison noted that the real division in the convention was between the planting interests of the South founded on slave labor and the commercial and industrial interests of the North—startling foresight discerning "the irrepressible conflict" which filled half a century with political controversy and tested the Constitution in the flames of a social revolution.

In all there were only six slave states, counting little Delaware, and they had neither wealth nor population comparable to the resources of the seven commercial states. Climate, soil, tradition, and labor supply seemed destined to make them producers of foodstuffs and raw materials to be exchanged in favorable markets for manufactured goods. Therefore, it was their prime concern to ship at the lowest possible freight rates in vessels sailing under any flag and to buy and sell on the most advantageous terms anywhere on earth. Weaker in number, they feared that the proposed Congress, dominated by a mere numerical majority, might lay an undue burden of customs duties and taxes upon them— the shifting of taxes being one of the grand devices of politics for the transfer of wealth from one class to another. They were also afraid that Congress, under capitalistic influences, would enact tariff legislation and navigation laws injurious to their enterprise.

On the other hand, the trading and industrial interests of the North, languishing under free trade, under financial disorders, and under English discriminations, saw their only hope for prosperity in protective tariffs and favorable commercial legislation. The issue was definite and familiar. It had been made clear in the contest with Great Britain when Parliament sought to restrain colonial legislatures and colonial trade with reference to the profits of British merchants, shippers, and manufacturers. It was to cut athwart the history of centuries to come.

Disputes arising from this inherent conflict of interests ran throughout the proceedings of the convention even when questions apparently remote from the main issue were on the carpet. Especially were they animated on matters of representation and taxation, those sore points in the revolutionary struggle. Anxious to secure a strategic position in the new government through the largest possible strength in the lower house, southern planters proposed to count slaves as people in distributing Representatives on the population basis. At the same time, aware that their states had fewer inhabitants than the commercial commonwealths of the North, the planters urged that direct taxes be apportioned only on the basis of the free white population. For equally obvious reasons most of the Northern delegates wanted just the opposite of these two propositions. So on this issue a compromise was the last resort. Adopting a well-known expedient the convention agreed on treating three-fifths of the slaves as people for both reckonings, representation and direct taxation.

In framing the provisions relative to the regulation of commerce, the same clash of opinion appeared. If the new government was to have the power to control trade and make treaties with foreign nations, it might prohibit the importation of slaves and enter into commercial agreements detrimental to the planting interest. Here also an accommodation was evidently imperative and it took the form of two provisions: the importation of slaves was not to be forbidden before the lapse of twenty years and a two-thirds vote in the Senate was to be required for the ratification of treaties. An additional concession was made to the South in the clause providing for the return of fugitives bound to servitude—all the more readily because this was highly useful in the North where the restoration of runaway servants was also acceptable to masters.

During the arguments that sprang from the clash of economic interests, the ethics of slavery itself was broached though at no time did it rise to the position of a leading issue. Taking advantage of the occasion several members of the convention denounced chattel bondage in uncompromising language. Gouverneur Morris, of Pennsylvania, condemned it as a nefarious institution and a curse to the states in which it prevailed. Mason, of Virginia, a slaveholder himself, seeing nothing but evil in it, declared that it discouraged the arts and industry, led the poor to despise honest labor, and checked the immigration of whites whose work gave strength and riches to the land.

The voice of defense, raised in reply, came from the Far South. Spokesmen from South Carolina insisted that the whole economic life of their state rested on slavery and that, owing to the appalling death rate in the rice swamps, continuous importation was necessary. With cold optimism Oliver Ellsworth, of Connecticut, advised moderation. "The morality or wisdom of slavery," he said, "are considerations belonging to the states. What enriches a part enriches the whole. . . . As population increases, poor laborers will be so plenty as to render slaves useless."

Technically, Ellsworth was right, for slavery as an institution was not before the convention but some decision had to be made with respect to the importation of Negroes. On this point, too, conciliation was found expedient. Virginia and North Carolina, already overstocked, were prepared to end the traffic in African slaves but South Carolina was adamant. She must have new supplies by importation or she would not federate; hence the clause postponing action at least until 1808. These were the great compromises of the Constitution.

II. THE RISE OF NATIONAL PARTIES

THE controversy over the ratification of the federal Constitution had not died away when the country was summoned to take part in a contest over the election of men to direct the new government.

When the results of the poll were all in and the new government was organized, it was patent to everyone that the men who had made the recent constitutional revolution were carrying on the work they had begun in 1787. Washington, the chairman of the constitutional convention, was unanimously chosen President of the United States. Of the twenty-four Senators in the first Congress under the Constitution, eleven had helped to draft "the new charter of liberty." In the House of Representatives was a strong contingent from the body of framers and ratifiers, with the "father of the Constitution," James Madison, in the foreground. The Ark of the Covenant was evidently in the house of its friends; or, to put the matter in another way, the machinery of economic and political power was mainly directed by the men who had conceived and established it. And very soon the executive and judicial departments were filled with leaders who had taken part in framing or ratifying the Constitution.

For the most important post in his administration, namely, that of the Treasury, Washington chose Robert Morris, a member of the convention; when that gentleman declined, he turned to another colleague, Alexander Hamilton, a giant of Federalism. For the office of Attorney General, the President selected the spokesman of the Virginia delegation at the Philadelphia assembly, Edmund Randolph. As Secretary of War, he appointed another ardent advocate of the Constitution, General Knox, of Massachusetts. Only one high administrative command went to a statesman whose views on the new government were, to say the least, uncertain; Thomas Jefferson, who had been in Paris during the formation and adoption of the Constitution, was made Secretary of State in charge of foreign affairs. In the judicial department, there was not a single exception: all the federal judgeships created under the Judiciary Act of 1789, high and low, were given to men who had helped to draft the Constitution or had supported it in state conventions or in the ratifying campaigns. In his appointments to minor places in the government Washington was equally discreet; after attempting to conciliate a few opponents by offering them positions, he flatly declared that he would not give an office to any man who attacked the principles of his administration.

The first government was thus in no sense a coalition. When the paper document of Philadelphia became a reality, it lived on in the reason and will of the men who had constructed and adopted it. It was they who enacted the laws, enforced the decrees, raised the army, and collected the taxes, and so made the new Constitution an instrument of power in the direction of national economy and in the distribution of wealth. In their hands mere words on parchment were transformed into an engine of sovereign compulsion that could not be denied anywhere throughout the length and breadth of the land.

While creating the offices of the new government in detail and endowing them with the powers required to give effect to its decisions, Congress was well aware that it was necessary to soften some of the opposition to the new régime with measures of conciliation. The directors of federal affairs knew by what narrow margin the approval of the Constitution had been wrung from a reluctant people. They saw North Carolina and Rhode Island still outside the Union and unrepentant. They had before them a large number of amendments proposed by several of the state conventions and they were assured by any number of the critics that promises to carry some of the demands into immediate effect had been made in winning the votes necessary to ratification. All these amendments, as Congress could not fail to see, showed a fear of the federal government and suggested restraints on its authority. Although some were harmless enough, others betrayed the spirit of Daniel Shays, who, if vanquished, was by no means dead.

To allay, if not remove, the temper expressed in several of the propositions, Madison, therefore, presented in the House of Representatives, and the first Congress adopted, a series of amendments to the Constitution, ten of which were soon ratified and in 1791 became a part of the law of the land. Among other things, these amendments stipulated that Congress should make no law respecting the establishment of religion, abridging freedom of speech or press, or the right of the people to assemble peaceably and petition the government for a redress of grievances. Indictment by grand jury and trial by jury were guaranteed to all persons charged by federal officers with serious crimes. Finally, to soften the wrath of provincial politicians, it was announced in the Tenth Amendment that all powers not delegated to the United States by the Constitution or withheld by it from the states were reserved to the states respectively or to the people.

This overt declaration of the obvious was supplemented seven years later by the Eleventh Amendment, written in the same spirit, forbidding the federal judiciary to hear any case in which a state was sued by a citizen. Assured by the friendly professions of the national government and constrained by economic necessity, North Carolina joined the Union in November, 1789, and Rhode Island in May of the following year.

With the machinery of administration in operation and professions respecting natural rights duly made, the directors of the federal government were free to devote themselves to prime questions of financial, commercial, and industrial legislation. In fact, while the philosophers were discussing the constitutional amendments, Hamilton, Secretary of the Treasury, was formulating the great system and the collateral reports forever associated with his name. First upon his program was the funding of the entire national debt, domestic and foreign, principal and interest, at face value, approximating altogether $50,000,000; in other words, old bonds and certificates were to be called in and new securities issued. A part of this enormous sum was to bear interest at six per cent and a part at three per cent, while the interest on the remainder was to be deferred for ten years.

In the second place, Hamilton proposed that the national government assume at face value the revolutionary obligations of the states, amounting to about $20,000,000, and add them to the debt carried by the general treasury. In this fashion he intended to make secure the financial standing of the United States and force all the public creditors to look to the federal government rather than the states for the payment of the sums due them. To provide a capstone for his financial structure, Hamilton advocated the creation of a national bank in which the government and private investors were to be represented. Three-fourths of the capital stock of this institution was to consist of new six per cent federal bonds and the rest of specie. With a view to assisting the government and the security holders in buoying up the public credit, that is, the prices of federal bonds, provision was to be made for a sinking fund from which the Treasury could buy its securities in the market from time to time.

To sustain this magnificent paper edifice erected on the taxing power of the federal government, duties were to be laid on imports in such a manner as to encourage and protect American industry and commerce. Finally, the public lands in the West, which the Crown of Britain had once sought to wrest from colonial politicians, were to be sold and the securities of the federal government were to be accepted in payment.

It required no very profound economic insight to grasp the import of the Hamiltonian program: holders of the old debt—continental and state—were simply to exchange their depreciated paper at face value for new bonds bearing interest and guaranteed by a government that possessed ample taxing power. Prime public securities, such as were now to be issued, would readily pass as money from hand to hand, augmenting the fluid capital of the country and stimulating commerce, manufacturing, and agriculture. If the government bonds failed to realize all expectations in the line of capital expansion, notes issued by the United States bank were to supply the deficiency. At last American business enterprise, which had suffered from the want of currency and credit, was to be abundantly furnished with both and at the same time protected against foreign competion by favorable commercial legislation. Naturally those who expected to reap the benefits from Hamilton's system were delighted with the prospects. On the other hand, since the whole financial structure rested on taxation, mere owners of land and consumers of goods, on whom most of the burden was to fall, got it into their heads that they were to pay the bills of the new adventure.

As the issues raised by Hamilton's projects came before the people one by one, the tide of political passion rose higher and higher. It was well known that a large part, perhaps the major portion, of the old bonds, state and continental, had passed from the hands of the original purchasers into the coffers of shrewd and enterprising speculators. After the adoption of the Constitution became certain, far-sighted financiers sent agents all over the country, especially into the southern states, with bags of precious specie, bought enormous quantities of depreciated paper at a low figure—sometimes ten or fifteen cents on the dollar—and effected a great concentration of public securities in Philadelphia, New York, and Boston. Inevitably the cupidity of those who had risked their money in this speculation and the anguish of those who had sold their original certificates at merely nominal prices furnished the fuel for an explosion when Hamilton's fiscal plans appeared on the political carpet.

During the prolix and hot-tempered debates that marked the passage of Hamilton's measures through Congress, the country gradually divided into two parties, which grew steadily in coherence of organization and in definiteness of program. To speak more concretely, the antagonism between agriculture and business enterprise that had been so marked in colonial times and had found tense expression during the contest over the Constitution now bore fruit in regular political parties, each with a complete paraphernalia of leaders, caucuses, conventions, names, symbols, and rhetorical defense mechanisms. Candidates were nominated, policies proclaimed, newspapers edited, and spoils distributed with reference to the fortunes of one group or the other. All the passions that go with war were enlisted in contests that eventuated in a counting of heads.

As these two party factions in one form or another have continued to divide the nation, statesmen and theorists have felt called upon to expound the causes of such political antagonisms. Some agree with Macaulay in tracing the origins of party to instinctive differences among people. In every country, that celebrated Whig once declared, there is a party of order and a party of progress; the former, conservative in temper, clings to established things, while the latter, adventurous in spirit, is eager to make experiments. Long afterward a literary critic, Brander Matthews, applied the Macaulay doctrine of innate ideas to American politics; "intuitive Hamiltonians," he said, believe in government by the well-born, while "intuitive Jeffersonians" love and trust the common people. Still another explanation of American parties, one more commonly accepted by Fourth of July orators, is that formulated by James Bryce in The American Commonwealth: our parties originally sprang from differences of opinion concerning the nature and functions of the Union; one exalts federal authority, the other cherishes the rights of the states.

In reality, however, none of these simple explanations does more than skim the surface of politics. None throws any light on the origins of the innate tendencies, for example. With reference to that point all are as cryptic as the statement that God made Federalists and Republicans. Why did one group of politicians take a liberal view of the Constitution and another a narrow view? Whence came the intuitions that divide men? Have they existed since the dawn of history? Why did some trust the people and others fear them? Was it an accident that a New York lawyer stood at the head of the party which despised the masses and a Virginia slave owner led the party which professed democratic faith in the multitude?

The answers to these questions, as far as they are forthcoming at all, lie in the professions of politicians, reported in congressional debates, newspapers, letters, and partisan pamphlets of the Hamiltonian epoch, and if such evidence is to be accepted in court, the causes of the party division were more substantial than matters of temperament or juristic theory. By the time the partisan battle began to rage in full fury, the Federalists had a positive record of achievement to which they could point with pride and assurance. They had restored the public credit by funding the continental and state obligations at face value, incidentally enriching thousands of good Federalists in the process. They had protected American industry and shipping by appropriate economic discriminations against foreign enterprise.

In establishing a national bank and a mint for the coinage of metals, they had provided a uniform national currency for the transaction of business. They had devised a scheme of taxation easily yielding adequate revenues to sustain the huge national debt and all the capitalistic undertakings which rested upon that solid foundation. They had erected a system of national courts in which citizens of one state could effectively collect claims against citizens of other states and they had made it impossible for debtors to outwit their creditors through the medium of paper money and similar methods of impairing the obligation of contracts. They had begun to build an army and a navy, making the American nation so respected abroad that foreign powers no longer dared to treat its ministers with contempt, and giving the flag such substantial significance that the Yankee skipper felt proud and secure under it no matter whether he rode into the waters of European ports, traded rum for Negroes along the

African coast, or exchanged notions in Canton for tea and silks. That was an accomplishment measurable in terms of national honor and pride as clearly as in the outward and visible signs of economic prosperity.

Opponents of this general program, taking at first the negative title of Anti-Federalists and later the more euphonious name of Republicans, by no means attacked the idea of exalting American credit and improving the standing of the country among the nations of the earth. In detail, however, they dissented, with varying emphasis, from the propositions contained in the Federalist economic program. They wished to discharge the national debt but not in such a fashion as to enrich speculators or impose a heavy burden of taxation on the masses. Especially were they tender of the people engaged in agriculture. A permanent funded debt and a national bank founded on it, they complained, would tax the farmers and planters to sustain an army of bond holders and stock jobbers.

Speaking on this theme for southern citizens, one Anti-Federalist warned the House of Representatives that his constituents "will feel that continued drain of specie which must take place to satisfy the appetites of basking speculators at the seat of Government. . . . Connecticut manufactures a great deal. Georgia manufactures nothing and imports everything. Therefore, Georgia, although her population is not near so large, contributes more to the public treasury by impost." When the proposal to establish a national bank was before Congress, the same agrarian orator lamented in a similar strain that "this plan of a National Bank is calculated to benefit a small part of the United States, the mercantile interest only; the farmers, the yeomanry, will derive no advantage from it." When the unwrought-steel schedule of the tariff bill was under consideration, Lee, of Virginia, declared that "it would operate as an oppressive though indirect tax upon agriculture, and any tax, whether direct or indirect, upon this interest at this juncture would be unwise and impolitic."

Far from being the mere froth of excited politicians, this view represented the matured convictions of leaders given to deliberation and analysis. In several letters addressed confidentially to Washington, Jefferson expounded the economic grievances of his faction. He argued that the national debt had been unnecessarily increased; that the United States Bank had been created as a permanent engine of the moneyed interest for influencing the course of government; and that "the ten or twelve per cent annual profits paid to the lenders of this paper medium are taken out of the pockets of the people who would have had without interest the coin it is banishing; that all capital employed in paper speculation is barren and useless, producing like that on a gaming-table no accession to itself and is withdrawn from commerce and agriculture where it would have produced addition to the common mass; that it nourishes our citizens in habits of vice and idleness instead of industry and morality; that it has furnished effectual means of corrupting such a portion of the Legislature as turns the balance between the honest voters whichever way it is directed." Of all the mischiefs which Jefferson saw in the Federalist system, "none is so afflicting and fatal to every honest hope as the corruption of the legislature." Of course, Jefferson expressed his alarm over the liberal way in which the Constitution had been construed by the men who formulated and enacted Federalist policies into law, but the gravamen of his complaint was that Hamilton's economic measures exploited one section of society for the benefit of another.

Yet it is difficult to see why holders of government bonds were to be denounced for voting in favor of measures affecting their concerns while slave owners were to be pardoned for voting down the Quaker memorials against slavery presented to Congress on March 23, 1790. In fact, Jefferson himself frankly stated that he wanted "the agricultural interest" to govern the country and presumably to pursue policies advantageous to that social group. At bottom, accordingly, the dispute between parties was over economic measures rather than over questions of political propriety. On both sides the logicians were equally able and equally sincere; hence it seems reasonable to conclude that neither interpretation of the Constitution, liberal or strict, flowed with the force of exigent mathematics from the language of the instrument itself.

Nevertheless, the politicians and statesmen of the period made much of their appeals to correct views of the Constitution. Leaders of the Federalist party had been largely responsible for the framing and adoption of that document; they understood it; and they demonstrated with a great show of learning that it authorized whatever they wanted it to sanction. The opposition employed the same appeal—for contrary ends. "It is unconstitutional," was the cry that rose daily from the Anti-Federalist ranks as they sought to dethrone Hamiltonism. "Let us return to the Constitution!" exclaimed John Taylor when closing a vitriolic indictment of the Secretary's program and policies.

III. AGRICULTURAL IMPERIALISM AND THE BALANCE OF POWER

IF THE philosophical Jefferson and his official family thought that they could settle down in political power to the enjoyment of peace, light taxes, and arcadian pleasures, they were soon disillusioned. The agricultural interest, which they so proudly represented, was no provincial estate sufficient unto itself. On the contrary, it depended for its prosperity upon the sale of its produce in the markets of the Old World while its advance guard on the frontier cherished imperial designs upon the neighboring dominions of England and Spain.

Therefore American agriculture vibrated in its fortunes with every turn in the European balance of power, never more precisely than in the third year of Jefferson's administration when the fury of the Napoleonic tempest was again unleashed across the sea. No theory of isolation could protect it from the shock of a struggle for empire that extended from

London to Ceylon, from Moscow to Mexico City, from Copenhagen to Cape Town, encircling the globe with fire. America as well as Europe was set afloat. Within a few years the Republicans in control of the federal government, buffeted by gales from abroad and by passions at home, were exercising powers greater than any ever claimed by Hamilton and defending the constitutionality of laws which they had once rejected. And in this swift whirl of fact and philosophy, their opponents, the Federalists, were forced into a narrow and crabbed provincialism that made Jefferson's juristic argument against the United States Bank seem broad and generous in comparison.

It has long been the fashion of historians to cite this reversal of fortunes in demonstrating the mutability of human affairs and the hollowness of political professions. Do not the items stand written clearly in the bond? The Republicans had proclaimed their unshakable faith in a narrow interpretation of the Constitution; in 1803 they purchased Louisiana—an act which Jefferson himself called a violation of the supreme law; a few years later they invoked the power of regulating commerce to justify a measure abolishing it and a "force bill" carrying that embargo into effect. Celebrating the virtues of agriculture, they had scorned the arts of trade; yet they vowed that their war on Great Britain was made with a view to upholding American commercial rights upon the high seas. They had opposed a national Bank and a protective tariff; but, at the close of their experiment in war, they resorted to both expedients in spite of their legal scruples.

And on the other side was the record of the Federalists. They had proclaimed their steadfast faith in a liberal view of the Constitution; but they could find no warrant in the parchment for the Louisiana purchase or the embargo. They had taken pride in cherishing the arts of trade; yet they voted against the war on England which was supposed to sustain the inviolability of American commerce. The reversal of politics, considered in terms of political rhetoric, seemed to be absolute.

Considered, however, in economic terms, it was a reversal of means not ends. If the purchase of Louisiana was unconstitutional, it at least added millions of acres of rich farming lands to be developed by Jefferson's beloved "agricultural interest." In the sphere of politics it also meant, as the Federalists said, the overbalancing of "the commercial states" by agricultural commonwealths. If in form the war on England was declared for commercial motives, it was in reality conceived primarily in the interests of agriculture.

This fact the scholarly researches of Julius W. Pratt have demonstrated in a convincing fashion. Agriculture just as shipping suffered from British depredations, for American exports were, in the main, not manufactures but the produce of farms and plantations. The men who voted in 1812 for the declaration of war on England represented the agrarian constituencies of the interior and their prime object was the annexation of Florida and Canada. Hence the opposition of the commercial sections to an armed conflict waged for the purpose of adding more farmers and planters to the overbalancing majority was at bottom no deep mystery.

Nor was the reversal of the Republican position on finance shrouded in obscurity. The second United States Bank, established by that party, did not grow out of a desire to draw the banking fraternity to the support of the government as in Hamilton's time but in truth sprang from a struggle to free the federal treasury from abject dependence on eastern financial interests and rescue the currency from the chaos created by the war. And finally, the protective tariff adopted by the Republicans in 1816 was defended by the spokesman of the planting interest, John C. Calhoun, on the ground that tariff schedules, when properly made, would provide a home market for cotton, corn, and bacon. At that time New England banks, strong enough to stand alone, welcomed no new rival in the hands of Jeffersonian politicians; and New England capitalists, largely engrossed in the carrying trade, did not look with favor on customs duties that promised to cut it down. If reference be had, therefore, to the substance of things desired, some of the ambiguity of jurisprudence seems to be removed and the continuity of economic forces once more demonstrated.

The first great stroke of Republican policy in the sphere of foreign relations, namely, westward expansion by the purchase of the Louisiana territory in 1803, was no bolt out of the blue either for the planters and farmers of the West or for Jefferson, who professed to cherish their interests. A decade before that event there were hundreds of American pioneers in the Spanish territory beyond the Mississippi; near the close of the eighteenth century the bishop of Louisiana reported that "the Americans had scattered themselves over the country almost as far as Texas and corrupted the Indians and Creoles by the example of their own restless and ambitious temper." Already promoters in the West had their eyes fixed on Mexico and were blowing up colorful dreams of imperial annexations to be realized in that direction.

Already the war in Europe had forced the fate of the West upon the attention of the federal government. The first phase of that struggle had opened, as we have seen, in 1793, while Thomas Jefferson was still serving as Secretary of State under President Washington, in a strategic post of observation from which he discovered many things. Especially did he grasp the meaning of the fact that, in the general scramble for spoils among the powers of the Old World, England might wrest Louisiana from the feeble grasp of the Spanish monarch—a menace to the United States to be avoided at all costs. Though he retired from the State Department in 1793, Jefferson retained his keen interest in the advancing frontier and continued to appreciate its importance.

During the intervening years until his inauguration as President, events flowed swiftly in the regions beyond the Alleghenies as a steady stream of settlers moved westward with the sun. Kentucky was admitted to the Union as a state in 1792 and Tennessee in 1796, both of them good agricultural communities that gave electoral votes to Jefferson in 1800.

Ohio, then rapidly filling up, was to have a voice in the next presidential election. The whole West was vibrant with prospects of great agricultural enterprise and the leaders who directed affairs in the Mississippi Valley knew what they wanted. They were unanimous in their resolve that the Mississippi must be kept open to American trade all the way to the Gulf of Mexico; and those with the largest imagination, as we have just said, were prepared for imperial undertakings beyond the mighty river. If Jefferson was inclined to hold back and deal timidly with foreign powers, he could not escape the firm pressure of his frontier constituents. In fact the very existence of the western farmers and planters, to say nothing of handsome earnings, depended upon the navigation of the Mississippi without let or hindrance.

Down the river to New Orleans they floated their tobacco, corn, hemp, wheat, pork, and lumber for shipment to the towns on the eastern seaboard or the markets of the Old World. To them this outlet to the sea was as important as the harbor of Boston to the merchants of that metropolis. For their bulky produce, transportation over muddy roads across the mountain barrier was almost prohibitive in its cost. Tea, coffee, cloth, and nails might come to them that way but, before the age of steamboats and improved roads, farm produce had to find a less expensive and more practical route. Therefore, in their search for a livelihood, in their quest for profitable enterprise, the men on the frontier were compelled to keep open the port of New Orleans. Moreover, if their restless spirit of migration was not to be quenched forever on the east bank of the Mississippi, then their next march would carry them beyond the borders of the existing American dominion. By 1800 Kentucky had grown too civilized for Daniel Boone; and signs of the onward surge were clearly evident.

Accordingly, the frontiersmen watched with eagle eyes the fortunes of the King of Spain to whom at the close of the Seven Years' War in 1763 had fallen the prize of Louisiana. While he controlled New Orleans, there was little to fear. No doubt he resented the constant activity of Americans on the banks of the Mississippi; no doubt he grew angry when he read in the reports of his governors that these aggressive aliens looked greedily upon his untilled lands; but he was powerless to hold them in check.

In the summer of 1802 a crisis was precipitated: a royal order from Spain in July closed the port of New Orleans to American produce. Hard on the heels of this news came a confirmation of the rumor that Napoleon had really wrested Louisiana from Spain. At any time, therefore, the French flag might be raised on the American border; for a temporary lull in the European War—effected by the treaty of Amiens signed in the spring of that year—promised the Corsican an opportunity to tempt fortune next in the New World. In a few months "the scalers of the Alps and the conquerors of Venice" might appear in New Orleans, Natchez, and St. Louis. Their capacity for action was notorious.

Immediately the West was ablaze with excitement and alarm. Immediately a turbulent call to arms resounded along the frontier; expeditions were organized to prevent the landing of French troops; the legislators of Kentucky passed resolutions of protest against "invasion," pledging their lives and fortunes to sustain their rights; petitions for immediate aid flooded in upon the philosopher in the White House. Whatever his inclination, Jefferson was thus made aware that willful and irascible leaders in the West would open New Orleans by force if the federal government could not open it by negotiation.

If Jefferson's natural love of tranquillity and his affection for a strict construction of the Constitution had been ten times as great, the clamor of the West would have compelled him to act. He knew a political storm when he saw it on the horizon; so he urged his ebullient frontier constituents to restrain their ardor until he could try the resources of diplomacy.

Then he set the machinery in motion at Paris, thinking all the time of the produce dammed up at New Orleans rather than of the expansion of America in the abstract. The crisis, he evidently thought, was to be considered in terms of corn, tobacco, and bacon. "The cession of Louisiana and the Floridas by Spain to France," he wrote to Livingston, the American minister in Paris, "works sorely in the United States. It completely reverses all the political relations of the United States and will form a new epoch in our political course. . . . There is on the globe one single spot the possessor of which is our natural and habitual enemy. It is New Orleans through which the produce of three-eighths of our territory must pass to market." Spain might have retained it in her weakening hands for years, he went on to say, but the occupation of New Orleans by France would be a menace that could not be ignored. Thus driven by realities Jefferson instructed Livingston to sound Napoleon on the possibility of buying New Orleans and also the Florida territory east of the Mississippi—on the assumption that the latter had gone to France with the Louisiana region.

With characteristic abruptness, Napoleon decided to sell to the United States every inch of the territory so recently wrung from Spain and instructed his minister of foreign affairs to open negotiations for that purpose. A few hours later Livingston was suddenly confronted by the astounding offer of the whole Louisiana domain. For a moment he was bewildered because he had no orders authorizing him to buy an empire; but his courage being equal to the occasion, he accepted the proposal. Monroe, who appeared on the scene at this moment, added his approval; and on April 30, 1803, the treaty of cession was signed by the negotiators. According to its terms, the Louisiana Territory, as received from Spain, was to be transferred to the United States in return for $11,250,000 in six per cent bonds plus the discharge of certain claims held by American citizens against France—a purchase price amounting to $15,000,000 in all. When the deed was done Livingston exclaimed that the action would in time transform vast solitudes into flourishing communities, reduce England from her still dominant position in American affairs, and give the United States a position of first rank among the great powers of the earth.

IV. NEW AGRICULTURAL STATES

DURING the years between the inauguration of George Washington and the retirement of James Monroe, the "agricultural interest" was enlarging its area, multiplying its adherents, and increasing its wealth. When the first President of the United States took the oath of office in Wall Street, there were thirteen states in the Union; within a little more than three decades nine new commonwealths had been erected in the Valley of the Mississippi—Kentucky, Tennessee, Ohio, Louisiana, Indiana, Mississippi, Illinois, Alabama, and Missouri—and two on the outskirts of New England—Vermont and Maine. In the same eventful period the population of the country multiplied nearly three times; at its close there were more inhabitants in Kentucky and Tennessee than in Massachusetts, Rhode Island, Connecticut, and Vermont combined. With the movement of peoples and the rise of new communities went of course a westward shift in the center of political gravity.

At the end of Monroe's administration Virginia, mother of Presidents, had to yield the scepter. Four years afterward Massachusetts was also forced to abdicate when her conservative son, John Quincy Adams, who had won the palm by an accident in the grand scramble of 1824, was swept from the White House before the flood of western Democrats headed by Andrew Jackson of Tennessee. The political forces of agriculture which had driven from power Hamilton's party of finance, commerce, and industry in 1800 had now been made apparently invincible by recruits from the frontier.

No wonder the statesmen of "wealth and talents" were in despair as they read the handwriting on the wall. At the Hartford convention a decade before, the assembled Federalists had prophesied that the admission of new western states would destroy the delicate balance between the planting and the commercial sections, that the planting interest allied with the western farmers would for a time govern the country, and that finally the western states, multiplied in number and augmented in population, would control the interests of the whole. To ward off this disaster the soothsayers of calamity had then offered ingenious paper projects in the form of constitutional amendments but words could not stifle the earth hunger of the multitudes nor bar the gates to them.

Through the years the tide of migration rolled westward, leaving in its wake widespreading farms and plantations whose owners, organized in political communities, worked hard at getting and using their full share of political power in the government of the nation. And their labors were not without reward. Of the fourteen Presidents of the United States elected between the passing of John Quincy Adams and the coming of

Theodore Roosevelt, all except four were either born in the Mississippi Valley or were, as residents, from early life identified with its people and its interests.

This westward migration—far greater in volume than the invasion that peopled the hills of New England and the lowlands of Virginia—was in one respect distinguished from other significant movements of colonizing races. The English settlements of the Atlantic seaboard were established under the patronage of powerful companies or semi-feudal proprietors encompassed by the protecting arm of a strong and watchful government. In striking contrast, the movement that carried American civilization beyond the Appalachians was essentially individualistic. No doubt, land companies helped to blaze the westward way, but they were few in number and their rôle in the process of occupation was relatively unimportant, especially after the initial steps were taken. It must be conceded also that little associations of neighbors from time to time detached themselves from the older Atlantic communities and went in groups over the mountains, but their adventures, like the undertakings of corporations, were mere eddies in the swarming migration that filled the continental empire. In the main, the great West was conquered by individuals or, to speak more accurately, by families.

When pioneers from English communities on the coast first began to open paths toward the Mississippi, the western region was a wilderness in which several seaboard colonies had conflicting legal rights under charters and grants from kings of England. Though the claimants, for many reasons, including the royal proclamation of 1763 closing the frontier to easy settlement, did little to develop their estate, its value was appreciated, if not by the commonalty, at least by statesmen and by investors with an eye to fortunate land speculations.

By no accident, accordingly, on the outbreak of the Revolution, George Rogers Clark, at the head of an armed expedition, was dispatched into the West for the purpose of wresting from the Ohio country the grip of England. As contemplated, the stroke was effective. While negotiating the treaty of peace with Great Britain at the close of the war for independence, the American delegation was able to clinch the achievement by fixing the western boundary of the United States at the Mississippi River.

Meanwhile, a lively contest arose in America over the fruits of victory. The politicians in control of the states that had claims, good and bad, naturally wanted to direct the disposal of the western lands and to recoup from that source at least some of the expenses of the struggle against Britain. But the politicians in other states, bitterly resenting this monopoly, declared that the Northwest had been won by common sacrifices and demanded equal shares in the fruits of victory. Finally, after much wrangling the principle of national ownership was adopted and the several claimants, sometimes with specific reservations, ceded their holdings to the United States.

The government to which this huge domain was transferred, namely, the Congress created by the Articles of Confederation, though too feeble to execute any grand plan of colonization, prepared the way for individual and corporate action by creating some of the conditions necessary to effective occupation. By two remarkable ordinances enacted in 1784 and 1785 it set momentous precedents for the Northwest Territory.

In the first of these decrees the Congress enunciated the fateful principle that the territories to be organized in the West should be ultimately admitted to the Union as states enjoying all the rights and privileges of the older commonwealths—not kept in the position of provinces in another Roman Empire ruled by pro-consuls from the capital. The second ordinance made provision for the official surveys which were to carve out farms, towns, counties, and states on a rectangular, or checker-board, pattern. With respect to actual settlement the Congress also arranged for the sale of lands so that pioneers and speculators could acquire holdings by lawful procedure and acquire titles of unimpeachable validity.

The rolling tide of migration that swept across the mountains and down the valleys, spreading out through the forests and over the prairies, advanced in successive waves. In the vanguard was the man with the rifle—grim, silent, and fearless. He loved the pathless forest, dense and solitary, carpeted by the fallen leaves of a thousand years and fretted by the sunlight that poured through the Gothic arches of the trees, where the wild beast slunk through the shadows, where the occasional crash of a falling branch boomed like thunder, and where the camp fire at night flared up into the darkness of knitted boughs as the flaming candles on the altar of a cathedral cast their rays high into the traceries of the vaulted roof.

Unsocial as the rifleman was in his hunting habits, he generally had a family on or near the frontier. With the aid of his wife and children, he threw up a rude shelter, often open on one side like the cabin in which Lincoln's mother died. He girdled and killed a few trees near by and laid a rail fence around his lot. There the family planted a "truck patch" of corn, beans, turnips, cabbage, and potatoes. While the hunter was searching for game in the forests or fishing in some neighboring stream, the wife and children vigorously hoed among the tangled roots and tough grasses of the garden. When autumn came the crops were harvested; the corn was stored in a rough crib; the cabbages, turnips, and potatoes, bedded in straw, were buried in great mounds from which the winter's supply could be taken. Wood for the big fireplace of sticks and clay came from the forest's edge. In all its phases the mode of living was crude but it was far removed even so from the depths of primitive culture.

In the wake of the man with a rifle came the seekers of permanent homes. In the Northwest, and usually in the Southwest, the leader in this next phase of occupation was the man with a plow, or, to speak more correctly, the family with established habits of domestic economy—the farming group who understood and loved the steady and sober industry of the field, the housewife who was a mistress of the thousand arts that created comfort, security, and refinement, and the rollicking children who made the frontier ring with merriment and who helped to enrich their parents as they grew in years. Immigrants of this type soon built a fourth side to their abode and set in glass windows; within a short time they substituted well-constructed frame or brick dwellings for their first log cabins. They cleared broad acres for tilling and combined with their neighbors to open roads through the woods, fling rude bridges across streams, and build churches and schoolhouses.

As the settlements of the county expanded into compact farms they made provision for local government, erecting a courthouse and log jail and choosing officers to administer rough and ready justice in civil and criminal cases. Before the first generation was ready to surrender to the children, the county seat had usually grown into a thriving village where, as a traveler through the Ohio country in 1836 declared, "broadcloths, silks, leghorns, crapes, and all the refinements, luxuries, elegancies, frivolities, and fashions are in vogue." A few of the more ingenious men developed into manufacturers and millers on a small scale; business enterprise with all its implications commenced.

To the south of the Ohio River, the settlers who followed the hunters were generally white farmers, akin in spirit and purpose to those who peopled the Northwest Territory. But close behind these home builders, especially into the wider valleys and broader plains, came masters with their slaves, buying up, uniting, and enlarging the holdings of their forerunners. In this way one of the distinctions that marked the old South from the Northwest was widely carried into the lower Mississippi Valley. Though, as southern observers were wont to say, western masters were shrewder and less punctilious than the grand gentlemen of the Virginia and Carolina lowlands, they were all united by ties of common interest, particularly on points touching their "peculiar institution."

The economy of the new West, essentially agricultural, rested mainly upon a system of freehold farms. In the lower Mississippi Valley and in the Missouri country, it is true, the planters with their slaves early pushed out toward the frontier; but in large sections of Alabama, Tennessee, and Kentucky, and all through the Northwest Territory, where slavery was forbidden, the small farmer reigned supreme. In this immense domain sprang up a social order without marked class or caste, a society of people substantially equal in worldly goods, deriving their livelihood from one prime source—labor with their own hands on the soil.

For a long time there were in that vast region no merchant princes such as governed Philadelphia and Boston, no powerful land-owning class comparable to the masters of Hudson Valley manors. Even the slave owners of the gulf states, though sometimes richer than their brethren on the seaboard, were many years in acquiring the magnificent pretensions that characterized the gentry of Virginia and South Carolina. Sugar makers and cotton growers of the Southwest gave their section no Washingtons, Randolphs, Madisons, and Monroes. Jefferson Davis belonged to the second generation of Mississippi planters and by the time he grew to manhood his class was marching swiftly to its doom.

V. THE APPROACH OF THE IRREPRESSIBLE CONFLICT

Had the economic systems of the North and the South remained static or changed slowly without effecting immense dislocations in the social structure, the balance of power might have been maintained indefinitely by repeating the compensatory tactics of 1787, 1820, 1833, and 1850; keeping in this manner the inherent antagonisms within the bounds of diplomacy. But nothing was stable in the economy of the United States or in the moral sentiments associated with its diversities.

Within each section of the country, the necessities of the productive system were generating portentous results. The periphery of the industrial vortex of the Northeast was daily enlarging, agriculture in the Northwest was being steadily supplemented by manufacturing, and the area of virgin soil open to exploitation by planters was diminishing with rhythmic regularity—shifting with mechanical precision the weights which statesmen had to adjust in their efforts to maintain the equilibrium of peace. Within each of the three sections also occurred an increasing intensity of social concentration as railways, the telegraph, and the press made travel and communication cheap and almost instantaneous, facilitating the centripetal process that was drawing people of similar economic status and parallel opinions into coöperative activities. Finally the intellectual energies released by accumulating wealth and growing leisure—stimulated by the expansion of the reading public and the literary market—developed with deepened accuracy the word-patterns of the current social persuasions, contributing with galvanic effect to the consolidation of identical groupings.

The fact that free-soil advocates waged war only on slavery in the territories was to Jefferson Davis conclusive proof of an underlying conspiracy against agriculture. He professed more respect for the abolitionist than for the free-soiler. The former, he said, is dominated by an honest conviction that slavery is wrong everywhere and that all men ought to be free; the latter does not assail slavery in the states—he merely wishes to abolish it in the territories that are in due course to be admitted to the Union.

With challenging directness, Davis turned upon his opponents in the Senate and charged them with using slavery as a blind to delude the unwary: "What do you propose, gentlemen of the Free-Soil party? Do you propose to better the condition of the slave? Not at all. What then do you propose? You say you are opposed to the expansion of slavery. . . . Is the slave to be benefited by it? Not at all. It is not humanity that influences you in the position which you now occupy before the country. . . . It is that you may have an opportunity of cheating us that you want to limit slave territory within circumscribed bounds. It is that you may have a majority in the Congress of the United States and convert the Government into an engine of northern aggrandizement. It is that your section may grow in power and prosperity upon treasures unjustly taken from the South, like the vampire bloated and gorged with the blood which it has secretly sucked from its victim . . . You desire to weaken the political power of the southern states; and why? Because you want, by an unjust system of legislation, to promote the industry of the New England states, at the expense of the people of the South and their industry."

Such in the mind of Jefferson Davis, fated to be president of the Confederacy, was the real purpose of the party which sought to prohibit slavery in the territories; that party did not declare slavery to be a moral disease calling for the severe remedy of the surgeon; it merely sought to keep bondage out of the new states as they came into the Union—with one fundamental aim in view, namely, to gain political ascendancy in the government of the United States and fasten upon the country an economic policy that meant the exploitation of the South for the benefit of northern capitalism.

But the planters were after all fighting against the census returns, as the phrase of the day ran current. The amazing growth of northern industries, the rapid extension of railways, the swift expansion of foreign trade to the ends of the earth, the attachment of the farming regions of the West to the centers of manufacture and finance through transportation and credit, the destruction of state consciousness by migration, the alien invasion, the erection of new commonwealths in the Valley of Democracy, the nationalistic drive of interstate commerce, the increase of population in the North, and the southward pressure of the capitalistic glacier all conspired to assure the ultimate triumph of what the orators were fond of calling "the free labor system." This was a dynamic thrust far too powerful for planters operating in a limited territory with incompetent labor on soil of diminishing fertility. Those who swept forward with it, exulting in the approaching triumph of machine industry, warned the planters of their ultimate subjection.

Seward knew from experience that a political party was no mere platonic society engaged in discussing abstractions. "A party," he said, "is in one sense a joint stock association, in which those who contribute most direct the action and management of the concern. The slaveholders contributing in an overwhelming proportion to the capital strength of the Democratic party, they necessarily dictate and prescribe its policy. The inevitable caucus system enables them to do this with a show of fairness and justice." This class of slaveholders, consisting of only three hundred and forty-seven thousand persons, Seward went on to say, was spread from the banks of the Delaware to the banks of the Rio Grande; it possessed nearly all the real estate in that section, owned more than three million other "persons" who were denied all civil and political rights, and inhibited "freedom of speech, freedom of press, freedom of the ballot box, freedom of education, freedom of literature, and freedom of popular assemblies. . . . The slaveholding class has become the governing power in each of the slaveholding states and it practically chooses thirty of the sixty-two members of the Senate, ninety of the two hundred and thirty-three members of the House of Representatives, and one hundred and five of the two hundred and ninety-five electors of the President and Vice-President of the United States."

Becoming still more concrete, Seward accused the President of being "a confessed apologist of the slave-property class." Examining the composition of the Senate, he found the slave-owning group in possession of all the important committees. Peering into the House of Representatives he discovered no impregnable bulwark of freedom there. Nor did respect for judicial ermine compel him to spare the Supreme Court. With irony he exclaimed: "How fitting does the proclamation of its opening close with the invocation: 'God save the United States and this honorable court. . . .' The court consists of a chief justice and eight associate justices. Of these five were called from slave states and four from free states. The opinions and bias of each of them were carefully considered by the President and Senate when he was appointed. Not one of them was found wanting in soundness of politics, according to the slaveholder's exposition of the Constitution, and those who were called from the free states were even more distinguished in that respect than their brethren from the slaveholding states."

Having described the gigantic operating structure of the slavocracy, Seward drew with equal power a picture of the opposing system founded on "free labor." He surveyed the course of economy in the North—the growth of industry, the spread of railways, the swelling tide of European immigration, and the westward roll of free farmers—rounding out the country, knitting it together, bringing "these antagonistic systems" continually into closer contact. Then he uttered those fateful words which startled conservative citizens from Maine to California—words of prophecy which proved to be brutally true—"the irrepressible conflict."

This inexorable clash, he said, was not "accidental, unnecessary, the work of interested or fanatical agitators and therefore ephemeral." No. "It is an irrepressible conflict between opposing and enduring forces." The hopes of those who sought peace by appealing to slave owners to reform themselves were as chaff in a storm. "How long and with what success have you waited already for that reformation? Did any property class ever so reform itself? Did the patricians in old Rome, the noblesse or clergy in France? The landholders in Ireland? The landed aristocracy in England? Does the slaveholding class even seek to beguile you with such a hope? Has it not become rapacious, arrogant, defiant?" All attempts at compromise were "vain and ephemeral." There was accordingly but one supreme task before the people of the United States—the task of confounding and overthrowing "by one decisive blow the betrayers of the Constitution and freedom forever." In uttering this indictment, this prophecy soon to be fulfilled with such appalling accuracy, Seward stepped beyond the bounds of cautious politics and read himself out of the little group of men who were eligible for the Republican nomination in 1860.

Given an irrepressible conflict which could be symbolized in such unmistakable patterns by competent interpreters of opposing factions, a transfer of the issues from the forum to the field, from the conciliation of diplomacy to the decision of arms was bound to come. Each side obdurately bent upon its designs and convinced of its rectitude, by the fulfillment of its wishes precipitated events and effected distributions of power that culminated finally in the tragedy foretold by Seward. Those Democrats who operated on historic knowledge rather than on prophetic insight, recalling how many times the party of Hamilton had been crushed at elections, remembering how the Whigs had never been able to carry the country on a clean-cut Webster-Clay program, and counting upon the continued support of a huge array of farmers and mechanics marshaled behind the planters, imagined apparently that politics—viewed as the science of ballot enumeration—could resolve the problems of power raised by the maintenance of the Union.

And in this opinion they were confirmed by the outcome of the presidential campaign in 1852, when the Whigs, with General Winfield Scott, a hero of the Mexican war, at their head, were thoroughly routed by the Democratic candidate, General Franklin Pierce of New Hampshire. Indeed the verdict of the people was almost savage, for Pierce carried every state but four, receiving 254 out of 296 electoral votes. The Free-Soil party that branded slavery as a crime and called for its prohibition in the territories scarcely made a ripple, polling only 156,000 out of more than three million votes, a figure below the record set in the previous campaign.

With the Whigs beaten and the Free-Soilers evidently a dwindling handful of negligible critics, exultant Democrats took possession of the Executive offices and Congress, inspired by a firm belief that their tenure was secure. Having won an overwhelming victory on a definite tariff for revenue and pro-slavery program, they acted as if the party of Hamilton was for all practical purposes as powerless as the little band of abolitionist agitators. At the succeeding election in 1856 they again swept the country —this time with James Buchanan of Pennsylvania as their candidate. Though his triumph was not as magisterial as that of Pierce it was great enough to warrant a conviction that the supremacy of the Democratic party could not be broken at the polls.

During these eight years of tenure, a series of events occurred under Democratic auspices, which clinched the grasp of the planting interest upon the country and produced a correlative consolidation of the opposition. One line of development indicated an indefinite extension of the slave area; another the positive withdrawal of all government support from industrial and commercial enterprise. The first evidence of the new course came in the year immediately following the inauguration of Pierce.

In 1854, Congress defiantly repealed the Missouri Compromise and threw open to slavery the vast section of the Louisiana Purchase which had been closed to it by the covenant adopted more than three decades before. On the instant came a rush of slavery champions from Missouri into Kansas determined to bring it into the southern sphere of influence. Not content with the conquest of the forbidden West, filibustering parties under pro-slavery leaders attempted to seize Cuba and Nicaragua and three American ministers abroad flung out to the world a flaming proclamation, known as the "Ostend Manifesto," which declared that the United States would be justified in wresting Cuba from Spain by force—acts of imperial aggression which even the Democratic administration in Washington felt constrained to repudiate.

Crowning the repeal of the Missouri Compromise came two decisions of the Supreme Court giving sanction to the expansion of slavery in America and assuring high protection for that peculiar institution even in the North. In the Dred Scott case decided in March, 1857, Chief Justice Taney declared in effect that the Missouri Compromise had been void from the beginning and that Congress had no power under the Constitution to prohibit slavery in the territories of the United States anywhere at any time. This legal triumph for the planting interest was followed in 1859 by another decision in which the Supreme Court upheld the fugitive slave law and all the drastic procedure provided for its enforcement. To the frightened abolitionists it seemed that only one more step was needed to make freedom unconstitutional throughout the country.

These extraordinary measures on behalf of slavery were accompanied by others that touched far more vitally economic interests in the North. In 1859, the last of the subsidies for trans-Atlantic steamship companies was ordered discontinued by Congress. In 1857, the tariff was again reduced, betraying an unmistakable drift of the nation toward free trade. In support of this action, the representatives of the South and Southwest were almost unanimous and they gathered into their fold a large number of New England congressmen on condition that no material reductions should be made in duties on cotton goods. On the other hand, the Middle States and the West offered a large majority against tariff reduction so that the division was symptomatic.

Immediately after the new revenue law went into effect an industrial panic burst upon the country, spreading distress among businessmen and free laborers. While that tempest was running high, the paper money anarchy let loose by the Democrats reached the acme of virulence as the notes of wildcat banks flooded the West and South and financial institutions crashed in every direction, fifty-one failing in Indiana alone within a period of five years. Since all hope of reviving Hamilton's system of finance had been buried, those who believed that a sound currency was essential to national prosperity were driven to the verge of desperation. On top of these economic calamities came Buchanan's veto of the Homestead bill which the impatient agrarians had succeeded in getting through

Congress in a compromise form—an act of presidential independence which angered the farmers and mechanics who regarded the national domain as their own inheritance.

To this confusion in party affairs, the intellectual and religious ferment of the age added troublesome factional disputes. A temperance element, strong enough to carry prohibition in a few states, was giving the politicians anxiety in national campaigns. A still more formidable cabal, the Know Nothing, or American Party, sprang up in the current opposition to foreigners, the papacy, infidelity, and socialism. Combining the functions of a party and a fraternal order, it nominated candidates for office and adopted secret rites, dark mysteries, grips, and passwords which gave it an atmosphere of uncertain vitality. Members were admitted by solemn ceremony into full fellowship with "The Supreme Order of the Star-spangled Banner," whose "daily horror and nightly specter was the pope." When asked about their principles, they replied mysteriously: "I know nothing." Appealing to deep-seated emotions, this movement showed strength in many localities and was only dissolved by the smashing energy of more momentous issues.

The signal for a general realignment of factions and parties was given by the passage of the Kansas-Nebraska bill of 1854 repealing the Missouri Compromise. In fact, while that measure was pending in Congress a coalescing movement was to be observed: northern Whigs persuaded that their old party was moribund, Democrats weary of planting dominance, and free-soilers eager to exclude slavery from the territories began to draw together to resist the advance of the planting power. In February of that year, a number of Whigs and Democrats assembled at Ripon, Wisconsin, and resolved that a new party must be formed if the bill passed.

When the expected event occurred, the Ripon insurgents created a fusion committee and chose the name "Republican" as the title of their young political association. In July, a Michigan convention composed of kindred elements demanded the repeal of the Kansas-Nebraska act, the repeal of the fugitive slave law, and the abolition of slavery in the District of Columbia. This convention also agreed to postpone all differences "with regard to political economy or administrative policy" and stay in the field as a "Republican" party until the struggle against slavery extension was finished. All over the country similar meetings were mustered and the local cells of the new national party rose into being. Meanwhile the old Whigs who wanted peace and prosperity were floating about looking for any drifting wreckage that might hold them above the waves.

As the election of 1856 approached, the Republicans made ready to enter the national field. After a preliminary conference at Pittsburgh, they held a national convention at Philadelphia and nominated for the presidency, John C. Frémont, the Western explorer, a son-in-law of Benton, the faithful Jacksonian Democrat. In their platform they made the exclusion of slavery from the territories—and of necessity its economic and political implications—the paramount issue. So restricted, the platform offered no prizes to regular Whigs, no tariff, banking, or currency reforms; rather did it appeal to the farmers of the Jeffersonian school—men who were not slave owners and did not expect to enter that class, men who were determined to keep slavery out of the territories and to make the federal domain an estate for free farmers.

Lest there be some misunderstanding, they made it clear throughout their campaign that they were not trying to revive the Federalist or the Whig party. They were conscious of the fact that the name "Republican" of which they boasted was the device chosen by Jefferson for his embattled farmers and used by his followers until they fell under the sway of Jackson. "There is not a plank in our platform," exclaimed one of the Republican orators from Wisconsin before the great accommodation of 1860, "which does not conform to the principles of Jefferson; the man who, of all others, has ever been regarded as the true representative of the Republican party of this country. He was its representative in the Congress of 1776. He was its leader and representative in 1800; he was its true representative in 1812; he is the true representative of the Republican party to-day. We stand, Sir, upon his doctrines and we fight for his principles. We stand upon no sectional platform; we present no sectional issues . . . and we are coming to take possession of this government, to administer it for the whole country, North and South; and suffer monopolists neither of the North or the South to control its administration and so shape its action as to subserve the interests of the aristocratic few." On this platform those who opposed the plutocracy of the East and the planting aristocracy of the South could easily unite.

Replying to the Republican challenge the Democratic organization granted to its pro-slavery wing almost every demand. In its platform of 1856 it reiterated as a matter of course its fixed agricultural creed: no protective tariffs, no national banks, no industrial subsidies, and no Hamiltonian devices. It then commended the bargain of 1850, endorsed slavery as an institution, approved the repeal of the Missouri Compromise, and proposed that the new states to be admitted to the Union should come in with or without slavery as their constitutions might provide. In exchange the northern wing received honorific compensation in the nomination of James Buchanan of Pennsylvania. The South thus got the platform; the North, the candidate.

Defied by the Democrats in front and menaced by the Republicans on the left, the old Whigs, who hated the bother of slavery agitation and merely wanted to get government support for business enterprise, were sorely perplexed. They saw their southern brethren drawn away by the Democratic gift of the Kansas-Nebraska bill and yet they could not find in the Republican platform a promise of protection for industry or a pledge of currency reform. On the face of things, a combination with either of these political associations was impossible and so the Whigs decided to tempt the fates again and alone. At a convention held in Baltimore, they condemned "geographical parties," expressed a reverence for the Constitution and the Union, and nominated Millard Fillmore, a man "eminent for his calm and pacific temperament." As Fillmore had already been blessed by the American, or Know Nothing, party, there was some prospect of effecting a formidable bloc under his leadership.

When the votes were counted in the autumn of 1856, it was clear that a great majority of the people were opposed to anti-slavery agitation in every form. Not only was Buchanan elected by a safe margin on a strong slavery program; he and Fillmore together polled nearly three million votes against less than half that figure cast for Frémont. In other words, Garrison had been at work for a quarter of a century when, by a decision of more than two to one, even the mildest plank in the anti-slavery platform was overwhelmingly repudiated by the country at large. Still Frémont's poll revealed an immense gain in the number of free-soilers as compared with their trivial strength at previous contests, demonstrating in a striking manner that the fight for the possession of the territories, with all it implied in terms of political and economic power at Washington, could not be avoided. Especially did it show the Whigs that they would have to work out a new combination of forces if they expected to get business enterprise on an even keel again.

Fortunately for them, the way to the solution of their problem was pointed out by the election returns: Fillmore had received 874,000 votes, a number which, added to Frémont's total, would have elected a candidate. Given these figures, the question of how to unite free-soil farmers and timid apostles of prosperity became therefore the supreme issue before the political leaders who took their bearings after the storm of 1856 in the hope of finding some method of ousting the Democrats at the next tourney. Neither group could win without the other; the union of either with the planting aristocracy was impossible. Obviously an accommodation—a readjustment of the balance of power—and the right kind of candidate offered to Whigs and free-soil Republicans the only assurance of ultimate victory.

All the while the conflict was growing more furious. Advocates of protection, taking advantage of the panic which followed the tariff revision, organized a stirring campaign to wean workingmen from their allegiance to a free-trade Democracy. Advocates of a sound currency protested against the depreciated notes and the wildcat banks that spread ruin through all sections of the land. The abolitionists maintained their fusillade, Garrison and Phillips, despite their pessimism, resting neither day nor night. Going beyond the bounds of mere agitation, the slavery faction of Missouri in its grim determination to conquer Kansas for bondage and northern abolitionists in their equally firm resolve to seize it for freedom convulsed the country by bloody deeds and then by bloody reprisals. In a powerful oration, "The Crime against Kansas," done in classical style but bristling with abuse of the slavery party, Charles Sumner threw Congress into a tumult in 1856 and provided a text for the free-soilers laboring to wrest the government from the planting interest. Before the public excitement caused by this speech had died away, the attention of the nation was arrested by a series of debates between Lincoln and Douglas held in Illinois in 1858—debates which set forth in clear and logical form the program for excluding slavery from the territories and the squatter-sovereignty scheme for letting the inhabitants decide the issue for themselves.

Then came the appalling climax in 1859 when John Brown, after a stormy career in Kansas, tried to kindle a servile insurrection in the South. In the spring of that year, Brown attended an anti-slavery convention from which he went away muttering: "These men are all talk; what we need is action—action!" Collecting a few daring comrades he made a raid into Harper's Ferry for the purpose of starting a slave rebellion. Though his efforts failed, though he was quickly executed as a "traitor to Virginia," the act of violence rocked the continent from sea to sea.

In vain did the Republicans try to treat it as the mere work of a fanatic and denounce it as "among the gravest of crimes." In vain did Lincoln attempt to minimize it as an absurd adventure that resulted in nothing noteworthy except the death of Brown. It resounded through the land with the clangor of an alarm bell, aggravating the jangling nerves of a people already excited by fears of a race war and continued disturbances over the seizure of slaves under the fugitive slave act—disorders which sometimes assumed the form of menacing riots.

The turmoil in the country naturally found sharp echoes in the halls of Congress. Buchanan's policy of aiding the slavery party in its efforts to get possession of Kansas and the taunting action of the free-soilers in their determination to save it for liberty, gave abundant occasions for debates that grew more and more acrimonious. Indeed the factions in Congress were now almost at swords' points, passion in argument and gesture becoming the commonplace of the day.

When Senator Sumner made a vehement verbal attack on Senator Butler of South Carolina in 1856, Preston Brooks, a Representative from the same state and a relative of the latter, replied in terms of physical force, catching Sumner unawares and beating his victim senseless with a heavy cane. Though the act was not strictly chivalrous—for Sumner, wedged in between his chair and his desk, could not defend himself— admiring South Carolinians gave Brooks a grand banquet and presented him with a new cane bearing the words: "Use knockdown arguments." On both sides of the Senate chamber all the arts of diplomacy were discarded, and the meanest weapons of personal abuse brought into play. Douglas called Sumner a perjurer who spat forth malignity upon his colleagues. The prim, proud Senator from Massachusetts, conscious of possessing a mellow culture, replied by likening Douglas to a "noisome, squat and nameless animal" that filled the Senate with an offensive odor. Things were even worse in the lower house. Without exaggeration did Jefferson Davis exclaim that members of Congress were more like the agents of belligerent states than men assembled in the interest of common welfare—an utterance that was startlingly accurate—born of prophetic certainty. Every shocking incident on the one side only consolidated the forces on the other. By 1860 leaders of the planting interest had worked out in great detail their economic and political scheme—their ultimatum to the serried opposition—and embodied it in many official documents.

In brief, the federal government was to do nothing for business enterprise while the planting interest was to be assured the possession of enough political power to guarantee it against the reënactment of the Hamilton-Webster program. Incidentally the labor system of the planting interest was not to be criticized and all runaway property was to be returned. Anything short of this was, in the view of the planting statesmen, "subversive of the Constitution."

The meaning of the ultimatum was not to be mistaken. It was a demand upon the majority of the people to surrender unconditionally for all time to the minority stockholders under the Constitution. It offered nothing to capitalism but capitulation; to the old Whigs of the South nothing but submission. Finally—and this was its revolutionary phase—it called upon the farmers and mechanics who had formed the bulk of Jacksonian Democracy in the North to acknowledge the absolute sovereignty of the planting interest. Besides driving a wedge into the nation, the conditions laid down by the planters also split the Democratic party itself into two factions.

During the confusion in the Democratic ranks, the Republicans, in high glee over the quarrels of the opposition, held their convention in Chicago—a sectional gathering except for representatives from five slave states. Among its delegates the spirit of opposition to slavery extension, which had inspired the party assembly four years before, was still evident but enthusiasm on that ticklish subject was neutralized by the prudence of the practical politicians who, sniffing victory in the air, had rushed to the new tent. Whigs, whose affections were centered on Hamilton's program rather than on Garrison's scheme of salvation, were to be seen on the floor. Advocates of a high protective tariff and friends of free homesteads for mechanics and farmers now mingled with the ardent opponents of slavery in the territories. With their minds fixed on the substance of things sought for, the partisans of caution were almost able to prevent the convention from indorsing the Declaration of Independence. Still they were in favor of restricting the area of slavery; they had no love for the institution and its spread helped to fasten the grip of the planting interest on the government at Washington. So the Republican convention went on record in favor of liberty for the territories, free homesteads for farmers, a protective tariff, and a Pacific railway. As the platform was read, the cheering became especially loud and prolonged when the homestead and tariff planks were reached. Such at least is the testimony of the stenographic report.

Since this declaration of principles was well fitted to work a union of forces, it was essential that the candidate should not divide them. The protective plank would doubtless line up the good old Whigs of the East but tender consideration had to be shown to the Ohio Valley, original home of Jacksonian Democracy, where national banks, tariffs, and other "abominations" still frightened the wary. Without Ohio, Indiana, and Illinois, the Republican managers could not hope to win and they knew that the lower counties of these states were filled with settlers from the slave belt who had no love for the "money power," abolition, or anything that savored of them. In such circumstances Seward, idol of the Whig wing, was no man to offer that section; he was too radical on the slavery issue and too closely associated with "high finance" in addition. "If you do not nominate Seward, where will you get your money?" was the blunt question put by Seward's loyal supporters at Chicago. The question was pertinent but not fatal.

Given this confluence of problems, a man close to the soil of the West was better suited to the requirements of the hour than a New York lawyer with somewhat fastidious tastes, obviously backed by fat purses. The available candidate was Abraham Lincoln of Illinois. Born in Kentucky, he was of southern origin. A son of poor frontier parents, self-educated, a pioneer who in his youth had labored in field and forest, he appealed to the voters of the backwoods. Still by an uncanny genius for practical affairs, he had forged his way to the front as a shrewd lawyer and politician. In his debates with Douglas he had shown himself able to cope with one of the foremost leaders in the Democratic party. On the tariff, bank, currency, and homestead issues he was sound. A local railway attorney, he was trusted among businessmen.

On the slavery question Lincoln's attitude was firm but conservative. He disliked slavery and frankly said so; yet he was not an abolitionist and he saw no way in which the institution could be uprooted. On the contrary, he favored enforcing the fugitive slave law and he was not prepared to urge even the abolition of slavery in the District of Columbia. His declaration that a house divided against itself could not stand had been counterbalanced by an assertion that the country would become all free or all slave—a creed which any southern planter could have indorsed. Seward's radical doctrine that there was a "higher law" than the Constitution, dedicating the territories to freedom, received from the Illinois lawyer disapproval, not commendation.

Nevertheless Lincoln was definite and positive in his opinion that slavery should not be permitted in the territories. That was necessary to satisfy the minimum demands of the anti-slavery faction and incidentally it pleased those Whigs of the North who at last realized that no Hamiltonian program could be pushed through Congress if the planting interest secured a supremacy, or indeed held an equal share of power, in the Union. Evidently Lincoln was the man of the hour: his heritage was correct, his principles were sound, his sincerity was unquestioned, and his ability as a speaker commanded the minds and hearts of his auditors. He sent word to his friends at Chicago that, although he did not indorse Seward's higher-law doctrine, he agreed with him on the irrepressible conflict. The next day Lincoln was nominated amid huzzas from ten thousand lusty throats.

A large fraction of Whigs and some fragments of the Know Nothing, or American, party, foreseeing calamity in the existing array of interests, tried to save the day by an appeal to lofty sentiments without any definitions. Assuming the name of Constitutional Unionists and boasting that they represented the "intelligence and respectability of the South" as well as the lovers of the national idea everywhere, they held a convention at Baltimore and nominated John Bell of Tennessee and Edward Everett of Massachusetts for President and Vice-President. In the platform they invited their countrymen to forget all divisions and "support the Constitution of the country, the union of the states, and the enforcement of the laws." It was an overture of old men—men who had known and loved Webster and Clay and who shrank with horror from agitations that threatened to end in bloodshed and revolution—a plea for the maintenance of the status quo against the whims of a swiftly changing world.

A spirited campaign followed the nomination of four candidates for the presidency on four different platforms. Huge campaign funds were raised and spent. Besides pursuing the usual strategy of education, the Republicans resorted to parades and the other spectacular features that had distinguished the log-cabin crusade of General Harrison's year. Emulating the discretion of the Hero of Tippecanoe, Lincoln maintained a judicious silence at Springfield while his champions waged his battles for him, naturally tempering their orations to the requirements of diverse interests. They were fully conscious, as a Republican paper in Philadelphia put it, that "Frémont had tried running on the slavery issue and lost." So while they laid stress on it in many sections, they widened their appeal.

In the West, a particular emphasis was placed on free homesteads and the Pacific railway. With a keen eye for competent strategy, Carl Schurz carried the campaign into Missouri where he protested with eloquence against the action of the slave power in denying "the laboring man the right to acquire property in the soil by his labor" and made a special plea for the German vote on the ground that the free land was to be opened to aliens who declared their intention of becoming American citizens. Discovering that the homestead question was "the greatest issue in the West," Horace Greeley used it to win votes in the East. Agrarians and labor reformers renewed the slogan: "Vote yourself a farm."

In Pennsylvania and New Jersey, protection for iron and steel was the great subject of discussion. Curtin, the Republican candidate for governor in the former state, said not a word about abolishing slavery in his ratification speech but spoke with feeling on "the vast heavings of the heart of Pennsylvania whose sons are pining for protection to their labor and their dearest interests." Warming to his theme, he exclaimed: "This is a contest involving protection and the rights of labor. . . . If you desire to become vast and great, protect the manufactures of Philadelphia. . . . All hail, liberty! All hail, freedom! freedom to the white man! All hail freedom general as the air we breathe!" In a fashion after Curtin's own heart, the editor of the Philadelphia American and Gazette, surveying the canvass at the finish, repudiated the idea that "any sectional aspect of the slavery question" was up for decision and declared that the great issues were protection for industry, "economy in the conduct of the government, homesteads for settlers on the public domain, retrenchment and accountability in the public expenditures, appropriation for rivers and harbors, a Pacific railroad, the admission of Kansas, and a radical reform in the government."

With a kindred appreciation of practical matters, Seward bore the standard through the North and West. Fully conversant with the Webster policy of commercial expansion in the Pacific and knowing well the political appeal of Manifest Destiny, he proclaimed the future of the American empire—assuring his auditors that in due time American outposts would be pushed along the northwest coast to the Arctic Ocean, that Canada would be gathered into our glorious Union, that the Latin-American republics reorganized under our benign influence would become parts of this magnificent confederation, that the ancient Aztec metropolis, Mexico City, would eventually become the capital of the United States, and that America and Russia, breaking their old friendship, would come to grips in the Far East—"in regions where civilization first began." All this was involved in the election of Lincoln and the triumph of the Republican party. Webster and Cushing and Perry had not wrought in vain.

The three candidates opposed to Lincoln scored points wherever they could. Douglas took the stump with his usual vigor and declaimed to throngs in nearly every state. Orators of the Breckinridge camp, believing that their extreme views were sound everywhere, invaded the North. Bell's champions spoke with dignity and warmth about the dangers inherent in all unwise departures from the past, about the perils of the sectional quarrel. When at length the ballots were cast and counted, it was found that the foes of slavery agitation had carried the country by an overwhelming majority. Their combined vote was a million ahead of Lincoln's total; the two Democratic factions alone, to say nothing of Bell's six hundred thousand followers, outnumbered the Republican army. But in the division and uproar of the campaign Lincoln, even so, had won the Presidency; he was the choice of a minority—a sectional minority at that—but under the terms of the Constitution, he was entitled to the scepter at Washington.

VI. THE SECOND AMERICAN REVOLUTION

In the spring of 1861 the full force of the irrepressible conflict burst upon the hesitant and bewildered nation and for four long years the clash of arms filled the land with its brazen clangor. For four long years the anguish, the calamities, and the shocks of the struggle absorbed the energies of the multitudes, blared in the headlines of the newspapers, and loomed impressively in the minds of the men and women who lived and suffered in that age. The agony of it hung like a pall over the land. And yet with strange swiftness the cloud was lifted and blown away. Merciful grass spread its green mantle over the cruel scars and the gleaming red splotches sank into the hospitable earth.

It was then that the economist and lawyer, looking more calmly on the scene, discovered that the armed conflict had been only one phase of the cataclysm, a transitory phase; that at bottom the so-called Civil War, or the War between the States, in the light of Roman analogy, was a social war, ending in the unquestioned establishment of a new power in the government, making vast changes in the arrangement of classes, in the accumulation and distribution of wealth, in the course of industrial development, and in the Constitution inherited from the Fathers. Merely by the accidents of climate, soil, and geography was it a sectional struggle. If the planting interest had been scattered evenly throughout the industrial region, had there been a horizontal rather than a perpendicular cleavage, the irrepressible conflict would have been resolved by other methods and accompanied by other logical defense mechanisms.

In any event neither accident nor rhetoric should be allowed to obscure the intrinsic character of that struggle. If the operations by which the middle classes of England broke the power of the king and the aristocracy are to be known collectively as the Puritan Revolution, if the series of acts by which the bourgeois and peasants of France overthrew the king, nobility, and clergy is to be called the French Revolution, then accuracy compels us to characterize by the same term the social cataclysm in which the capitalists, laborers, and farmers of the North and West drove from power in the national government the planting aristocracy of the South. Viewed under the light of universal history, the fighting was a fleeting incident; the social revolution was the essential, portentous outcome.

To be sure the battles and campaigns of the epoch are significant to the military strategist; the tragedy and heroism of the contest furnish inspiration to patriots and romance to the makers of epics. But the core of the vortex lay elsewhere. It was in the flowing substance of things limned by statistical reports on finance, commerce, capital, industry, railways, and agriculture, by provisions of constitutional law, and by the pages of statute books—prosaic muniments which show that the so-called civil war was in reality a Second American Revolution and in a strict sense, the First.

The physical combat that punctuated the conflict merely hastened the inevitable. As was remarked at the time, the South was fighting against the census returns—census returns that told of accumulating industrial capital, multiplying captains of industry, expanding railway systems, widening acres tilled by free farmers. Once the planting and the commercial states, as the Fathers with faithful accuracy described them, had been evenly balanced; by 1860 the balance was gone.

A few days after Lincoln's election, namely, on November 10, the state legislature of South Carolina, without a dissenting voice, called a popular convention to choose the course appropriate to the emergency. In December the convention met in a thrill of excitement. The galleries and lobbies of the assembly hall were crowded with ladies in gala attire, soldiers in bright new uniforms, judges, editors, and officers, all in high spirits and sanguine as to the outcome. The delegates were nearly all old men or men beyond the middle years, too old to fight but too proud to let the Lincoln menace pass without an answer. Divine blessings were invoked, the issue was submitted to debate, and then by a unanimous vote South Carolina declared her independence. As soon as the momentous verdict was rendered, a shout of triumph ran through the streets of Charleston and the night was made joyous with merrymaking, enlivened by song and wine, dancing and fireworks. Those wiseacres who thought they saw dark shadows in the background slunk away or held their tongues. The jubilee was perfect.

As in the time of the nullification struggle, South Carolina now called upon her neighbors to follow her example; and before Lincoln was inaugurated six of them—Florida, Georgia, Alabama, Mississippi, Louisiana, and Texas—had proclaimed their union with the northern states at an end. Though in Alabama and Georgia a respectable minority was opposed to secession, in the other four states only a few malcontents could be mustered to resist the flushed and confident majority. Having declared their independence, the seceded states, acting on a summons from Mississippi, sent delegates in February, 1861, to Montgomery, Alabama, where a plan of union was adopted and preparations were made for the establishment of a new general government.

This was the posture of affairs when Lincoln took the oath of office on March 4, 1861. Virginia, North Carolina, Tennessee, and Arkansas trembled in the balance. Conventions had been called in these states but they had all refused to take the fatal step, preferring to await the course pursued by the incoming President. In Virginia, North Carolina, and Tennessee there was a large majority against secession on the issues presented before Lincoln's inauguration. Though they all upheld slavery, their economy was more diversified than that of the cotton belt; they had wide upland sections occupied by small farmers who had no special love for the planting aristocracy at the head of southern affairs.

Even after Fort Sumter fell, when the call for blood was running through the land, there was still a formidable opposition to secession in each of these states. In North Carolina, the federal faction resorted to the tactics of indifference and obstruction; in Virginia, it managed to tear away several disaffected counties, organize them into the new state of West Virginia, and enter the Union as a separate commonwealth; in Tennessee, it furnished thousands of soldiers for the northern army and kept whole counties in constant turmoil. Hence it happened that Lincoln on the day of his coming to power found secession menacing but by no means triumphant. The chemicals for a crisis were prepared but some stroke was necessary to explode them.

From the early days of November, 1860, to March 4, 1861, while planters prepared for the worst, the government at Washington drifted, helpless in the conflicting currents. According to the terms of the Constitution, Lincoln could not be inaugurated until the day lawfully appointed, and so for four critical months the Democratic party, which had been split wide by the campaign and defeated at the polls, continued to hold the reins of power. Its titular leader, President James Buchanan, had no popular mandate to deal with the question of secession. Nor had he any overmastering will of his own in the premises. Obviously bewildered by the stirring events taking place about him, he exclaimed in one breath that the southern states had no right to withdraw from the Union and in the next that he had no power to compel them to retain their allegiance. His Cabinet crumbled away, his host of advisers wrangled among themselves, and inaction seemed to him the better part of valor—at least it could be defended on the ground that nothing should be done to embarrass the incoming President.

On every side were heard the buzzing voices of politicians attempting to forecast the future, effect compromises, soothe angry passions. The Congress which assembled in December had no mandate from the election of the preceding month; the House had been chosen two years earlier and the Senate piecemeal over a period of six years. Congressmen were as perplexed as the President. To the public generally it seemed as if the solid earth were dissolving.

The new President took a positive stand on the nature of the Union: it was perpetual and no state could lawfully withdraw from it. He was equally firm in declaring that he would enforce the Constitution and the statutes against states that sought to violate or defy the law but his tone was conciliatory and he closed with a simple and moving appeal to sentiments of union, peace, and friendship.

Beyond all dispute Lincoln's problems in those tense days were stupendous. He spoke for a minority. He was no dictator standing for a triumphant majority and commissioned to carry out its appointed task. On the contrary he was aware, as southern planters were aware, that the North was torn by factions and he had no way of discovering how the bulk of his own party wanted him to act in the crisis. He knew that the anti-slavery sentiment in the country, though strong, was limited in its appeal; that, except in the hearts of the abolitionists, it was timid; that the Quakers who professed it were in general against emancipation by war.

Moreover abolitionists were divided on secession. Henry Ward Beecher, when informed that the southern states were withdrawing from the Union, burst forth: "I do not care if they do." Horace Greeley wrote in the Tribune: "If the cotton states shall decide that they can do better out of the Union than in it, we insist on letting them go in peace. The right to secede may be a revolutionary one but it exists nevertheless." A wide belt of slave states had not seceded: a single utterance or act by Lincoln savoring of a war on slavery would have sent them all into the arms of the Confederacy. Nor could Lincoln count with certainty on undivided economic support above the Potomac. Ardently as they desired the preservation of the great customs union, northern business interests did not want war, save in the last bitter extremity. With respect to this problem Greeley estimated that southern debtors owed at least $200,000,-000 to creditors in New York City alone, drawing from his figures the conclusion that a resort to arms meant general ruin in commercial circles. Unless human experience was as naught, the watchword of the solemn hour was Caution. For good reasons, therefore, all practical men, including Jefferson Davis on the one side and Abraham Lincoln on the other, feverishly sought some middle ground of compromise.

Why was the fatal blow that substituted armed might for negotiation ever struck? According to all outward and visible signs the opposing sections might have stood indefinitely in the posture of expectancy. Why did any one seek to break the spell? In whose brain, in the final analysis, was made the decision which directed the hand to light the powder train and blow up the wall of doubt that divided peace from war? No unanimous verdict on that point has yet been rendered by a court of last resort; one more question of war guilt remains unsolved.

It has been said that Lincoln, by deciding to send relief to Fort Sumter in the harbor of Charleston, splashed blood on his own head. The answer to such a thesis is that the relief sent to the beleaguered fort consisted mainly of provisions for a starving garrison and offered no direct menace to the Confederacy. It has been alleged that the inner leaders of the Confederacy, feeling the ground slipping from under them, thought bloodshed necessary to consolidate their forces and bring the hesitant states into their fold. The answer commonly made to this argument is that President Davis, in his final instructions to General Beauregard, commanding the Confederates at Charleston, spoke merely in general terms about the reduction of Sumter and advised action only if certain conditions of evacuation were rejected.

As a matter of fact, Major Anderson, in charge of Union forces, offered a compromise which should have been sent to Davis for review but Beauregard's aides, spurred on by an ardent secessionist from Virginia, made the decision on their own account in favor of audacity and at 4:30 on the morning of April 12, started the conflagration by firing on Fort Sumter. This bombardment and the surrender of the fort had just the effect foreseen by the extremists: the South, by striking the first blow and hauling down the Stars and Stripes, kindled the quivering opinion of the North into a devouring flame. Lincoln's call for volunteers and answer of force by force pushed Virginia, North Carolina, Tennessee, and Arkansas into the Confederacy. The die was cast.

The long conflict which ended in the downfall of the Confederacy thus had many phases. It was waged on land and sea by arms, in the capitals of Europe by diplomacy, and in the sphere of morals by propaganda, publicity, and coercion. Descriptions of the war itself must be entrusted to those who have charted the science of military tactics or mastered the art of depicting tragedy and romance. Since every one of its great battles has been the subject of fierce debate among experts, the layman does well to leave the technical issues to them. In the large, however, the problem for the South was mainly that of defense, although one heroic effort was made to push the war into the enemy's domain by a thrust into Pennsylvania—a thrust parried at Gettysburg in July, 1863. On the other hand, the problem of the North, to state it simply, was one of invasion and conquest. Lincoln's task was that of beating southern armies on their own soil or wearing them down to exhaustion.

Geography, as often happens, gave a distinct turn to the military process. The Appalachian mountains, stretching through the Confederacy into Alabama, divided the theater into two immense sections, in each of which, east and west, were prizes sought by northern armies. If Richmond, the confederate capital, could be taken by a bold stroke, the moral effect would be electric of course. If a wedge could be driven down the Mississippi Valley to the Gulf, the Confederacy would be severed and the southwest cut off from the center of power. Moreover victories in the west were necessary to hold the wavering states of Kentucky and Missouri in line with the Union. All this was patent to Lincoln and his advisers and on such theories they started operations in both areas.

To the armies of the western arena, victory came first. In February, 1862, General Grant captured Fort Donelson on the Cumberland River, offering to his defeated foeman the ultimatum: "No terms except unconditional and immediate surrender." At Shiloh, Murfreesboro, Vicksburg, Chickamauga, Chattanooga, and other points desperate fighting occurred, with varying results, but with an unmistakable drift. Within little more than a year after the fall of Donelson, the Mississippi Valley was open to the Gulf. "The Father of Waters again goes unvexed to the sea!" exclaimed Lincoln when he heard of the surrender of Vicksburg on July 4, 1863. The initiative in the West had passed to the Union commanders who continued to hammer the wedge, making wider and wider the rift between the two sections of the Confederacy. In the autumn of the next year, Sherman was at Atlanta and soon on his devastating march to the sea. To the complaint against his ruthless severity, he had an emphatic answer: "War is hell!" On Christmas day, Savannah was in his hands; the ocean was open before him.

Contrasted with the successes in the West, Union operations in the East during the first two years of the war presented an almost unbroken series of misfortunes. Hurried into action against better counsels by the popular cry, "On to Richmond," the federal army rushed into the enemy's country in July, 1861, to meet a terrible disaster at Bull Run. For four years periodical advances were made on Richmond without important military results. General after general—McClellan, Pope, Burnside, Hooker, and Meade—was tried and found wanting; none could administer the fatal blow. Their highest achievements amounted to little more than successful defense. McClellan checked General Lee at Antietam in September, 1862; and Meade paralyzed his northward thrust at Gettysburg in July of the following year; but nothing decisive was accomplished. At last in February, 1864, Lincoln turned to General Grant whom he placed in command of the armies of the Union. After surveying the ground, the new military master, supported by unlimited supplies, commenced a pitiless drive on Lee's army in Virginia. Though every inch of ground was stubbornly contested, the relentless pressure told in the end. Richmond fell, the Confederacy collapsed, Lee surrendered at Appomattox on April 9, 1865. The war was over.

To this outcome the contest on the sea, though less dramatic than that on the land, bore a vital relation. There, too, the task was cut out by remorseless fact: the South, an agricultural region, was largely dependent upon Europe for manufactured goods and in turn had to pay its bills in cotton and other raw materials. Once more, therefore, the sea power loomed large on the horizon of those who weighed national destinies. Quick to perceive it, Lincoln, on April 19, 1861, proclaimed a blockade against southern ports and, to make his order more effective, proceeded to increase the naval forces depleted by neglect. As time moved on, the iron grip of the northern patrol upon the sea-borne trade of the Confederacy grew tense. Only once within the four years was the blockade in serious peril—in the spring of 1862 when the confederate ironclad, the Merrimac, steamed out into Hampton Roads, crushed two federal vessels as if they were paper, and spread consternation far and wide in the Union ranks. At that very moment, however, a northern ironclad, the Monitor, was ready for the test and met it, ending the depredations of the Merrimac. A new epoch in sea fighting was opened; the success of the blockade was assured; the fate of the Confederacy was sealed.

Day and night, through winter and summer, the war vessels of the Union patrolled the coast, performing a relentless routine that was only now and then enlivened by an exciting chase when a blockade runner hove in sight. Though many adventurers, European and southern, equipped swift ships and risked lives and fortunes trying to break the cordon, the unresting vigilance of the federal navy steadily raised the hazards of the game. In 1860, the value of the cotton exported amounted to about two hundred million dollars; two years later it had fallen to four millions. Correlatively the foreign trade of the Confederacy in commodities of every kind was also cut to trifling proportions. Near the end of its career, the Richmond government could not get enough high-grade paper for its bonds and notes or enough iron to keep up the tracks and rolling stock of its railways. Southern businessmen no doubt showed great energy and capacity in building plants and furnishing supplies but they could not repair the industrial neglect of two centuries during the four years of the war.

The armed combat which called forth so much heroism and sacrifice was accompanied by all those darker manifestations of the human spirit that always mark great wars: corruption in high places, cold and cynical profiteering, extravagance, and heartless frivolity. Before six months had passed, the air of Washington was murky with charges of fraud. "We are going to destruction as fast as imbecility, corruption, and the wheels of time can carry us," said a discouraged Senator. A congressional investigation revealed startling facts: contractors had made fat profits; they had charged outrageous prices; they had deliberately cheated the government by the delivery of inferior goods. The trail led in the direction of the War Department; thereupon Lincoln removed the Secretary, a machine politician from Pennsylvania, and with a touch of poetic justice sent him as minister to the court of the Tsar. An eminent authority estimated that from one-fifth to one-fourth of the money paid out of the federal treasury was tainted with the tricks of swindlers.

Troubles of the same nature plagued the South. Richmond newspapers were full of complaints about robberies by "official rogues." A Georgia editor lamented that "quartermasters and commissaries grew rich by speculation and robbery." In fact allegations of this type became so numerous that the confederate congress enacted a special law against knavery in the bureaus charged with buying war materials. But apparently the disease could not be stamped out; for one competent southern writer attributed the downfall of the Confederacy to the curse of corruption. Men of more moderate temper on both sides ascribed the evils that worried their respective governments more to inefficient administration than to the inordinate rapacity of merchants and capitalists.

Notwithstanding the poverty of the Richmond government, chances to make huge profits and live on the fat of the land were also abundant in the South. Blockade-running presented prizes especially tempting: one ship alone yielded to her owners seven hundred per cent profit before she was captured. Some of the railways paid dividends ranging from thirty to sixty per cent and politicians waxed rich from army contracts. "The passion for speculation," cried President Davis in 1863, "has seduced citizens of all classes from a determined prosecution of the war to a sordid effort to amass money." Though the curtailment of foreign commerce made it difficult to import European finery, editors daily lamented that, while confederate soldiers were dying for the lack of medicines, the shops of the cities made more extensive displays of foreign fabrics than ever before.

Over against stories of profiteering and luxurious displays were equally insistent tales of poverty and suffering among the working classes. It is easy to pile up illustrations from the daily press. To be sure, the wages of skilled artisans, especially in the North, rose rapidly and gross figures were often cited to silence the mutter of misery; but a scientific study of the facts long afterward showed conclusively that earnings did not keep pace with commodities and that the loud protests of factory operatives had a basis in reality. As a matter of course also the prices of agricultural produce shot upward but they did not tally in any way with the cost of the manufactured goods which the farmers had to buy. On the whole therefore the balance tipped sharply in favor of the entrepreneur. Prices were not checked by government intervention; loose buying in huge quantities for war purposes tended to push them still higher; while rich winnings escaped heavy taxation to pay current bills. In the general ruin at the end, southern profiteers lost most of their ill-gotten gains but northern capitalism certainly grew fat on Caesar's meat.

All the passions of the war inevitably got into politics, giving intensity to emotions naturally bitter enough. Never for an instant was Lincoln allowed to forget politics, either by his followers or by his opponents. At the outset, he was simply besieged by office-seekers. "I seem like one sitting in a palace, assigning apartments to importunate applicants while the structure is on fire and likely soon to perish in ashes," he said in his direct way a short time after his inauguration; and until the last shadows fell, job hunters asking for places in the administration and in the army tormented his waking hours. Nearly every action, civil or military, had to be taken with reference to politics. No matter what he did, Lincoln came under the censure of editors who had no respect for the bounds of propriety. On one occasion, a New York paper went so far as to inquire: "Mr. Lincoln, has he or has he not an interest in the profits of public contracts?" and then without giving any evidence, answered its own query in the affirmative. Members of his Cabinet esteemed him lightly and thought themselves far wiser than he; one of them, Chase, Secretary of the Treasury, thought it not unworthy of his honor to carry on a lively backstairs campaign to wrest the presidency from Lincoln in 1864.

Attacked on all sides, Lincoln held true to his central idea of saving the Union and when the end of his first term arrived the Republicans decided that they would not "swap horses while crossing a stream." Taking the name Union Party as their title, they renominated Lincoln for President and selected as his associate a southern man, a Unionist from Tennessee, Andrew Johnson. Having to meet this call for an endorsement of the administration, northern Democrats, in their platform, denounced the war as a failure, advocated an immediate peace, and favored a restoration of the federal system—with slavery as before. Choosing as their candidate, General McClellan, who was in their eyes "a military hero," they tried to carry the country by means of drum and trumpet, expedients that had so often brought victory in the past.

But the answer of the people at the polls was decisive. The Republicans, besides reëlecting Lincoln, returned enough Senators and Representatives to force Congress to adopt the Thirteenth Amendment abolishing slavery forever within the jurisdiction of the United States. The war was to go on, therefore, until peace could be won by the sword. Thus the voters vindicated the great mystic in the White House, disclosing as if by some subtle instinct the fateful mission of their generation.

When at the close of the great tragedy, the statisticians came upon the scene to make their calculations, the world was astounded to read the record of the awful cost in blood and treasure. Comprehensive and accurate figures were not available and the most cautious estimates varied but there were gross totals that staggered the mind. On the northern side, the death roll contained the names of three hundred and sixty thousand men and the list of wounded who recovered two hundred and seventy-five thousand more. On the southern side, about two hundred and fifty thousand men had given their lives to the lost cause and an unknown number had been wounded. According to a conservative reckoning, therefore, six hundred thousand soldiers had paid the last full measure of devotion.

Neither the losses nor the costs of the war, not even the heroic deeds on the field of battle—so lovingly described in a thousand memoirs and histories—were after all the final phases of the great process that flowed through the years of the conflict and transformed American society. From one standpoint they were means to ends, ends that usually outran the purposes and visions of the masses who played their several rôles in that long drama. Viewed in the large, the supreme outcome of the civil strife was the destruction of the planting aristocracy which, with the aid of northern farmers and mechanics, had practically ruled the United States for a generation. A corollary to that result was the undisputed triumph of a new combination of power: northern capitalists and free farmers who emerged from the conflict richer and more numerous than ever. It was these irreducible facts, as already noted, that made the Civil War a social revolution.

And that revolution was thoroughgoing. Beyond a doubt the ruin of the planting class through the sweep of the war was more complete than the destruction of the clergy and the nobility in the first French cataclysm because the very economic foundations of the planting system, including slavery itself, were shattered in the course of events. In wide regions of the South, estates had been devastated by fire and pillage, buildings had decayed, tools and livestock had wasted away. The bonds and notes of the Confederacy had fallen worthless in the hands of their holders and there was little fluid capital available for the restoration of agriculture to its former high position. To pile calamity on calamity, the old debts due northern merchants and capitalists, long overdue indeed, could now be collected by distraint through the medium of the federal courts sustained by northern bayonets. To complete its ruin, the planting aristocracy was subjected to the military dominion of the triumphant orders ruling through Washington while its own leaders, with some exceptions, were excluded by law from places of trust and influence in their respective states as well as in the national government. Finally the new combination was supported by the emancipated bondmen into whose hands the ballot was thrust by the white victors.

A crucial stroke in this revolution—though by no means as significant as sometimes suggested—was the confiscation or, to use a more euphonious term, the abolition of the planter's property in labor. Whatever may be the ethical view of the transaction, its result was the complete destruction of about four billion dollars' worth of "goods" in the possession of slave owners without compensation—the most stupendous act of sequestration in the history of Anglo-Saxon jurisprudence. Even that was not drastic enough for some radicals. Extremists wanted to make the execution still more crushing by transferring to the slaves the estates they tilled but this was too much for the temper of those who directed the course of federal affairs in Washington.

While the planting class was being trampled in the dust—stripped of its wealth and political power—the capitalist class was marching onward in seven league boots. Under the feverish stimulus of war the timid army marshaled by Webster in support of the Constitution and Whig policies had been turned into a confident host, augmented in numbers by the thousands and tens of thousands who during the conflict made profits out of war contracts and out of the rising prices of manufactured goods. At last the economic structure of machine industry towered high above agriculture—a grim monument to the fallen captain, King Cotton. Moreover, the bonds and notes of the federal government, issued in its extremity, furnished the substance for still larger business enterprise. And the beneficent government, which had carefully avoided laying drastic imposts upon profits during the war, soon afterward crowned its generosity to capitalists by abolishing the moderate tax on incomes and shifting the entire fiscal burden to goods consumed by the masses.

To measurable accumulations were added legal gains of high economic value. All that two generations of Federalists and Whigs had tried to get was won within four short years, and more besides. The tariff, which the planters had beaten down in 1857, was restored and raised to the highest point yet attained. A national banking system was established to take the place of the institution abolished in 1811 by Jeffersonian Democracy and the second institution destroyed by Jacksonian Democracy in 1836. At the same time the policy of lavish grants from the federal treasury to aid internal improvements so necessary to commerce was revived in the form of imperial gifts to railway corporations; it was in the year of emancipation that the construction of the Pacific railway, opening the overland route to the trade of the Orient, was authorized by the Congress of the United States. With similar decisiveness, the federal land question which had long vexed eastern manufacturers was duly met; the Homestead Act of 1862, innumerable grants to railways, and allotments to the states in aid of agricultural colleges provided for the disposal of the public domain. As a counter stroke, the danger of higher wages, threatened by the movement of labor to the land, was partially averted by the Immigration Act of 1864—an extraordinary law which gave federal authorization to the importation of working people under terms of contract analogous to the indentured servitude of colonial times.

While all these positive advantages were being won by capitalists in the halls of Congress, steps were taken to restrain the state legislatures which had long been the seats of agrarian unrest. By the Fourteenth Amendment, proclaiming that no state should deprive any person of life, liberty or property without due process of law, the Supreme Court at Washington was granted constitutional power to strike down any act of any state or local government menacing to "sound" business policies. Finally the crowning result of the sacrifice, the salvation of the Union, with which so many lofty sentiments were justly associated, assured to industry an immense national market surrounded by a tariff wall bidding defiance to the competition of Europe.

While business enterprise received its share of the advantages accruing from the Second American Revolution, other elements in the combination of power effected in 1860—namely the free farmers of the West and the radical reformers of the East—also had their rewards. On the outbreak of the war, their old opponents on the land question were no longer in a position to dictate. The planters of the South were out of the political lists and northern mill owners, who had feared that free farms would lure away wage-workers, were shown the possibilities of a counterpoise in the promotion of alien immigration. If some were unconvinced by such reasoning, they could at least see that the agrarian element in the Republican party was too strong to be thwarted by the business wing. So eventually in 1862 the hard contest over the public domain came to an end with the passage of the Homestead Act which provided for the free distribution of land in lots of one hundred and sixty acres each to men and women of strong arms and willing hearts, prepared to till the soil. In this action, the appealing slogan, "Vote yourself a farm," was realized and before the ink of Lincoln's signature was dry the rush to the free land commenced.

To northern farmers who had no thought of going to the frontier, the war likewise brought marked advantages. Especially did the Mississippi Valley, former home of agrarian discontent and Jacksonian Democracy, reap immense gains in inflated prices paid for farm produce, in spite of the mounting cost of manufactured goods. At one time wheat rose to more than two dollars and a half a bushel and other commodities followed its flight. From overflowing coffers debt-burdened tillers of the soil who had once raged against the money-power now discharged their obligations in Greenback "legal tenders" received for the fruits of their labor. The more fortunate farmers collected large returns from rising land values, accumulated capital, and became stockholders in local railway and banking enterprises. For many years a prosperous farming class, tasting the sweets of profit, could look upon the new course of politics and pronounce it good. There was discontent, no doubt, and a reaction against industrialism was bound to come but the political union of 1860, though strained, was never successfully broken.

VII. THE TRIUMPH OF BUSINESS ENTERPRISE

THE Second American Revolution, while destroying the economic foundation of the slave-owning aristocracy, assured the triumph of business enterprise. As if to add irony to defeat, the very war which the planters precipitated in an effort to avoid their doom augmented the fortunes of the capitalist class from whose jurisdiction they had tried to escape. Through financing the federal government and furnishing supplies to its armies, northern leaders in banking and industry reaped profits far greater than they had ever yet gathered during four years of peace. When the long military struggle came to an end they had accumulated huge masses of capital and were ready to march resolutely forward to the conquest of the continent—to the exploitation of the most marvelous natural endowment ever bestowed by fortune on any nation.

History was repeating old patterns in a new and more majestic setting. In the development of every great civilization in the past, there had come to the top groups of rich and enterprising businessmen devoted to commerce, industry, and finance. The sources of their fortunes varied and their modes of acquisition differed from age to age, but they formed a dynamic element in every ancient society that passed beyond the primitive stage of culture and everywhere they advanced with deadly precision on the classes which derived their sustenance from agriculture. In the documents which record the rise of civilization in Egypt, Babylonia, and Persia and in the trading centers of Tyre, Sidon, and Carthage, the immense operations of businessmen can be traced, though priests, singers, poets, philosophers, and courtiers were the chief masters of the written word.

Even in Athens, acclaimed the cultural center of antiquity, the directors of trade and industry played a powerful rôle that can be discerned through the thick layers of clerical and classical tradition.

Nor were the noble Romans from Remus to Cicero merely engaged in demonstrating their excellence in law or their proficiency in arms. Long before the era of the republic had drawn to a close, the forum at the capital had become the center for the greatest network of commerce and finance that the genius of man had yet woven out of economic enterprise. When the ears of antiquarians are correctly attuned, they can hear the clank of the money-changer's metal above the measured periods of Marcus Aper, Cicero, and Julius Secundus.

As medieval civilization rose on the ruins of the Roman system, businessmen appeared once more at the center of things. The Italian fortunes that fertilized sources of letters and art in Venice, Florence, and Genoa and sustained the Renaissance, which in turn introduced the modern age, were made mainly by trade, barter, and industry.

When again a new epoch was opened by mechanical inventions, when Arkwright, Crompton, Watt, and Stephenson turned the medieval civilization upside down, the businessman rose to heights undreamed by his predecessors.

Compared with their historic forerunners, the triumphant businessmen of America had a freer field and a richer material endowment. Their planting opponents were laid lower in the dust by one revolutionary stroke than the nobility of France or the landed gentry of England by the upheavals which had broken their ranks. In the United States, no royal families, no great landed aristocracy, no heavily endowed clergy owned the forests, plains, and mountains where lay the natural resources so necessary to the development of business. More than one-half of the whole area of the country, to be exact, 1,048,111,608 acres, belonged to the government in 1860—a benevolent government in the hands of friends, ready to sell its holdings for a song, to give them away, or to let them pass by mere occupation. The rest belonged in large part to farmers and could be easily bought, leased, or rented for mineral exploitation. So no ancient titles, parchments, and seals prevented an enterprising individual from getting at the materials for his operations; vast mining royalties did not flow into the coffers of an opposing class to enrich it and give more substance to its power in the state. In short, much of the land for industrial exploitation could be had for the asking or at the price of a little political manipulation; the rest could be obtained in a fairly easy market.

Equally available were willing hands to develop the natural endowment. On the shores of the Old World stood a limitless supply of laborers, reared to manhood and womanhood at the expense of their mother countries, awaiting an opportunity to take part in the American advance; and competing steamship companies were now prepared to bring them across at a mere fraction of the passenger rate imposed by shipmasters in the days of Alexander Hamilton.

The American stage furnished by nature to businessmen for the fulfillment of their customary rôle was magnificent beyond comparison. Counting Alaska, it embraced 3,600,000 square miles—an area nearly equal to that of all Europe. Within the geographical limits of the domain beyond the Mississippi, the entire Roman Empire, so marvelously described in the first chapter of Gibbon's imperishable work, could be comfortably tucked.

There are, of course, good grounds for differences of opinion as to the names to be enrolled first in the peerage of the new industrial age;

yet none will exclude from it Jay Gould, William H. Vanderbilt, Collis P. Huntington, James J. Hill, and Edward H. Harriman of the railway principality; John D. Rockefeller of the oil estate; Andrew Carnegie of the steel demesne; Jay Cooke and J. Pierpont Morgan of the financial seigniory; William A. Clark of the mining appanage; or Philip D. Armour of the province of beef and pork. To draw the American scene as it unfolded between 1865 and the end of the century without these dominant figures looming in the foreground is to make a shadow picture; to put in the presidents and the leading senators—to say nothing of transitory politicians of minor rank—and leave out such prime actors in the drama is to show scant respect for the substance of life.

From a review of the American business peerage, it appears that the eleven men just named had so many things in common that they can be treated collectively. All were of north European stock, mainly English and Scotch-Irish; Gould alone, according to Henry Adams, showing a "trace of Jewish origin." The old planting aristocracy of the South furnished no major barons of business. Of the group here brought under examination only two, Morgan and Vanderbilt, built their fortunes on the solid basis of family inheritances while only one had what may be called by courtesy a higher education: Morgan spent two years in the University of Göttingen. Carnegie began life as a stationary engineer; Jay Cooke as a clerk in a general store in Sandusky; Jay Gould as a surveyor and tanner; Huntington, Armour, and Clark as husky lads on their fathers' farms; Hill as a clerk for a St. Paul steamboat company; Harriman as an office boy in a New York broker's establishment; and Rockefeller as a bookkeeper in Cleveland.

All but Carnegie, who was tinged with skepticism, were apparently church members in good and regular standing. Jay Cooke, his biographer tells us, was "a liberal patron of the Evangelical Christian Church and of those who preached its doctrine." He was a strict and conscientious observer of the Sabbath, displaying during the Civil War a great deal of anxiety about "the laxity of Lincoln and Grant on the Sunday question." In addition to setting apart one-tenth of the profits from his business for charitable uses, Cooke gave bells, steeples, organs, Sunday-school books, rectories, and silver communion services to churches, while bestowing generous subsidies on deserving ministers—at least until he was overwhelmed by bankruptcy. He taught a Sunday-school class at great personal sacrifice and, although he disliked ritualistic controversies, was loyal to the Episcopalian Church unto his death. His faith he summed up in the words: "We must all get down at the feet of Jesus and be taught by no one but Himself." Rockefeller was a no less active and devoted member of his church, the Baptist denomination. Armour gave liberally to a non-sectarian Sunday school. Hill, though a Protestant, settled more than half a million dollars upon a Catholic seminary, thinking that the papal organization was best fitted for the task of bringing immigrant workingmen under civic discipline in America. "What will be their social view, their political action, their moral status, if that single controlling force should be removed?" he once asked in cautious tones. Morgan seems to have been reticent on religious as well as other matters but his semi-official "Life" shows him contributing generously to the Episcopalian Church of which he was a consistent member.

Above all else, the new economic barons were organizers of men and materials—masters of the administrative art—who saw with penetrating eyes the wastes and crudities of the competitive system in industry and transportation. Possessed of a luminous imagination they could think imperially of world-spanning operations that lifted them above the petty moralities of the village-smith or of the corner-grocer. In coöperation with tireless workers in science and invention, they wrought marvels in large-scale production, bringing material comfort to millions of people who never could have wrung them barehanded from the hills and forests. "Two pounds of ironstone mined upon Lake Superior," to use a single illustration, "and transported nine hundred miles to Pittsburgh; one pound and one-half of coal, mined and manufactured into coke, and trans-ported to Pittsburgh; one half-pound of lime, mined and transported to Pittsburgh; a small amount of manganese ore mined in Virginia and brought to Pittsburgh—and these four pounds of materials manufactured into one pound of steel, for which the consumer pays one cent." With natural pride did Andrew Carnegie, the recorder of this achievement, put it among the wonders of the world. Compared with the complicated Pittsburgh operation, the deeds of the pyramid builders—who merely commanded under the lash armies of slaves to drag by brute force huge blocks of stone into one enormous pile—sink into banalities, inviting respect neither for the intelligence displayed nor for the object in view.

In this development industry had moved swiftly through three stages. The little old-fashioned mill on the river's bank turned by a lumbering water wheel, marking the first step in machine manufacture, had given way to the immense plant driven by engines or turbines of gigantic power. Then in turn the isolated establishment under the ownership of a single master or a few masters had surrendered to the corporation. At the end of the century three-fourths of the manufactured products came from factories owned by associations of stockholders; in each great in-dustry was a network of federated plants under corporate direction; by 1890 combination was the supreme concept of the industrial magnate. Oil products, iron, steel, copper, lead, sugar, coal, and other staples were then in the hands of huge organizations that constituted, if not monopo-lies, efficient masters of their respective fields. During the following decade, the work of affiliation went forward with feverish haste, cul-minating in the billion dollar United States Steel Corporation of 1901.

Since generalizations about the barons of capitalist enterprise give but a pale and colorless picture of their cyclopean operations, one con-crete and detailed analysis seems worth a volume of miscellanies. And the best example of all is offered by the oil business, for in its development is illustrated in clear and vivid outline the whole gigantic process—industrial, political, and legal—which followed the overthrow of the planters and revolutionized the heritage bequeathed by Washington, Jefferson, and Jackson. In the unfolding of this single industry, we see modern science, invention, business acumen, economic imagination, and capacity for world enterprise at work creating material goods and organizing human services to supply not only every nook and cranny of this country but the uttermost parts of the earth with useful commodities of a high standard.

In the record of this industry lies the story of aggressive men, akin in spirit to military captains of the past, working their way up from the ranks, exploiting natural resources without restraint, waging economic war on one another, entering into combinations, making immense fortunes, and then, like successful feudal chieftains or medieval merchants, branching out as patrons of learning, divinity, and charity. Here is a chronicle of highly irregular and sometimes lawless methods, ruthless competition, menacing intrigues, and pitiless destruction of rivals. Private companies organize armed guards and wage pitched battles over the possession of rights of way for pipe lines. Men ordinarily honest are seen slinking about in the cover of night to destroy property and intimidate persons who refuse to obey their orders. Agreements are made with railway companies to obtain secret rebates on shipments of oil and, what is more astounding, rebates on the shipments of rival concerns. Newspapers are purchased; editors are hired to carry on propaganda and to traduce respectable citizens whose sole offense is the desire to handle an independent business. The most astute counsel, occupying conspicuous positions in public service and social esteem, are employed to sustain the rights of defendants in litigation.

In the same chronicle, the relations of economics and politics are unfolded. The sources of attacks on trusts are exposed. Combinations and their enemies are seen operating in legislatures and courts, drawing lawmakers, governors, and judges into one structural pattern. Bribery, intrigue, and threats are matched by blackmail until the closest observer often fails to discover where honor begins and corruption ends. Public policies, lawmaking, and judicial reasoning become unintelligible except in relation to the interests of oil producers, shippers, and refiners.

Meanwhile, as this running warfare goes on from year to year, the production, refining, shipment, and selling of oil concentrate in the hands of one gigantic combination. Legislatures assail it; courts declare it dissolved; but its economic power is steadily augmented. And all through this drama, from the start, dishonesty, chicane, lying, vulgarity, and a fierce passion for lucre are united with an intelligence capable of constructing immense agencies for economic service to the public and a philanthropic spirit that pours out money for charitable, religious, educational, and artistic plans and purposes.

With the high velocity that marked the advance of manufacturing and the extractive industries, the system of transportation passed through many phases during this period. Naturally the first railroad builders had concentrated their efforts on short lines between important cities, such as Baltimore and Washington, Philadelphia and Reading, Boston and Springfield, New York and New Haven; for the prospects of profitable business on such roads were good, the terrain offered no great obstacles, the capital could be obtained with relative ease. By 1860, nearly all the important cities of the East were connected by one or more tracks and the railway leaders were taking up the next obvious task: that of uniting short lines and forming continental projects. Indeed by that time the chief seaboard cities were already linked with Chicago and St. Louis by various systems and the call for the advance to the Pacific was heard in the land.

This movement the Civil War expedited rather than checked. During the gloomiest days of the conflict, as we have seen, Congress gave a strong impetus to it by authorizing railway companies to bridge the gap between the Atlantic and the Pacific. That undertaking, pushed with lightning speed, heralded still more magnificent adventures. Congress now granted public lands to railway corporations in imperial domains; states, cities, and counties bonded themselves for staggering debts to get rail connections; farmers and merchants along projected lines invested their savings in securities; and European capitalists were induced to take heavy risks. Sustained by lavish financial backing, construction and consolidation swept on at a magic pace up and down the continent.

Fifteen years after the completion of the first road to California, the Southern Pacific had linked New Orleans with the Coast; the Atchison, Topeka and Sante Fé had united the waters of the Mississippi with the Western Ocean; and the Northern Pacific had cut a path from the Great Lakes to Puget Sound. By 1890, America had 163,562 miles of railways, more than all Europe had and indeed nearly half the mileage of the world. At that date, the nominal capital represented by the business had reached a total of almost ten billion dollars or about one-sixth of the estimated national wealth—easily twice the value of all the slaves on whose labor the planting aristocracy of the South had once built its political power. Moreover the process of consolidation had gone so far that seventy-five companies, out of about sixteen hundred, dominated more than two-thirds of all the mileage in the country.

Notwithstanding the high degree of concentration thus attained, there was evidently room for still greater confederacies, promising returns still more colossal to their architects. Besides the lure of larger profits, the casualties of competition were driving railway promoters to seek closer affiliations; rate cutting, rebating, and promoters' wars, coupled with periodical panics, had brought financial difficulties even to the strongest lines. Only one American railroad listed on the London Exchange in 1889 was paying dividends on its common stock; within less than fifteen years more than four hundred companies, representing two and a half billions in capital, had perished in bankruptcy.

It was such calamities, no less than colossal ambitions, that moved the empire builders, like Morgan, Harriman and Hill, to attack the problem of unification, thereby opening a new era in transportation. Certainly it was just such economic anarchy that brought the first of these three giants to the conclusion in 1885 that he must "do something about the railroads" and led him in the short space of seventeen years to gather under his control thirteen systems having a mileage of fifty-five thousand and a capital of three billion. With the same volcanic energy and feudal ruthlessness Harriman united thousands of miles under his sovereignty and was in a fair way to encircle the globe when death overcame him. He made his most daring stroke in combining the Union Pacific and the Southern Pacific—more than fifteen thousand miles—and he had his eyes on Siberia when the long shadows closed upon him.

The work of the railway men, like that of the oil magnates, involved political complications; but the former, compelled to deal with organized farmers and manufacturers, were subjected to a control far more stringent than that imposed upon the oil interests. In fact they were harassed almost beyond endurance, so they thought, by the hue and cry of shippers and travelers and threatened on all sides by prosecutions under the Sherman Anti-Trust law enacted in 1890.

Even Morgan and Hill, powerful as they were, could not escape political entanglements. After effecting a vast consolidation of the Northern Pacific, the Great Northern, and the Chicago, Burlington and Quincy under the Northern Securities Company chartered in New Jersey, they found themselves face to face with the redoubtable Theodore Roosevelt in the White House, a man who genuinely loved a good fight. "If we have done anything wrong," said Morgan to the President, "send your man (meaning Attorney-General Knox) to my man (naming one of his lawyers) and they can fix it up." But Morgan was not now dealing with Grover Cleveland. Roosevelt replied: "That can't be done"; and pressed the suit until the Supreme Court in 1904 by a decision of five to four declared the merger illegal. "It really seems hard," complained Hill on hearing the outcome, "when we look back upon what we have done . . . that we should be compelled to fight for our lives against political adventurers who have never done anything but pose and draw a salary."

Faced always by the danger of dissolution at the hands of the government, subjected to the rule of "reason" in fixing rates, and compelled to deal with national trade unions in arranging wage schedules, promoters and organizers in the railway sphere at length found the range of their activities materially limited. Moreover the collapse of many a grand structure, such as the New York, New Haven and Hartford system, bringing sickening losses to "innocent investors," intensified the rising hostility of the public in every direction and drew the net of official control still tighter. With the pleasures and profits of the game abated and its hazards raised, railway construction and consolidation were brought almost to a standstill.

Yet the evils of disjointed and conflicting lines inadequate to the requirements of national transportation remained painfully manifest— so impressive to the doubting Thomases among manufacturers and farmers that Congress in the Railway Act of 1920 actually sought to encourage more and greater railway federations under government supervision. By that time the capital of the lines, real and fictitious, was set down at more than twenty billion dollars.

With the consolidation of industries and railways and the necessary financial maneuvers went a fundamental shift of economic authority from promoters to financiers. In the old days of petty industry, the master of each plant extended his operations by means of his savings and profits, supplemented occasionally by loans from local bankers. The latter stood, so to speak, on the edge of the industrial realm; the isolated bank, employing neighborhood savings and deposits, served the isolated plant. In those more primitive times, opportunities for investment were limited mainly to government bonds and the stocks of minor canal, turnpike, industrial, shipping, and railway concerns; accumulations of capital were small and the area of speculation, except in public lands, was narrowly bounded. It was perfectly natural, therefore, that local sovereignty in industry should be associated with states' rights in banking politics; that attempts of Federalists and Whigs to force the barriers of tomorrow by creating a permanent national banking system should be effectively blocked by the Democratic party.

Broadly speaking, such was the state of affairs when the Civil War broke rudely in upon the old order, setting in train forces that changed the face of things within a few years. The very financing of the conflict itself taught countless thousands, through public drives and the ownership of "baby bonds," the mysteries of interest and saving while the profits of war manufacturers furnished vast reservoirs of active capital seeking general investment, thus amalgamating local publics into a national public. Far from stopping at the close of the military struggle this process was quickened by the sale of securities for the building of continental railways supported by national credit, which in turn paved the way for the sale of securities issued by distant industrial corporations.

As such transactions multiplied and opportunities to amass new capital by the manipulation of paper increased, the New York Stock Exchange raised its economic forum to the position of an all-American tribunal. Thus localism in finance broke down and the banks of the strategic cities, meeting the new demand, began to operate on a national scale, somewhat as the Bank of the United States was operating when destroyed by Jackson's farmer-labor party. It was to their hoardings, to their stock and bond departments, that promoters of railways and industrial corporations now had to turn for assistance; and in the course of time bankers learned that they could in reality become masters of the economic scene—were in some measure forced to assume that rôle. If industrial magnates could visit them, they could pay visits in return. In the exchange of courtesies, it was soon discovered that the weapon of the hour was finance and that the possession of the weapon had passed to the bankers.

With financial control, managerial sovereignty was transferred from the operators of industries and railways to the directors of capital accumulations—a fact illustrated in a striking fashion when Morgan brought about the union of fifteen great railway organizations and created a steamship trust, a harvester trust, the United States Steel Corporation, and numerous other combinations less pretentious in scope. By the end of the century the government of American railways and staple industries, with exceptions of course, had been lost by the men who had grown up in the roundhouses and the mills through all the technical processes. On the whole, the high command in the empire of business was now in the hands of great banking corporations, and captains of industry were as a rule no longer evolved by natural selection; they were chosen by the dominant bankers who served as financial guardians.

And these dominant bankers were so united by treaties of alliance and by conversations, to use the language of diplomacy, that the boundaries of their respective dominions were difficult to delimit. In 1911, Morgan's semi-official biographer, after enumerating the giant banks under his sovereignty, placed his total banking power at more than a billion dollars and the assets of the railway and industrial corporations under his paramount influence at ten billions. About the same time, the authority on trusts, John Moody, recorded that two mammoth financial complexes —the Morgan and Rockefeller interests—had gathered under their suzerainty a network of enterprises which constituted "the heart of the business and commercial life of the nation."

Of course there was always warfare on the borders of this new Roman empire; novel industries were continually springing up with the progress of invention; and minor princelings and earls, as long as they restrained their pretensions, enjoyed a high degree of local autonomy. But new enterprises of any moment found it hard, if not almost impossible, to obtain a foothold without paying tribute to the grand seigneurs; certainly no large issue of stocks and bonds could be floated in defiance of their orders.

By the end of the nineteenth century the hegemony of American financiers was supreme at home and they were ready for foreign conquests. It was in 1899 that Morgan and Company floated the first significant foreign loan ever issued in America, the bonds of the Mexican republic. This was followed in two years by a fifty million loan to the government of Great Britain to help pay the expenses of conquering the Boer republics. Soon after this came another opportunity, the Russo-Japanese War; while the Tsar's agents were begging and borrowing in Paris and London, fiscal agents of Tokyo, in dire straits for money, were copiously supplied by New York banking houses until the danger point was reached. So American capital contributed to the extension of English supremacy in

Africa and Japanese supremacy over Manchuria. A little later with the aid of President Roosevelt, China was forced to grant American bankers a share in a fifty million dollar loan negotiated with Germany, France, and England; the House of Morgan floated it. In the meantime American capital directed by New York bankers poured down into the Caribbean, making smooth the path of American dominion there.

Roads from four continents now ran to the new Appian Way—Wall Street—and the pro-consuls of distant provinces paid homage to a new sovereign. The land of Washington, Franklin, Jefferson, and John Adams had become a land of millionaires and the supreme direction of its economy had passed from the owners of farms and isolated plants and banks to a few men and institutions near the center of its life.

VIII. THE RISE OF THE NATIONAL LABOR MOVEMENT

INHERING in the onward flow of stubborn facts which shook to pieces the planting aristocracy and assured the triumph of business enterprise were the inevitable factors foreseen by southern statesmen—a growing army of wage workers haunted by poverty, an increasing solidarity among skilled craftsmen, and periodical uprisings of labor in industry and politics. While vainly attempting to stem the course of machine production and natural science, Calhoun had warned his countrymen against their fated fruits. "It is useless to disguise the fact," he announced from his place in the Senate while Lincoln was yet a young man. "There is and always has been in an advanced stage of wealth and civilization a conflict between capital and labor. . . . We have, in fact, but just entered upon that condition of society where the strength and durability of our political institutions are to be tested."

Within little more than a decade after Lincoln's death, to be precise in 1877—the very year in which the last northern bayonet was withdrawn from the capital of Calhoun's state—the social order of the victors was threatened by a violent railway strike stretching from Pennsylvania to Texas. More years rolled on and the Congress of the United States, under the command of labor leaders sitting in the gallery with stop watches in their hands, dictated to the owners of railways the hours of work for their trainmen. And a successor of Thomas Jefferson signed the bill.

Business enterprise quickened into life by the demand for military supplies [in the Civil War] called to loom and forge and throttle thousands of new laborers from the farms of America and from the fields and shops of the Old World, unorganized, unacquainted with trade union principles, and frequently accustomed to low economic standards. Financing its armies mainly by bond issues and inflated currency, without taking effective action to control prices in any sphere, the federal government allowed the cost of living to shoot skyward like a rocket. It cannot be denied that wages moved in the direction of prices but they lagged far behind and at no time during the armed conflict did they fairly correspond with the level of commodities or place labor in the happy realm of those who gathered great fortunes from the necessities of the perilous hour. If the war assured employment, it also raised the cost of everything the workers had to buy and sharpened their struggle for existence.

To meet a crisis of this kind labor was ill-prepared. In 1861, only a few of the standard crafts were organized into unions, amalgamated on a national scale, able to lay down terms in the market place. More than that, there was among the unions so organized no common association to operate throughout the country, no federation of all organized labor to give solidarity to opinion and power to demands. It was not until rising prices began to pinch severely and the closing of the war began to send wages down, that working people, driven by hardships, commenced to draw together in large bodies. Between 1861 and 1865 the number of local unions multiplied nearly fourfold; at the end of the decade, the number of strategic crafts nationally organized had risen to at least thirty, claiming a total strength of more than two hundred thousand enrolled members.

Keeping pace with the prosaic process of forming local and national trade unions, though often unconnected with it, ran a series of industrial struggles which menaced the structure of the capitalist system and seemed about to fulfill at times the prophecy of the planters that another irrepressible conflict would plague the victors. In 1873, while the hero of Appomattox was still President of the United States, a devastating panic arrived, scattering unemployment, poverty, and bitterness of soul in its wake. Late in the following year the anthracite regions of Pennsylvania were terrorized by crimes of violence which threatened the social order of the state. During the boom which accompanied the Civil War those districts had been flooded by unskilled laborers, many of whom were homeless and reckless characters; and mining had been carried on in feverish haste under conditions that made the lot of slaves on Jefferson Davis's plantation seem pleasant by comparison. Though efforts to organize regular unions with a view to raising standards had failed, secret societies, known as the Molly Maguires, sprang up in the leading anthracite centers, followed by numerous outrages in which mine owners, foremen, and bosses were cruelly beaten, in some cases murdered in cold blood.

For months this terror reigned, defeating all attempts to ferret out the guilty, until by prolonged intrigue a detective wormed his way into the inner ring, and in 1875 sprang a deadly trap, revealing the operations of the conspirators, and sending several to the gallows and others to prison. When duly unfolded at the trial of the criminals, the story proved to be a curious mixture of industrial strife and private revenge, forming an important episode in the relations of capital and labor, a phase of a raw and unrelieved war over the distribution of wealth, comparable in its lawlessness, though more cruel, to the physical contests that took place between capitalists sparring for supremacy in the early days of oil and railway consolidation.

In the midst of the excitement over the Molly Maguires came a far more ominous struggle—a railway strike that involved more than one hundred thousand workers, paralyzed nearly all the lines between the Atlantic coast and the Mississippi, and reached out into allied industries. This explosion, like the upheaval in the anthracite districts, had been long in gathering and before it was over made manifest all the elements common to modern industrial conflicts. It opened in a determined resistance to falling prices. After the collapse of the war inflation in the devastating panic of 1873, railway companies began to reduce wages by successive orders, ending in the summer of 1877 with a horizontal cut of ten per cent, apparently effected by concert. In connection with the wage reductions, many managers, plainly declaring their intention to smash trade unions, adopted the practice of discharging without ceremony all the men who dared to serve on grievance committees. On the other side, the Brotherhood of Locomotive Engineers, founded in 1863, made rapid progress in organizing highly skilled engine drivers and in lining up brakemen, conductors, and trackmen until by 1875 it could boast of fifty thousand members, a reserve fund of a million dollars, and many a decree dictated to railway presidents in minor disputes.

To the fuel for a conflagration already collected, a match was applied on July 17, 1877, when some employees of the Baltimore and Ohio, having appealed in vain to the company for relief from a cut in their wages, stopped work and called upon their comrades to prevent the movement of trains. Apparently without prearrangement and without any active direction from the officials of the Brotherhood, the strike spread rapidly all over the East.

Cessation of work was followed by the mobilization of the state militia at strategic centers, and the appearance of the state militia was frequently in turn a herald of open warfare. In Baltimore nine strikers and bystanders were killed soon after the soldiers came upon the scene. In Pittsburgh a regular pitched battle was fought; when the militiamen marched into the midst of the assembled strikers, they encountered a resistance which developed into a guerrilla war ending in several deaths and the destruction of the railway station, roundhouses, and hundreds of freight cars, causing losses running into the millions. The striking workmen of Columbus made a tour of the city, using intimidation to close industrial plants on every side. At Buffalo and Reading, skirmishes with the militia resulted in many casualties. In Chicago, where the police tried to break up a meeting of strikers in the streets, an all-day battle took place in which nineteen persons were killed and a large number wounded. When a huge crowd of labor sympathizers jeered and challenged the police in St. Louis, the latter retaliated by arresting all the trade union delegates mobilized at the central labor hall to discuss the situation. Even far away on the Pacific Coast were heard echoes of the strife as workers and vigilant committees came into combat.

For two weeks this nation-wide struggle between strikers and soldiers continued, until finally the militia, supplemented at many points by federal troops, succeeded in getting the upper hand. The governor of Pennsylvania, for example, by sending a detachment of armed men over the railway between Philadelphia and Pittsburgh and by threatening "a sharp use of the bayonet and musket," set trains in motion to the West. By similar methods in course of time the strike was broken everywhere, forcing most of the workers to resume their places at reduced wages or on the former terms.

This deadly grapple between capital and labor, the most serious and most extensive in the history of the country, exhibited in its progress the gravest aspects of economic warfare. On the one side, the railway managers declared that they would not allow labor to lay down the law to them, asserting that wage reductions were made necessary by the state of business. On their side, labor men replied that they would not submit to dictation by the managers, that their wages were below the point of decent existence, that the railway companies, besides watering their stocks, had been guilty of perpetrating frauds on the public, and that railway directors rode about the country in luxurious private cars proclaiming their inability to pay living wages to hungry working men.

According to a judicious reporter who surveyed the field during this conflict, all the elements usually arrayed against capitalists were found in action: railway strikers, miners, and other industrial workers in various parts of the country whose wages were "oppressively low," trade unionists in general who naturally sympathized with their brethren at war, communists who hoped "for no immediate benefit from the strike unless it should lead to a general social revolution and disruption of property tenures," idle laborers of the tramp class accepting temporary jobs as strike-breakers; and the criminal fringe rejoicing in any disorder offering an opportunity for revenge and robbery. Every engine of agitation was also employed. While the strike was in progress, "knots of men gathered in all the large towns and industrial sections to listen to harangues upon the oppressions of capital, the social revolution, and the labor republic." At a monster mass meeting held under socialist auspices in Tompkins Square, New York City, on the evening of July 25, eight or ten thousand people cheered impassioned speeches by labor orators; and this was followed the next night by a similar gathering in Cooper Union under trade union management.

In the course of the warfare the public was deluged by propaganda. Whenever a fray ended in bloodshed, the press published charges and countercharges of the kind that have since become familiar items in the records of industrial conflicts. According to the employers, the strikers were guilty of starting each riot. According to the strikers, the blame rested on the militia and the proof lay in the fact that nearly all the deaths were among the ranks of workmen. Popular sympathy for labor was enlisted by pictures of starving women and children. Appeals were made on behalf of the suffering, collections for them were taken at public meetings, and farmers sent food from their fields by the wagon load.

In no small measure the industrial disputes associated with the advance of capitalism were due to the flat refusal of employers to recognize labor organization as an inescapable outcome of the economic process and to accept collective bargaining as a peaceful mode of reaching agreements on hours and wages. During the contest of 1877, the uncompromising resolve of the leading railway managers to brook no interference with their business helped to precipitate the strike and then to embitter the warfare that ensued. The same factor weighed heavily in the Homestead affair of 1892 and still more heavily in the convulsive struggle at Chicago two years afterward. Although the capitalists of nearly every great industry had by that time protected themselves by combinations against falling prices and the stress of competition—against the law of supply and demand—neither they nor their spokesmen were willing, as a rule, to concede to labor the same right or necessity.

In their opposition to collective bargaining, they were supported by many learned economists who, after more or less research, discovered that trade unions violated the natural right of men to buy and sell labor and "other commodities" to the best possible advantage.

To all political economists, however, these infallible dogmas were not as plainly revealed. At Johns Hopkins University, for instance, Richard T. Ely, fresh from long and laborious studies in the Old World, was teaching historical rather than pontifical economics; and in his book on the American labor movement issued in 1886, he seemed to recognize in the formation of trade unions a drift of things quite as decisive as the facts covered by Sumner's prelatical dicta. And one of his associates, John R. Commons, much to the dismay of several college presidents, was distributing the news abroad that the organization of labor was as natural as flowing water —a means of raising the standard of life for the masses and a procedure worthy of approval in polite society.

The way being thus broken, other recruits from the middle classes joined the pioneer professors in asserting that employers should recognize unions and accept the practice of collective bargaining. "I believe in strikes. I believe also in the conservative value of the organization from which strikes come," declared the eminent Episcopal Bishop, Henry Codman Potter, in 1902. Sentiment was suffusing iron law, in spite of all the warnings.

By that time the National Civic Federation, composed of capitalists, labor leaders, and professional people, and dedicated to the fostering of harmony between organized capital and organized labor had begun to function. Marcus A. Hanna, master in industry, finance, and politics, had joined it and was pointing out what seemed to be the handwriting on the wall. Once outlawed and hunted to its lair, trade unionism was now mounting high on its dusty way toward reputability. The president of the American Federation of Labor had the support of many professors and was dining with magnates in New York. There were Mirabeaus of industrial democracy at the court of capitalism.

IX. THE TRIPLE REVOLUTION IN AGRICULTURE

TRIUMPHANT business enterprise, with its rush and roar of train and mill, its ostentatious display of overtopping riches, and its convulsive struggles with organized labor, gave the dominant tone to the intellectual and moral notes of the nineteenth century's closing decades, leading those who cast horoscopes in the national watchtower to neglect the quiet places of the countryside. Nothing could have been more natural. The great fortunes of the new bourgeois were heaped up in the urban centers where their retainers and vassals gathered to serve them. Of necessity, the culture that wealth attracted and fostered took on the flavor of the metropolis rather than the country house. In the cities were the industries and their hordes of employees, the newspapers, writers, publishers, libraries, parliaments, forums of discussion, and makers of opinion.

What is more, there was not, and never had been, in the United States a landed aristocracy exactly comparable to the social orders of that type in other civilizations. But in America, as we have said, there never had been any such class dominant throughout the country. Practically all the soil of New England and the Middle States was divided into relatively small farms, owned by the freeholders who tilled them, the handful of great proprietors in the Hudson River Valley forming an exception of diminishing importance. Though embracing many families of seasoned stock and long monopolizing the politics of the section, the landed gentry of the South never had a capital of concentration comparable to Rome, Berlin, Paris, London, or Tokyo and after the Second American Revolution the whole class lay prostrate before victorious capitalism.

And yet, through the furious years of the commercial development that followed the Civil War, American agriculture, so little noticed in the writings of philosophers and economists, underwent a transformation hardly less dynamic than the revolution that overtook manufacturing and transportation; and remained at the end of the century a productive estate of the highest importance for the whole of American civilization. While the cities were growing like magic, the countryside was also growing in strength. The total population of the United States in 1850 was less than thirty millions; the first census of the twentieth century reported more than fifty millions living on farms or in villages sustained by agriculture.

America had not yet, like England, devoured her farms—drawn three-fourths of her people into industrial cities. Neither had her felicity become primarily contingent upon the casualties and caprices of foreign and imperial trade or in any respect dependent on the sale of gray shirtings to savages in Africa or Brummagem trinkets to them that sit in darkness. Until near the end of the century, the domestic market maintained by agriculture, with farming people as great purchasers, absorbed practically all the products of American mills and mines.

In short, the expansion of agriculture almost paralleled the expansion of industry. During the era that lay between Lincoln's first election and the outbreak of the [first] World War, the mere increase in the number of farms was more than twice the total number of homesteads and plantations brought under cultivation between the landing of the Pilgrims and the victory of the Illinois rail-splitter at the polls. In round numbers, there were two million farms in the United States in 1860; fifty years afterward there were more than six million.

Comparatively speaking, the new farming homesteads added to the national heritage in the age of business enterprise were alone greater in number than all the industrial workers enrolled upon the books of the American Federation of Labor at the moment of its supremest strength. Expressed in terms of area, the additional farms brought under cultivation embraced over three hundred million acres of improved land or a dominion larger than the productive area of France and Germany combined. During that span of years the output of wheat rose from 173,000,000 bushels to nearly 700,000,000 bushels—one-sixth the total crop of the world.

Frequently overlooked by those who imagined that prosperity and power were the fruits of urban genius alone, agriculture in reality furnished the nutriment for flourishing industry and profoundly altered the relations of the United States with the countries of the Old World. Produce from the farms supplied huge quantities of freight for the railways, thus becoming one of the main supports for that important branch of American capitalism. It fed the armies of factory workers and by a rising purchasing power steadily enlarged the demand for the commodities they manufactured. It yielded materials for domestic packing and canning industries and tonnage for fleets of merchant vessels in the seven seas. A heavy element in the discharge of American debts to European capitalists, it thus aided in the rapid promotion of economic independence for the United States.

While heaping its produce higher and higher, American agriculture underwent a triple revolution no less Sibylline in its social implications than the conquest of manufacture by science and the machine. First of all, this era of triumphant progress in agriculture witnessed the dissolution of the slave-owning aristocracy—a landed estate—with a correlative influence on Negroes, white farmers, southern economy, and national politics. Next, it saw the long process of colonization and settlement opened at Jamestown in 1607 brought to a close by the exhaustion of the arable land on the far frontier with its sharp repercussion on labor, farm values, tenantry, and migration. Finally, this era marked the absorption of agriculture into the industrial vortex, endlessly sustained by capitalism, science, and machinery.

By this triple revolution, basic problems of population, food supply, and social policy were raised for the consideration of economists and statesmen. At the end of the epoch the protests of the agrarian or the discontented laborer could no longer be silenced by the command to go West and exploit the fertility of fresh soil. Within less than a hundred years after Jefferson's death, his "republic of free and independent farmers" had come to the end of its rope and it was far from clear by whose hands the soil of America would be tilled at the close of another century. The experience of Rome, France, Germany, Denmark, England, Italy, and China began to have an import for those who searched the future.

In order of time, the agricultural revolution in the South occupied first place and it displayed the most spectacular features.

Working for three hundred and sixty thousand slave owners of varying fortunes were about four million slaves. These bondmen were not only chattels; they were Negroes whose original ancestors had been imported from the forests of Africa. Whether handicapped or not by innate disabilities for life in America, as frequently argued, they certainly had never been subjected to any such cultural discipline as the European peasant or artisan and they seldom had been inspired through opportunity, property, and competition to raise themselves in the economic scale by industry and thrift. Whether bond or free, they were poorly equipped for developing prosperity on the land.

Outnumbering the slave owners and their chattels were the free farmers of the South whose families constituted at least two-thirds of the total white population. Of this group, the majority, industrious and self-respecting, lived in the broad belt of upland that stretched all round the coastal plain; and though deficient in formal education, these sturdy tillers of the soil showed capacity for raising their standard of living. Hanging on the lower ranges of the yeomen, but usually widely separated from them in cultural equipment, were the "poor whites," despised alike by master and slave. Scattered over barren pinelands and in mountain notches they waged a spiritless battle for existence against poverty and the hookworm. Economically futile, the poor whites were politically as negligible as the indentured servants of colonial times, from whom a large part had descended.

When the curtain was rung down at Appomattox all the parties to the southern triangle were forced to adapt themselves to novel conditions of life and labor. The planters, burdened by debt, restricted in their enterprises by lack of capital, and stripped, for the most part, of their complaisant labor supply, such as it was, had to devise other methods of cultivation than those they had practiced—or forsake agriculture completely for business, industry or the professions. Some who chose the first of these alternatives tried to hold their domains intact by employing their former slaves as wage earners to till the soil, but this was a strange relation both for masters and servants and only the most skillful managers could make it very productive. Other planters sought to keep their estates together by resorting to the practice of renting; dividing their land into convenient plots, they now leased it to white farmers or freedmen, receiving in return either cash or a share of the produce.

Since money was scarce, the "cropping" system was generally the method chosen. In that case the planter furnished the land and often a part of the capital while the tenant supplied the labor and occasionally some of the equipment; at the end of the year the fruits of the combination were divided according to the terms of the contract. In this fashion a tenant or cropper economy with its social implications supplanted tillage by slaves throughout immense areas formerly occupied by unified plantations under superior direction. Moreover, since the Negro or poor white seldom had any money in hand, he was usually under the necessity of receiving an advance of capital from his landlord and was thus tied to his patron by a chain of debts that never could be broken, unscrupulous landowners often taking advantage of both poverty and ignorance of bookkeeping and law.

Tested by results, none of the methods adopted by the planters was remarkably efficient. In truth the War had brought to a head a long-impending crisis in southern economy as well as the conflict between the sections of the country—an economy based on the exploitation of virgin soil by slave labor that was already staggering under heavy burdens when the Second American Revolution struck it a mortal blow.

Unwilling to cope with the hazards of agriculture in the new conditions, a large number of planters surrendered in despair and went into business or industry. Selling their estates on the auction block, often at ruinous prices, to capitalists who felt competent to make the wage or renting system work or disposing of their property in small plots to the white farmers on their borders, these planters turned high abilities once devoted to agriculture to the service of business enterprise their ancestors had so despised. Moreover, a large number of the planters, particularly the younger generation, abandoning their estates, moved from the South to northern cities, particularly the Democratic stronghold of New York, where they helped to give direction and tone to business and society.

No doubt the general course of economic affairs was unfavorable to the Negro as a farmer. The changing technique of agriculture in an age of machinery and science baffled the men and women of the colored race as well as their untutored white neighbors. Familiar with only two or three staple crops, limited in their skill to the primitive tillage of plow and hoe, they clung with pathetic devotion to tradition. They had raised three-fourths of all the cotton grown in the days of slavery, they knew how to plant, cultivate, and harvest it, they found it a commodity for which they could always get some cash at the end of the season, and they kept loyally in the way of their ancestors.

But they had not advanced very far in their freedom when they encountered formidable obstacles to continued and easy progress, namely, exhaustion of the soil, necessity for scientific fertilization, the ravages of the boll weevil, and the competition of Texas cotton culture under the stimulus of other labor, particularly Mexican. Though Booker T. Washington and his valiant assistants made heroic efforts to meet the novel problems by education and annual conferences, the direction of the current was against them. By the end of the century only one-half of the cotton crop was produced by Negro labor. Nor were the freedmen more fortunate in the higher mechanical pursuits. In slavery they had enjoyed relatively little opportunity to test their powers as artisans; and after emancipation lack of training, deficiency in aptitude, or the jealousy of white workers—or all three—prevented them from going far in the skilled trades. Given these realities, the inevitable drift of Negroes from the land and domestic employment was toward the lower ranges of industry; only four per cent of the Negroes were in the higher mechanical ranks thirty-five years after Lincoln's death.

If the mass of the colored population in the South took small notice of such matters, restive individuals made use of the discriminations to stir a resentment that reacted unfavorably on southern agricultural economy, especially as avenues of escape were now opening northward. The enormous growth of northern industry, the increasing demand for unskilled labor, the relatively high wages offered by business enterprise, and above all the curtailment of European and Asiatic immigration multiplied the opportunities available to that portion of the negro race energetic enough to cast aside the hoe and incur the risk of migration to the cities beyond the Ohio and the Potomac.

The velocity of this movement from the land was augmented after the [first] World War when negro soldiers, drafted into the "army of democracy," returned from camp and trench where, inspired by the lofty ideals of President Wilson, their Commander-in-chief, they had acquired sentiments that made them unwilling to wear with complacency the former badges of servitude. Moved by new theories and encouraged by active propaganda, multitudes of Negroes now chose the hard struggle of northern cities rather than the more leisurely and perhaps more healthful life on southern fields and in southern homes where reminders of fixed discriminations met them at every hand.

Whatever the interpretation of the southern tendencies, there was no question about the reality of the second phase in the triple agricultural revolution, namely, the final closing of the frontier, the disappearance of cheap or free land. By 1900, the outstanding characteristic of American development, colonization and settlement, was brought to a dead stop and American society finally reduced to the economic laws of older societies, a dénouement startling in its swiftness. In 1827, the Secretary of the Treasury had reported that "it would take five hundred years to settle the public domain"; after that declaration the state of Texas and the fruits of the Mexican War were added to the possessions of which he spoke.

And yet within the brief space of seventy years the impossible had happened. In 1860, the free soilers voted themselves farms, to use the current phrase, and while their opponents in the South were engrossed in the war for southern independence, they legalized their expectations. In 1862, Congress passed the Homestead law and the Morrill Act assigning to each state a share of the public lands, proportioned to its representation in Congress, for the support of agricultural and mechanical education.

The rush for which preparation was thus made exceeded every estimate. Within thirty years after the enactment of the Homestead law all the choice arable land on the continental domain had been staked out and occupied. By 1890, according to the historians of the West, the frontier had disappeared; the federal government had no more rich farming land to give away. Even wide semi-arid plains where the buffalo and the cowboy once roamed at will were being swiftly enclosed by wire fences; dry farming was being introduced on lands once scorned by the pioneer; and a clamor for appropriations to irrigate the deserts was already raised in Washington. A grand drama had come to an end; the doors of a great economic theater were closing. The United States was at last beginning to encroach upon marginal land and to pass into a stage which Europe and the Orient had reached centuries before.

The shock of this stupendous climax was felt throughout America and indeed throughout the world. No longer was the native farmer to enjoy the advantage of mining virgin soil and underselling his competitors in the Old World working fields that had been tilled for ages. No longer could the wage earners of the eastern cities or the laborious peasants of other hemispheres look for freedom and a secure living on the ample domain of the United States. No longer were members of Congress to rise on the floor and advocate the settlement of the West by Orientals. The world's chief outlet for economic unrest was now shut and no political legerdemain could open it again. The frontier which had nourished the pioneering spirit and given such a peculiar flavor to the social order for three centuries had vanished forever; there were to be no more Boones, Houstons, and Frémonts; the long wagon trains of homeseekers had gone down over the western horizon for the last time.

And with the passing of romance slowly dawned an age of realism. The army of untrained and wasteful farmers who had prospered by raising huge crops on virgin soil, in spite of their methods, could never again take refuge from themselves by leaving the exhausted lands of their first settlements for new sections in the West. At last they had to face the science of farming and marketing; and the politicians who now spoke for them in Congress stood in the presence of economic problems that could no longer be exorcised by the cabalistic phrases of Andrew Jackson, Abraham Lincoln, or William Jennings Bryan. Whether they could acquire new habits and discover new modes of agriculture was hidden somewhere in the depths of the twentieth century.

The third phase of the revolution in agriculture was the subjection of the farmer to the processes of capitalist economy—a movement accelerated by the destruction of the slave plantation and the exhaustion of free land on the frontier. A striking characteristic of the old farming unit had been its capacity for self-sufficiency—an ideal that was never fully realized, of course, but none the less gave a decided bent to rural life. Bread came from the corn and wheat fields; milk, butter, cheese, and meat from the pasture; clothing from the backs of the growing flock; wood from the forest; sugar from the maple grove; and leather from the neighboring tanyard. Horses and oxen raised on the farm furnished the motor power and a few simple and inexpensive tools made up the mechanical equipment. Of the annual produce a certain amount was sold to bring in cash for current expenses including taxes and some was exchanged at the village store for necessities not made at home. The essence of that system, like the economy of the middle ages, was production for use rather than for exchange or profit and the psychology of that mode of life inhered in all its transactions.

Into this order so often idealized by the sentimentalist, the American inventor and manufacturer thrust their instruments with ruthless might. Their reaper had started a revolution on the land before the Civil War and the range of its coming empire had been indicated by the establishment of the McCormick works in Chicago. But that crude affair, which merely cut the grain and left it unbound in piles, was superseded in the seventies and eighties by the automatic self-binder and later, in the Far West, by a machine that cut, threshed, and bagged wheat ready for market all in a single operation. In 1870, the chilled steel plow, light and durable, was made available at a low cost to farmers long accustomed to the heavy, back-breaking implement of ancient memories. Swift in succession came mechanical corn planters and wheat drills that drove from the fields the men who dropped or sowed grain by hand to the song of the lark. Corn huskers, shellers, riding plows, hay loaders, potato diggers, tractors, gas engines, and other prime devices of the inventor made a change in the cultivation of the soil scarcely less profound than that wrought by the spinning jenny, the loom, and the blast furnace in the methods of manufacture. The man or woman with a hoe, bowed by the weight of centuries, now mounted a tractor and drove the furrow with the mechanical ease of the motorist. If, unlike the industrial operative, the farmer worked alone in the open country, still the automobile, telephone, and radio now gave him quick communication with the market, bank, and grange. Agriculture of the hoe and spade was reduced to a subordinate position in national economy.

Supplemented by other factors, the introduction of machinery made capital almost as important to the farmer as to the manufacturer. Formerly agricultural implements were simple and cheap, often home-made; for a thousand years the heavy hoe had served the Italian peasant; the ax, hoe, plow, and scythe had met most of the needs of the American farmer for two centuries. Then suddenly the bewildering variety of novel and expensive machinery was pressed upon him. He was urged to lay aside his scythe and cradle, which cost but a few dollars and lasted a lifetime, to buy in its place a self-binder which cost twenty times as much, was in need of constant repair, and wore out in three or four years of hard usage even if not left out in the rain and snow to rust and rot, as it often was. And as a matter of fact the farmer had no choice. The price of his grain in the market being fixed by the cost of production on the most fertile and best-equipped farms, he was compelled to buy machinery or to work for somebody who could, just as the handicraftsman had been at the start of the industrial revolution. Consequently the value of farm implements and machines per acre of land almost doubled between 1890 and 1910.

To the financial problems raised by the inventors were added economic difficulties springing from the rise in land values, especially after the closing of the frontier. So in the strategy of its advance, farming, like manufacturing, called for more and more capital, an ever larger investment to keep pace with competition—more debts and a closer reliance on banks and bankers. Swiftly and silently it became capitalistic in nature and spirit without at the same time acquiring the social technology which capitalism had evolved to marshal its forces, command governments, break into foreign markets, scale debts by facile bankruptcy, and engage the services of experts in production, promotion, and sales.

A second capitalist tendency in agriculture was the drift toward specialization in crops—a drift aided by the introduction of machinery, the stimulus of business enterprise, and the pressure of competition. In this run of things, King Cotton was not only restored to his throne, but was given a still greater monopoly in southern rural economy than he had enjoyed in earlier days. According to the returns of 1866, the cotton crop was reckoned at less than a million bales; five decades later it had risen to more than ten million bales; and cotton culture had encroached on the fields devoted to other southern staples.

In the process of concentration the live-stock industry, once widely scattered on the farms and plantations of the seaboard and middle west, fixed a seat of empire in the Missouri Valley. Sustained by immense energies and huge accumulations of capital, the cotton, corn, wheat, fruit, dairy, and live-stock industries now loomed like giants on the field of national enterprise. Now American farmers, dependent upon one or two specialties and forced to buy large quantities of supplies at stores, found their personal fortunes, like those of manufacturers and capitalists, linked with the caprices and casualties of domestic and foreign trade, though not yet primarily dependent on them. An epoch had come to an end and the iron gates were locked. Industrial capitalists were organized to make their own prices; industrial workers were organized to fix wages; whereas farmers, with the exception of a few powerful groups, were still incorrigible individualists at the mercy of the market. Throughout wide areas, the independent, self-sufficient farm unit of Lincoln's era had become a specialized concern producing for profit, forced to employ large capital in the form of machinery and fertilizers, compelled to compete with

European agriculture on more equal terms, and obliged to carry the weight of an increment in land values which had mounted with the years. With energetic members of the younger generation escaping to the cities to share in capitalist enterprise, with new racial stocks occupying ancestral homesteads, with a remorseless competition determining the prices of produce, with industrial capitalists and industrial workers compactly united to dictate terms on manufactured commodities, the economy and culture of historic American farming were crumbling into ruins.

In the economic changes on the land were implicit new attitudes toward the state and society. It is true that farmers had figured largely in politics from the earliest time in America, but mainly as a negative and dissolving force.

Casting about for methods of improving their economic status, agrarian leaders decided at last to learn lessons from dynamic capitalism itself —to attempt a control of prices through the union of producers on the land and to make a positive use of the engine of the state in the promotion of their interests. Under their direction the National Grange, founded in 1867, flourished, languished, and flourished again; at the end of half a century it could boast of a "powerful organization of farmers, active in thirty-three states, with its own press, its own body of organizers, its own lecturers, its own literature, poems, music, and traditions."

As in the labor movement there were special and general tendencies. While the industrial workers of the trades were drawing together in craft unions, wheat, cotton, and fruit growers also strove to stabilize production and control prices through the agency of organization. Though many of these efforts proved futile, others achieved permanent results. For example, a local association of orange growers appeared in California in 1888; it soon was followed by a district organization; in 1905 a federation was brought to pass; and in the course of a few years the California Fruit Growers' Association became as effective in its peculiar sphere as the Brotherhood of Locomotive Engineers in its domain.

Besides drawing together in unions and displaying an increasing consciousness of solidarity, farmers revealed a changing attitude toward the state—a resolve to use the government for group designs. As is so often the case in history, the idea had long preceded the deed. George Washington, that practical farmer and persistent experimenter, urged, in his annual message to Congress in 1796, a federal appropriation to stimulate enterprise and experiment in agriculture, to draw to the national center the results of individual skill and observation, and to spread the collected information far and wide throughout the nation. But the seed sowed by Washington fell on barren ground.

Nothing of note was done until the swelling tide of farmers enrolled under the new Republican pennant swept into Washington in the train of Abraham Lincoln. While the manufacturers were then getting their share of the Chicago bargain in tariffs and other specific aids, representatives of the farmers, going beyond the terms of the Homestead Act which merely threw open to the plow more bare land, carried through Congress that very same year a measure creating the bureau of agriculture—and also the Morrill law dedicating an immense area of the public domain to education in the agricultural and mechanical arts.

The constitutional barrier now being forced, the course of federal farm legislation widened, slowly at first because many, who favored protective tariffs for industries, shrank from "class measures" in favor of agriculture. In 1884, the bureau of animal industry was organized and given a regulatory power over important branches of rural economy. Three years later Congress, by the Hatch Act, provided for the establishment of experiment stations in each of the once sovereign states. Two years more passed and the bureau of agriculture became a Department raised to Cabinet rank.

The agrarian drive was now on in earnest. It furnished a great deal of the momentum behind the passage of the federal interstate commerce law of 1887 aimed at the control of common carriers. Its power was reflected in the rural free delivery act of McKinley's administration, the irrigation act of 1902, the farm credits legislation of the Wilson-Harding régimes, the coöperative marketing act of silent normalcy—all of which bore the impress of the agricultural solidarity. In the states as well as in the federal sphere, swelling pages of the statute books and mounting appropriations for boards and departments of agriculture recorded the insurgency of agrarian leaders. Before the twentieth century was well out on its course, farmers, while rejecting the doctrines of socialism, were, like all other powerful groups, in practice making use of the government to promote collective advantages and to force other interests into acceptable lines of action. Though the fickle tides of populism flowed and ebbed, the volume of farm legislation and the activities of administrative agencies showed no signs of retreat. Agriculture had passed out of the age of mere uproarious protest into the age of collective effort and constructive measures. That too was something to be observed by those who searched for omens.

Catalog

If you are interested in a list of fine Paperback
books, covering a wide range of subjects
and interests, send your name and address,
requesting your free catalog, to:

McGraw-Hill Paperbacks
1221 Avenue of Americas
New York, N.Y. 10020